M000268603

Ancient Laws and Contemporary Controversies

Ancient Laws and Contemporary Controversies

The Need for Inclusive Biblical Interpretation

CHERYL B. ANDERSON

OXFORD
UNIVERSITY PRESS
2009

OXFORD
UNIVERSITY PRESS

Oxford University Press, Inc., publishes works that further
Oxford University's objective of excellence
in research, scholarship, and education.

Oxford New York
Auckland Cape Town Dar es Salaam Hong Kong Karachi
Kuala Lumpur Madrid Melbourne Mexico City Nairobi
New Delhi Shanghai Taipei Toronto

With offices in
Argentina Austria Brazil Chile Czech Republic France Greece
Guatemala Hungary Italy Japan Poland Portugal Singapore
South Korea Switzerland Thailand Turkey Ukraine Vietnam

Copyright © 2009 by Oxford University Press, Inc.

Published by Oxford University Press, Inc.
198 Madison Avenue, New York, New York 10016

www.oup.com

Oxford is a registered trademark of Oxford University Press.

All rights reserved. No part of this publication may be reproduced,
stored in a retrieval system, or transmitted, in any form or by any means,
electronic, mechanical, photocopying, recording, or otherwise,
without the prior permission of Oxford University Press.

Library of Congress Cataloging-in-Publication Data
Anderson, Cheryl B., 1950–
Ancient laws and contemporary controversies : the need for
inclusive biblical interpretation / Cheryl B. Anderson.
p. cm.
Includes bibliographical references.
ISBN 978–0–19–530550–0
1. Bible—Criticism, interpretation, etc. 2. Bible—Evidences, authority, etc.
3. Law (Theology)—Biblical teaching. I. Title.
BS511.3.A54 2009
220.601—dc22 2009005362

9 8 7 6 5 4 3 2 1

Printed in the United States of America
on acid-free paper

A portion of chapter 2 was published earlier as the article "Biblical Laws: Challenging the Principles of Old Testament Ethics," in *Character Ethics and the Old Testament: Moral Dimensions of Scripture,* edited by M. Daniel Carroll R. and Jacqueline Lapsley (Louisville, KY: Westminster John Knox Press, 2007), and is used here by permission.

All Scripture quotations, unless otherwise noted, are from the New Revised Standard Version of the Bible, copyright © 1989 by the Division of Christian Education of the National Council of Churches of Christ in the USA, and are used by permission.

Acknowledgments

According to senior colleagues in my field, it is not uncommon for the project of a new faculty member's first sabbatical to be completed only some three to four years later during the second sabbatical. Such information has made me feel a lot better about the delay in completing this project. I started the research for this book in 2004 during my first sabbatical, aided by a faculty fellowship from the Association of Theological Schools for the project "Biblical Laws: Ancient Contexts and Contemporary Parallels." However, the book was completed during my second sabbatical, and that year's project title was "The Bible, HIV/AIDS, and African Peoples: Exploring African and African American Biblical Interpretation in the Midst of a Pandemic." For this work, I received funding from the Christian Faith and Life grant of the Louisville Institute and the Fulbright program of the U.S. government.

Although the projects for these two sabbaticals appear to be unrelated, on a deeper level there is a connection. As part of the year's sabbatical, I had contact with five African American churches that have exemplary AIDS ministries—Covenant Baptist Church in Washington, D.C.; Trinity United Church of Christ in Chicago, Illinois; Metropolitan Interdenominational Church in Nashville, Tennessee; and City of Refuge United Church of Christ and Glide Memorial United Methodist Church in San Francisco, California. In the process, I saw that these congregations do interpret the Bible inclusively and so confront on a daily basis the issues of ancient laws and contemporary controversies, as indicated by the title of this book. I hope that this work serves to support the courageous ministries of these congregations and their pastors.

From the initial stages, I knew that this project would take me into unfamiliar academic areas. Remembering the adage "If you want to learn a subject, teach it," I first offered the course Biblical Law and the Ethics of Biblical Interpretation in the fall semester of 2003. I then offered it in the spring semester of 2005 and again in the fall semester of 2006. Even though I was able to offer the course, I still needed specialists in various fields to actually help me teach it. I am extremely grateful to my New Testament colleagues at Garrett-Evangelical Theological Seminary, K. K. Yeo and Osvaldo Vena, for their willingness to be guest lecturers, as well as to the others who helped me over those years—Sujin Pak Boyer, A. Andrew Das, Josh Feigelson, D. Stephen Long, Benjamin Sommer, and Cristina Traina. However, neither these scholars nor the students involved should be held responsible for the uses to which I have put the knowledge that was shared.

Some of the ideas presented here originated in papers I delivered at the Oxford Institute of Methodist Theological Studies, a conference that takes place every five years in Oxford, England. In 2002, I gave a paper on John Wesley, Martin Luther King Jr., and the need for inclusive biblical interpretation; concepts from that paper appear here in chapters 5 and 7. More recently, in 2007, I gave a paper there on the liberationist critiques of the books of Ruth and Esther, and that paper constitutes the greater part of chapter 3. This same paper is also scheduled to be published in a volume edited by Jon Berquist and Alice Hunt. A substantial portion of chapter 2 on Old Testament ethics was originally given as a paper at the Society of Biblical Literature and was subsequently published in a volume edited by M. Daniel Carroll R. and Jacqueline Lapsley. Other audiences have heard portions of my thoughts in lecture series that I have given at Virginia Wesleyan University and Oklahoma City University, as well as at First United Methodist Church in Evanston, Illinois, and First Presbyterian Church (PCUSA) in Arlington Heights, Illinois.

The following scholars have provided comments on various segments of the manuscript: Bruce Birch, Barry Bryant, Charles Cosgrove, Steve de Gruchy, Jonathan Draper, Brenda Joyner, James Perkinson, Joerg Rieger, and Robert Vosloo. Their opinions were very important to me, and I did make changes accordingly, but once again, they should not be held responsible for the final product. I must also thank the anonymous reviewers who evaluated the original proposal and offered very constructive feedback. In addition, I appreciated the comments of the one reviewer who read an earlier version of the manuscript.

The entire manuscript was typed by Cindy Kaynor, and the editorial work was done by Diane Capitani, Lynne Deming, and Brooke Lester during the early, middle, and late stages of the writing process, respectively. Thank you all so very much. We make quite a production team! I must also acknowledge Carey Newman at Baylor University Press for helpful information received about the publishing industry and, of course, Cynthia Reid at Oxford University Press for taking on this project and for agreeing that it should be directed toward a general audience. By the way, I have a word of advice for that general audience. Given the numerous endnotes for each of the chapters, I recommend that you not refer to them while reading the chapter. Basically, you can ignore the reference numbers at the end of sentences as you read and then, only after you have finished the chapter, glance at the endnotes. The endnotes do not contain any information that you need to follow the discussion in the chapters themselves.

I would like to thank the faculty and administration of Garrett-Evangelical Theological Seminary for the support I have received as a faculty member—and for the ability to take sabbaticals. Also, I am grateful for all the help I have received from the staff of the United Library in general and from Dianne Robinson and Kathleen Kordesh in particular. They have been unfailingly able to get the resources I needed, no matter how obscure they were. Finally, as student assistants, Krista McNeil and Sarah Thullen were extremely helpful in the fall of 2007 as I wrote and prepared to travel to South Africa at the same time. Taken altogether, Garrett-Evangelical has been an extremely positive environment in which to work.

My first book was dedicated to my parents; but this one is dedicated to my brother, Warren Eugene Anderson. He has taught me by his example that mistakes and tragedies can become miracles and triumphs.

Only when a community operates on the assumption that there is always an abundance of God's grace can it be secure enough to open its boundaries to include another. An inclusive community must believe that Christ's compassion is boundless and God's love is so abundant that God can love everyone on earth—not just those of us who think we are doing what is right in God's sight, not just those who think and act like us. God's grace is extended to those with whom we do not get along, to those who we think are our enemies, to those who we think are sinners. That is why Christ came—to show us that God's grace is boundless. Jesus, who lived in the security of God's abundant grace, gave himself for us so that we could have life abundantly. Out of our gratefulness for God's graciousness, we respond with our good work, sharing God's grace with more and more people. When we realize that God's grace is so rich and full and abundant that there is enough for me and you and everyone and that there will always be leftovers, we will have the courage to imitate Christ, to give ourselves for others—to act inclusively.

Eric H. F. Law, *Inclusion: Making Room for Grace*

Contents

Ancient Laws and Contemporary Controversies

I

The Need for Inclusive Biblical Interpretation

During the summer of 2005, I was teaching a Bible study class with teenagers who would be high school seniors that fall. I had them do an exercise, the purpose of which was to encourage them, as people of faith, to read the biblical text carefully and ask crucial questions about the messages communicated. We read the Ten Commandments, and I pointed out how slavery is condoned, and we read Judges 19, a particularly heinous story about the gang rape of a woman, and I showed them how one of the underlying messages of the text is that it is better for a woman to be raped than a man. My goal was to get them to see that they already had a sense of who God is and how God is at work in the world that can help them to evaluate problematic biblical texts. For one female African American student in the class, the exercise was a total failure. At one point, she had had enough, and she blurted out, "This is the Word of God. If it says slavery is okay, slavery is okay. If it says rape is okay, rape is okay."

I had assumed that her identity as an African American and a female would have given her a different perspective on these texts about slavery and rape, but it did not. Her notion of absolute biblical authority was such that it took precedence over her own particularities. Since then, I have reflected on this incident and realized that her lack of self-awareness and her commitment to the Bible are actually related. When I lead discussions with the laity on biblical laws, I have noted that few of them—male or female—have ever thought about what a woman might think about some of these laws. For example,

Exodus 22:16–17 deems the rape of an unmarried female to have injured her father rather than the female herself, and Deuteronomy 22:28–29 requires an unmarried female who has been raped to marry her rapist. Clearly, these laws do not take into account the female's perspective. After a rape, she would undoubtedly see herself as the injured party and would probably find marriage to her rapist to be distasteful, to say the least. Arguably, there are cultural and historical reasons why such a law made sense at that time, such as providing a household for a woman who might not marry otherwise. Just the same, the law communicates the message that the faith tradition does not (and should not) consider the possibility that women might have different yet valid perspectives.

My point, more generally, is that the exclusions within the law correspond to the same exclusions within the church tradition and to developments in Christian ethics. As a result, some denominations reject the ordination of women by tradition and deem ethical roles for women to be those that restrict them to the home and procreation. The impact of such determinations is that the gifts women have for ministry are devalued and the great contributions that women have made historically to the life of the church are ignored. Ultimately, these traditions of the church do not take into account the perspectives of or their consequences for women.

Women are not the only group to be devalued in this way. A failure to consider the realities of other groups, such as slaves, is discernible. Exodus 21:20–21 provides that if a slave survives a day or two after having been struck by a slave owner, "there is no punishment; for the slave is the owner's property." There are also the indigenous groups of Canaan, and in Deuteronomy 7:1–2, the Israelites are told to "utterly destroy them" and "show them no mercy." From the perspective of women, foreigners, and those whose ancestors have been slaves or who are themselves economically exploited and marginalized today, these laws are problematic. Yet, in today's context, many Christians simply are not aware that such laws exist in the Bible. Even if Christians are aware of these laws, there is a tendency to just assume that they are either obsolete or irrelevant and so have no impact on us as contemporary Christians. Whether we recognize it or not, however, such laws and their underlying values shape how we think of our own lives of faith and the parameters of the contemporary Christian community. Essentially, a "true" Christian is one who excludes these other perspectives, as implied by these laws. In other words, the faith tradition itself has become defined by continuing those exclusions; therefore, whether a contemporary Christian community is deemed orthodox is based on how stringently it has adhered to excluding the particularities of the "Other." As saddened as I was by the teenager's response to my biblical exercise, I should not have been surprised. As someone from the more conservative evangelical circles, she had learned the underlying lessons well—differences in perspective of and consequences for certain groups are to be ignored and thereby erased—even when she, as an African American and a female, fell within two of those negatively impacted groups! According to her understandings, there was no room for her to be a self-aware female and African American *and* still be within the Christian tradition.

My encounter with this student was not the only time I have seen this relationship between "authentic" Christianity and exclusion. Recent news reports readily offer several examples. In the spring of 2007, a female faculty member at a Southern Baptist seminary in Texas was fired as part of a denominational "redirection" and closer adherence to 1 Timothy 2:12: "But I suffer not a woman to teach, nor to usurp authority over the man, but to be in silence" (King James Version).[1] Of course, the fact that the faculty member, who was herself a graduate of the seminary, as well as the students who had given her excellent teaching evaluations, might have a different perspective is simply not considered. Furthermore, the consequences of the seminary's decision on the female professor's family, both emotionally and financially, are not part of the decision-making process. For traditional (conservative) Christianity, different perspectives are not acknowledged, and the consequences for targeted groups cannot be considered. In the battles within the Southern Baptist denomination over these doctrinal issues, as one scholar is quoted in the article as having said, "attitudes toward women have become something of a badge that says which side of the battle you're on." Similarly, in the summer of 2007, Pope Benedict XVI announced the removal of restrictions on celebrating an old form of the Good Friday mass. This form of the mass, which had been sought by some traditionalist Catholics, includes prayers for the Jews "to be delivered from their darkness" and converted to Catholicism.[2] The national director of the Anti-Defamation League, an American-based Jewish advocacy group, commented on his disappointment and offense at the reinstatement of the liturgy. He is quoted as having said that "it was the wrong decision for the wrong time. It appears the Vatican has chosen to satisfy a right-wing faction in the church that rejects change and reconciliation." The conservatives, however, only want to reinstate their tradition, but that tradition excludes any consideration of its impact on another group.[3]

Also, the Local Law Enforcement Hate Crimes Prevention Act of 2007 (HR 1592, also known as the Matthew Shepard Act) was proposed in Congress; it would have expanded the 1969 federal hate-crime law to include crimes motivated by a victim's actual or perceived gender, sexual orientation, or gender identity. The bill did "not punish, nor prohibit in any way, name-calling, verbal abuse or expressions of hatred toward any group, even if such statements amount to hate speech. It covers only violent criminal acts."[4] In fact, language was later added to the proposed bill, which explicitly stated that conduct protected under the First Amendment free expression and free exercise clauses would not be subject to prosecution. Yet, according to press reports, conservative Christian leaders feared that the act would prevent them from expressing their biblically based condemnation of homosexuality. Because there was an express provision allowing the free exercise of religion, it seems that they were worried about something else. More than anything, the bill brought public attention to the kind of violence committed against those who are different according to conventional gender identity and sexuality criteria, and it implies that there is a connection between antigay rhetoric (even if not punishable under the bill) and the violence experienced by these individuals. It is far more likely that if such a bill had become law, there would be broader discussions about the harmful consequences of conservative biblical interpretations about sexuality. Because the conservative biblical tradition does not take into account considerations of the harm caused to a particular group, a bill that might force such an analysis had to be opposed.

Finally, there are consistent press reports about the controversy between the Episcopal Church in the United States and the worldwide Anglican Communion over the 2003 election as bishop of Gene Robinson, an openly gay male with a partner, and the election in 2006 of Katharine Jefferts Schori as the American denomination's first female presiding bishop. It is worth noting that both of these events have occurred at a time when not all Episcopalian dioceses in the United States even support the ordination of women as priests. Taken together, these developments have left some conservative Episcopalians feeling that the denomination "had gotten off track." As one conservative person is reported to have said, "The real issue is the abandonment of biblical teaching. The word of God is no longer taken as the word of God."[5] Once again, from the traditional perspective, the "Word of God" is equated with exclusion—excluding and restricting women and homosexuals in this case—and to allow them greater participation is seen as counter to God's will. A more progressive understanding, though, is that since Jefferts Schori and Robinson were elected through proper denominational procedures, their inclusion is a sign of God doing a new thing in our midst. Their new roles in the body of Christ, then, are signs of divine action rather than a rejection of the divine will.

Basically, the exclusion of certain groups and perspectives has become equated with the church's concept of right doctrine (orthodoxy). As a result, we have come to define ourselves by that which we exclude. Under these circumstances, to argue in favor of including the particularities of women, African

Americans, Jews, and homosexuals, as is done here, is to go against the tradition and to risk being labeled unchristian," "liberal," "too secular," or even somewhat heretical. Yet, for those of us who are committed to the church as well as the empowerment of marginalized groups, it is a risk that we must take. To that end, this current study attempts to develop an inclusive approach to biblical interpretation that remains committed to both the Christian tradition and the concept of biblical authority. Specifically, this interpretative approach is different from traditional approaches as it is both critical and inclusive. Because these are probably unfamiliar terms, a more detailed discussion of each is warranted.

An approach to biblical interpretation that is "critical" means that it requires any biblical text to be evaluated, rather than just accepted and obeyed, and that evaluation involves assessing its underlying ideologies.[6] In its simplest definition, "ideology" refers to "a ruling value system in a society that (1) people take for granted and (2) serves the interests of the powerful at the expense of the less powerful."[7] For example, patriarchy, a system that privileges men over women, is an ideology, and feminist biblical scholars have struggled for decades to unmask the patriarchal nature of biblical texts. As one feminist scholar wrote more than twenty years ago: "Not only is scripture interpreted by a long line of men and proclaimed in patriarchal churches, it is also authored by men, written in androcentric language, reflective of religious male experience, selected and transmitted by male religious leadership. Without question, the Bible is a male book."[8]

The problem, however, is that female readers of biblical texts learn to identify with that male perspective, through an effect referred to as immasculation, and so read texts in ways that are contrary to their own interests.[9] The high school senior who was in the Bible study class I mentioned earlier is a perfect example of such a reader. She has learned to read the Bible in a way that is counter to her own spiritual, emotional, and physical health and well-being. Just as feminists have been aware of male ideological interests in biblical texts, in recent years, additional groups have identified other patterns of dominance and subordination in these texts based on race, religion, former colonial or colonized nation status, and so forth. Consequently, "the common thread" running through all these forms of ideological criticism "is the assumption that texts are not value-neutral but, rather, reflect to different degrees the relations and structures of race, gender, and class, which empower some persons and disenfranchise others."[10]

A crucial element of a critical approach to biblical interpretation, then, is "the *conscientization of biblical interpreters*," a process that seeks to make both the privileged and the nonprivileged aware of the values of hierarchical systems in both written texts and the world around them that privilege some over others and that they have subsequently internalized.[11] Based on the work of the Brazilian educator Paulo Freire, such conscientization, or awareness, develops through a pedagogical model that seeks the liberation of the marginalized.[12] According to Freire, traditional educational models employ a "banking" concept where "education becomes an act of depositing, in which the students are the depositories and the teacher is the depositor." Under these circumstances, "knowledge is a gift bestowed by those who consider themselves knowledgeable upon those whom they consider to know nothing," and the students' role is restricted to "receiving, filing, and storing the deposits." As a result, students are robbed of opportunities for creativity and insights that would enable them to transform the very systems that disadvantage them.[13] In such educational systems, there is an inverse relationship between the students having received knowledge and their ability to transform their environments.

> The more students work at storing the deposits entrusted to them, the less they develop the critical consciousness which would result from their intervention in the world as transformers of that world. The more completely they accept the passive role imposed on them, the more they tend simply to adapt to the world as it is and to the fragmented view of reality deposited in them.[14]

Applying Freire's concepts to biblical traditions means that, under the "banking" educational model, the faithful cannot develop a critical consciousness needed to engage and transform the inequities around them. Furthermore, there are obvious similarities between Freire's "banking" model and traditional notions of biblical authority in the church, where believers simply are to receive and accept the knowledge presented. Therefore, a new concept of biblical authority must accompany critical biblical interpretation. Because biblical authority will be discussed more fully in chapter 6, suffice it to say here that biblical authority does not have to be synonymous with authoritarianism.[15] Rather than authority as domination, a critical and liberative approach to biblical interpretation defines authority as partnership,[16] where the voice of God emerges from Scripture in the context of dialogue within faith communities.[17] From this perspective, authority is relational rather than hierarchical.

In addition, the approach proposed here is inclusive, that is, it seeks to include persons and insights that are usually ignored. More specifically, "inclusion is a discipline of extending our boundary to take into consideration another's needs, interests, experience, and perspective, which will lead to clearer understanding of ourselves and others, fuller description of the issue at hand, and possibly a newly negotiated boundary of the community to which we belong."[18] In other words, a critical and inclusive approach recognizes the value of engaging the realities of those who have traditionally been marginalized. By doing so, however, new issues are raised about biblical texts themselves as a moral resource. Hearing the witness of women and the descendents of slaves should force us to question the subordination of women and the acceptance of slavery, among other things, in biblical texts. For this reason, Bruce Birch cautions us to remember that "Israel's story is not intended to model normative behavior in all its particulars."[19]

> Any adequate approach to the Old Testament as moral resource must seek not only to *retrieve* moral perspectives that inform our ethics but in some instances to *reclaim* the biblical text from elements that distort or limit its moral witness. Thus, for example, the Old Testament reflects, in much of its testimony, a subordinate view of women that is not in harmony with the broader vision of love, justice, and wholeness made clear throughout the Old Testament. This broader vision itself roots in God's activity and will, and the church must claim and apply that vision to issues of the subordination of women in ways that go beyond what the biblical community could have imagined. It was in a similar way that the church finally claimed its moral obligation to oppose slavery even though both the Old and New Testaments seem to accept its existence.[20]

Being open to inclusion, therefore, means that hard questions have to be asked about which biblical elements must be retrieved and those that must be reclaimed—and those are not easy questions to answer. It will mean recognizing that "although it is through Israel that God's word and will are mediated, Israel is not the perfect embodiment of the living out of that divine moral vision."[21] Furthermore, these kinds of questions have to be asked in today's context when easy answers are popular, and the faithful flock to churches with signs outside the door such as the one I saw years ago in Nashville: "The Bible doesn't just tell us how things were, it tells us how things should be."

Lest the contrary be assumed, there is a clear theological basis for a critical and inclusive approach to biblical interpretation. It "depends on two basic theological judgments: (1) that the Bible is a human witness to the divine word in which God's revelation is communicated but also distorted and (2) that God is against ideology, that is, opposed to those cultural norms, values, institutions, etc. that serve the interests of the more powerful at the expense of the less powerful."[22] Given this understanding of God and God's purposes in our world, an approach that is critical and inclusive constitutes a "hermeneutical principle,"[23] an interpretive framework through which meaning is derived from biblical texts and according to which texts can be evaluated. Such a hermeneutical principle is consistent with theological understandings that the Bible's authority has Jesus Christ, the incarnate Word, as its foundation. Correspondingly, the emphasis in considerations of biblical authority should be placed on Jesus, the Word made flesh, and not just on the Bible as a written document.

> The Bible shares the incarnational character of the One to whom it bears witness. It proclaims by its composition as well as its declarations that the Creator has chosen to be revealed in creation, even coming among us as one of us. But that manifestation does not exhaust or circumscribe the divine presence or power, and the word by which that action is recalled and re-presented is only the servant of the living Word. The words of God spoken to prophets and poets are essential to Christian faith and carry the authority of their Speaker, but the word of God cannot be contained in any document; nor can it be comprehended apart from the Word made flesh, which is both the center and the norm of Scripture.[24]

Defining the "Other": The Need to Make the Connections

Today, feminist biblical scholars are continuing to raise questions about gender constructions and traditional understandings of women in biblical texts. There are works on the subject of women in the Bible by Alice Ogden Bellis,[25] Gale Yee,[26] Frances Taylor Gench,[27] and Wilda Gafney,[28] to name just a few examples. Plus, there are works on biblical interpretations in the context of contemporary African American women (sometimes referred to as womanist readings),[29] Asian women,[30] and Latinas (sometimes referred to as *mujerista* readings).[31] But women are not the only ones with concerns. There are volumes that incorporate perspectives of race and ethnicity, such as *True to Our Native Land: An African American New Testament Commentary*[32] and *Ways of Being, Ways of Reading: Asian American Biblical Interpretation.*[33] Other volumes address issues of class, particularly the plight of the poor in the global south, such as the work by Ernesto Cardenal and Jorge Pixley in Nicaragua,[34] and, more recently, Gerald West in South Africa.[35] There are postcolonial interpretations by R. S. Sugirtharajah[36] and Fernando Segovia.[37] Two scholars, Musa Dube and Kwok Pui-lan, joined their interests in feminist *and* postcolonial readings of the Bible.[38] Furthermore, Tod Linafelt has edited two volumes that consider how Christians should read their texts and understand their relationship to Judaism in the aftermath of the Holocaust.[39] In addition, lesbian/gay/bisexual and transgender scholars offer "queer" readings of the Bible to challenge traditional interpretations that exclude them from faith communities.[40]

Feminist/womanist/*mujerista*? Gender/race/class? Postcolonial/post-Holocaust/queer? These definitely are not the same kind of biblical scholars that existed a generation ago! They are raising new issues and interpretations given their own particularities. It is a new day, and, for some, being confronted with these new voices, heard from those usually labeled "the Other," can be overwhelming—and a bit frightening. The postmodern condition is blamed, with its critique of universal claims and celebration of a multiplicity of textual meanings, and, without a stable (read, traditional) sense of meaning, the "anti-postmodern" scholars fear that intellectual and moral anarchy cannot be far behind.[41] It might help to know that these movements are not random ones, and they are in fact connected to one another.

To begin making the connections, we need to define the term "patriarchy." "Patriarchy" refers to entrenched social systems in which both men and women participate, and "a society is patriarchal to the degree that it promotes male privilege by being *male dominated, male identified,* and *male centered.*"[42] A system is male dominated when "positions of authority—political, economic, legal, religious, educational, military, domestic—are generally reserved for men, and women in such positions are thought to be exceptions."[43] A male-identified system associates notions of men and masculinity with core cultural ideas about what is considered good, desirable, preferable, or normal. In other words, the society's core values closely resemble the core values of masculinity and "the ideal man," such as strength, decisiveness, rationality, autonomy, self-sufficiency. In contrast, qualities such as cooperation, mutuality, compassion, intuitive and nonlinear ways of thinking, and emotional expressiveness "are all devalued *and* culturally associated with femininity and femaleness."[44] Patriarchy is also male centered because "the focus of attention is primarily on men and what they do" and is evident in all aspects of contemporary culture, from newspaper reporting to the subjects of popular movies.[45]

Most important, though, a patriarchal system, since it elevates one group (male) by subordinating another (female), has an obsession with control because "men maintain their privilege by controlling women and anyone else who might threaten it."[46] Such an emphasis on male control over females has two unfortunate side effects. First, as the controllers, men "come to see themselves as subjects who intend and decide what will happen, and to see the other as objects to act upon; consequently, the controlled are seen without the fullness and complexity that define them as human beings."[47] Second, "a woman perceived as controlling a man is typically labeled a 'castrating bitch' or a 'ball buster,' and the man she supposedly controls is looked down upon as 'henpecked,' 'pussy whipped,' and barely a man at all."[48] At its most basic level, therefore, patriarchy is a hierarchical system that privileges males who are to be the dominant ones over females who are to be subordinate.

In this patriarchal context, women are objects to be controlled; they are considered "second-class citizens" and not appreciated as full human beings. As a response, feminism can be explained by the bumper sticker definition: "Feminism is the radical notion that women are people."[49] Feminist biblical scholars, therefore, fight against the invisibility of women in both biblical texts and the life of the church, and they seek to retrieve biblical traditions that reflect female experiences and interpretations that attest to their own experiences of the divine in their own lives. However, in the United States of America today, a patriarchal society, the "normative" male has characteristics other than gender. He is also white (race), Christian (religion), heterosexual (sexuality), and Western (a colonial power). Under a system of dominance and subordination, all who are different from that "ideal male" are marginalized. Accordingly, racism, sexism, and classism are related. Each implies the right of one group to dominate another. For racism, that right is grounded in "the belief in the inherent superiority of one race over all others"; for sexism, in "the belief in the inherent superiority of one sex over the other"; for classism, in the belief in the inherent superiority of the rich over the poor.[50] At their core, therefore, the struggles against racism, sexism, and classism, usually referred to as contextual, feminist, and liberationist approaches, respectively, should be united in favor of social and religious systems that no longer disadvantage them.

Similarly, the normative male is heterosexual, and heterosexism "is a reasoned system of bias regarding sexual orientation; it denotes prejudice in favor of heterosexual people and denotes prejudice against bisexual and, especially, homosexual people."[51] Heterosexism "leads to the conviction that heterosexuality is *the* normative form of human sexuality; it is the measure by which all other sexual orientations are judged; and all sexual authority, value, and power are centered in heterosexuality.[52] Consequently, heterosexism is "analogous to racism and sexism," whereas homophobia "finds appropriate analogies in racial bigotry and misogyny."[53] Upon closer examination, it is clear that homophobia is directly related to socially constructed notions of gender.

> Whether gay or straight, people might be homophobic because they cannot think of male same-sex activity without also imaging men as physically vulnerable, as potentially subject to rape. They cannot think

> of female same-sex activity without imaging women as powerful, as potentially free of male control. Such images of male vulnerability and female strength challenge the heterosexist myth to which we have all grown accustomed.[54]

Obviously, in our patriarchal system, men are to be dominant and never subordinate, and women are to be subordinate and never dominant. As one writer has observed, "Without the existence of sexism, there could be no homophobia."[55] Considering the underlying rationale, therefore, to condemn homosexuality is to reassert that males should not be in a subordinate position and to reinscribe simultaneously the notion that it is the appropriate one for females.

Normative heterosexuality also serves to define racial/ethnic and religious boundaries, rendering such boundaries "sexualized perimeters."[56] In the United States, we have race- and class-based sexual standards, with white middle-class (heterosexual) men as the norm, that "tend to define African American and Latino men as excessively masculine and oversexed or 'hypersexual' and Asian men as insufficiently masculine and undersexed or 'hyposexual.'"[57] However, comparable use of sexualized boundaries can be found elsewhere.

> This pattern of contrasting valorized dominant group sexuality with devalued nondominant group sexualities can be found in descriptions of ethnic relations around the world. Sexual stereotypes commonly depict "us" as sexually vigorous (usually our men) and pure (usually our women), and depict "them" as sexually depraved (usually their men) and promiscuous (usually their women).[58]

We must not forget, though, that distinctions made between the sexuality of white men and nonwhite men, whether described as hypersexual or hyposexual, are basically rooted in notions of the normative white (heterosexual) male that also associate nonwhite males with the feminine.

> The truth is that all nonwhite males, or males of cultural groups not endorsed by the dominant culture, are also seen in some degree as "effeminate." Sometimes this involves the accusation that one is controlled by feeling or is less "rational" than males of dominant racial and cultural groups, or more animalistic, rhythmic, or childlike. The depth of the hatred toward women is clearly reflected in this projection of female stigma onto any males who need to be distanced from dominant norms of "real manhood" for purposes of social control.[59]

Such sexualized boundaries also define religious boundaries, and, since the normative male is Christian (usually Protestant), non-Christians are marginalized. As the Jewish scholar Daniel Boyarin writes:

> As I reflect on my coming of age in New Jersey, I realize that I had always been in some sense more of a "girl" than a "boy." A sissy who did not like sports, whose mother used to urge me, stop reading and go out and play, in fifth grade I went out for—ballet. (Of course I explained to the guys that it was a kind of sophisticated bodybuilding.) This in itself is rather a familiar story, a story of inexplicable gender dysphoria, but one that for me, even then, a rather happy ending. I didn't think of myself so much as girlish but rather as Jewish.[60]

The concept of the Jew as the outsider has implications not only for gender constructions but for the very existence of a non-Christian religion, Judaism. The Holocaust refers to the systematic killing during World War II by Nazi Germany of between 5 and 6 million Jews and other groups, including homosexuals.[61] Because of the Christian church's complicit behavior, some Christian scholars have been motivated since then to explore Christianity's claims of presumed inherent superiority to Judaism and, therefore, its right to dominance over and against Judaism.[62]

Similarly, post-Holocaust readings of biblical texts explore inclusive ways of reading texts that affirm the validity of both the Christian and Jewish traditions. Speaking more globally, however, other religions are implicated as well. We are in a setting in which the "war on terrorism" collapses easily into a war on Islam. Furthermore, contrary to popular belief, this "Christian country" has become the most religiously diverse nation in the world.[63] Because traditional (heterosexist) Christianity tries to assert superiority over all other religions, it is imperative that Christians of good conscience find ways to help Christianity take its place as one of many religions in a religiously pluralistic context.

Finally, the normative privileged male, who is white and heterosexual, is also from the West, also referred to as the First World. As opposed to populations from the Two-Thirds World or the global south, he is the cultural and economic heir of the colonial empires of earlier centuries and of global capitalism today. Postcolonial critiques explore the ways in which European and American territorial expansion and economic exploitation were and are currently accompanied and aided by the spread of Christianity. An oral tradition in southern Africa, for example, says that "when the white man came to our country he had the Bible and we had the land. The white man said to us, 'Let us pray.' After the prayer, the white man had the land and we had the Bible."[64] History shows that this relationship was not a coincidence: "Many of the missionaries became active agents as informants, instigators, fighters, and collaborators in the European conquest of African states."[65]

Once again, the dominance of the West and the spread of Christianity worked together to create "sexualized perimeters."[66] In her lecture "Changing the Missionary Position: Facing Up to Racism, Sexism, and Nationalism in G (LBT) Liberation," feminist theologian Laurel Schneider recognizes that the term "missionary position" "evokes the overt sexual image of intercourse, in particular the stereotypical, or rather Western normative position of heterosexual intercourse, with a man on top of a woman on her back." However, she argues, it is a sexual position that "also evokes the image of a familiar gender hierarchy, the sexual position of the man indicating dominance over the woman" where "men are on top and are 'active,' women are beneath them in a supporting, 'passive' role." But there is more to the story because this sexual position came to "symbolize for both Greeks and Romans social position," and it was "ultimately codified as the proper Christian order of things by the likes of St. Thomas Aquinas," making "the social position of active male dominance over passive female submission *the* Christian position, supported by the theological systems of the Church."[67]

In the context of colonial expansion, she continues, the logic of whiteness and heterosexual masculinity combine in such a way that "the whiteness of a man came to lie solely in his ability to dominate others, and the nonwhiteness of men rested squarely in their condition of being dominated."[68]

> The sexuality of race was made explicit in this equation of domination, and the "science" of race served to cement what the Church already had done, making the sexualized dynamic of dominance and submission *natural.* White supremacy in service first of European colonial expansion and American slavery and then in service of global capitalism lies at the heart of the race/sex co-constitution, a co-constitution that ultimately functions to preserve the power and privilege of white males in a symbolic and very material economy of human diversity, positioned for the maintenance of its own order and the benefit of a few.[69]

As an article by another feminist theologian, Mayra Rivera Rivera, demonstrates, this logic of whiteness = masculinity = domination and the corresponding labeling of indigenous people and their land as feminine = dominated applied to the efforts in the late nineteenth and early twentieth centuries of Protestant missionaries to Puerto Rico (which they renamed Porto Rico).[70] One of the written reports of these missionaries describes "Porto Rico" as follows: "Porto Rico rests upon the bosom of the tropic seas as beautiful, majestic and fruitful in all its natural gifts as when Columbus first discovered it; *waiting only* the assistance of law, sound government aided by intelligent industry, enterprise and moral transformation."[71]

Rivera notes that, from the missionaries' perspective, "Porto Rico (the land) appears as a beautiful female who invites (and incites) the manly colonizer and waits—docile and available, to be entered, inseminated, and owned."[72] In contrast, the missionaries described their work in the following way: "to harness, penetrate and possess."[73] As seen earlier, Western territorial expansion and domination were and continue to be gendered, resting on oppositional polarities of the dominant/masculine/Westerner over and against the subordinate/feminine/conquered land.

It is not hard to make the connection between the colonial and missionary paradigm of domination over native (nonwhite) peoples and their lands with the current ecological crisis. It follows, then, that the ecological crisis has both gender and racial dynamics. Concerning gender, Rosemary Radford Ruether wrote more than thirty years ago that "the concept of domination of nature has been based from the first on social domination between master and servant groups, starting with the basic relationship between men and women."[74] Consequently, Ruether argued, "women must see that there can be no liberation for them and no solution to the ecological crisis within a society whose fundamental model of relationships continues to be one of domination." Furthermore, she proposed that the women's movement join with the ecological movement to transform current social and economic relationships and their underlying values.[75]

Concerning race, the United Church of Christ issued a groundbreaking report on environmental racism in 1987, which identified race as more important in predicting the location of the nation's commercial hazardous waste facilities than household income, the value of homes, and the estimated amount of hazardous waste generated by industry. In the follow-up report, issued early in 2007, "people of color were found to be more concentrated around hazardous waste facilities than previously shown."

> Over nine million people (9,222,000) are estimated to live in circular host neighborhoods within 3 kilometers of the nation's 413 commercial hazardous waste facilities. Over 5.1 million people of color, including 2.5 million Hispanics or Latinos, 1.8 million African Americans, 616,000 Asians/Pacific Islanders and 62,000 Native Americans live in neighborhoods with one or more commercial hazardous waste facilities. Indeed these host neighborhoods are densely populated, with over 870 persons per square kilometer

> (2,300 per mi^2), compared to 30 persons per square kilometer (77 per mi^2) in non-host areas. Not surprisingly, 343 facilities (83%) are located in metropolitan areas.[76]

As seen previously, in a gender paradigm of domination/subordination, the privileged white male heterosexual is to dominate land and nonwhites, and that or those to be dominated are associated with the subordinate feminine. As the Native American theorist Andrea Smith notes, once nonwhite groups are marked as violable, by extension, the lands and territories they occupy become violable as well.[77]

In the preceding discussion, the connections between racism/sexism/classism and postcolonial/post-Holocaust/queer analyses have been made. In a patriarchal system that is heterosexist and male identified, these are the groups that are "other" than the "ideal" European or North American white heterosexual male, who is also economically privileged and Christian. To better describe the intersecting structures and systems of domination/subordination that are involved here, Elisabeth Schüssler Fiorenza has coined the term "kyriarchy" or "kyriocentrism," which she defines as "a complex pyramidal system of intersecting multiplicative social structures of supremacy and subordination, of ruling and oppression."[78] These interlocking dynamics mean that any one person can experience any combination of disadvantages, based on how different they are from the norm. For example, a poor black female who is Christian is disadvantaged because she is poor (not affluent), black (not white), and female (not male), but she has some advantages because she is Christian. A working-class white heterosexual male has privileges based on race (white) and sexuality (heterosexual) but disadvantages based on class. Similarly, a Jewish homosexual male is disadvantaged because he is Jewish (not Christian) and homosexual (not heterosexual) but advantaged because he is white.[79] Likewise, an affluent white female who is a lesbian has privileges because she of her class (rich) and her race (white), but she is disadvantaged because of her gender (female) and her sexuality (not heterosexual). Speaking personally, I have advantages because I am an educated professional, and I am an ordained minister in a mainline Protestant denomination (the United Methodist Church). As a seminary professor, I may not be affluent, by any stretch of the imagination, but I do have some advantages based on class. Another advantage I have is that I am a heterosexual in a system that privileges heterosexuality. At the same time, I face disadvantages because I am female (not male) and African American, a racial/ethnic minority in the midst of white Western hegemony. In these respects, we can see that the dynamics of domination/subordination are interlocking and multidimensional.

Questions are now being raised, however, about the dichotomous logic that underlies these classifications of race, gender identity, and sexuality. As demonstrated in the previous discussion, one is usually classified as white *or* black, male *or* female, heterosexual *or* homosexual. Since the 2000 census, activists have now made it possible for multiracial individuals to check as many race categories as apply; previously, they could only identify themselves as "other."[80] Along the same lines, transgender and bisexual individuals resist the construction of mutually exclusive categories for gender identities (male or female) and sexuality (heterosexual or homosexual). Therefore, these groups are contesting the binary nature of these constructions themselves and not just the different values placed on them in a patriarchal system. The focus of this study, though, will remain on the latter phenomenon, the system of privileges accorded these binary categories.

It is indeed surprising, given the commonalities, that those considered "the Other" do not have a shared platform of political action. Instead, each group only addresses its own concerns without acknowledging the struggles of another group. As Smith describes it, we are usually engaged in "oppression olympics," a situation that occurs when "we are too busy fighting over who is more oppressed."[81] The better approach is expressed by a pastor in the Los Angeles area: "Oppression is oppression is oppression.... Just because we're not the ones who are being oppressed now, do we not stand with those oppressed now? This is the biblical mandate. That's what Jesus is all about."[82]

Rather than fight against one another, marginalized groups should join together and work against systems that privilege the few at the expense of the many. As the activist Suzanne Pharr wrote:

> We must find ways to build coalition, to make broad social change for all of us. There are many more people who are considered the Other (though called, ironically, the minority) than those who are defined as the Norm. We must become allies in a movement that works against power and control by the few and for shared power and resources for the many. To do this work, we will have to build a program that provides an analysis of the oppressions, their connections, and together we must seek ways to change those systems that limit our lives.[83]

What kinds of changes would occur in a transformed society, one not defined by the dominance/subordination paradigm? One change might be that sexual ethics could be evaluated according to sexual authenticity and fidelity rather than public conformity to heterosexist norms.[84] Another change is that masculinity could be reconceptualized. As Warren Blumenfeld writes, men have to "keep it all together," and "cannot show vulnerability, awkwardness or doubts; we always have to be 'on top,' in bed and out." These perceptions result from current gender roles that "teach males to hold in contempt anything within themselves hinting at 'femininity.' We thus kill a vital portion of our being."[85] A new paradigm would allow men (and women) to integrate the feminine and masculine aspects that we all have and so lead healthier and more complete lives. Traditionalists fear that loosening the grip of heterosexism and its dominance/subordinate paradigm will lead to anarchy; but it is the only way for us to move toward a more just and sustainable world for all.[86]

The Need to Unmask Particularity

In earlier sections of this chapter, I equated conservative Christianity with the exclusion of certain groups—women, homosexuals, and Jews—and the corresponding failure either to consider their perspectives in determining church policy or to take into account the harmful consequences caused to them by traditional biblical interpretations. Now, the reason that is the case should have become clearer. In the context of a male dominant/female subordinate gender paradigm (the one held by conservative Christianity), these groups are equated with the feminine and are to be dominated. Conceptually, it does not matter that they might have different yet valid perspectives, or that they suffered harm because of that paradigm. They are rendered objects to be controlled, and the possibility of seeing them as full human beings does not arise.

I can understand why such a system is supported by those elite males and females who benefit from it to one degree or another. My question is about "the Others"; why do *they* support it? Audre Lorde noted that there is a *mythical norm* in America that "is usually defined as white, thin, male, young, heterosexual, Christian, and financially secure," and that "each one of us within our hearts knows 'that is not me.'"[87] If we know that this is not who we are, why do we continue to support the status quo? To answer that question, we need to return to the definition of "ideology" given earlier. Ideology refers to "a ruling value system in a society that (1) people take for granted and (2) serves the interests of the powerful at the expense of the less powerful."[88] Based on this definition, patriarchy is an ideology because it serves the interests of the powerful and people take it for granted. In other words, patriarchy serves the interests of the few but appears to be the natural and, therefore, expected state of affairs.

These conditions could not develop if the powerful admitted that they were only speaking from their own particularity and were not taking the circumstances of other human beings into account. That admission can never happen, however, because it would deprive the powerful of their authority. Consequently, biblical traditions and biblical interpretations are developed by the privileged elite, but that group has had to mask or cover over the relationship they have to the determinations they make. Using comparable rationales, the church and the academy have justified their interpretations by contending that those interpretations are "divine" or "objective," respectively. In fact, these interpretations only reflected their own perspectives and circumstances, but that tactic has been successful. Their views are the orthodox views, and any attempt to incorporate other human experiences into the deliberations can be rejected as "contrary to biblical teachings." Because the purpose of this study is to propose an inclusive way of interpreting the Bible that affirms particularity, I need to "unmask" the hidden particularity of traditional biblical interpretation.

Unmasking the Church

The easiest way for the privileged elite of the church to mask their particularities is to contend that their texts and biblical interpretations are of divine and not human origin. Of course, by all appearances, associating any tradition with God makes them appear more holy and therefore more appealing to believers. An added advantage, however, is that to affirm an entirely divine origin means that no human (and therefore no male) influence has to be acknowledged. The clearest example of this can be found in the fundamentalist doctrine of Scripture. According to Donald McKim's analysis, the fundamentalist view is based on a concept of biblical inspiration, found in the Chicago Statement on Biblical Inerrancy, which asserts "the whole of Scripture and all of its parts, down to the very words of the original, were given by divine inspiration."[89] In some fundamentalist circles, this is verbal inspiration, and it inspired not only the thoughts but the very words found in Scripture, which may even have actually been dictated by God to the biblical writers.[90] Because of their divine origin, then, the Scriptures not only contain but *are the Word of God*, "hence all their elements and all their affirmations are absolutely errorless, and binding the faith and obedience of men."[91]

Thanks to the classic and very popular Hollywood movie, the American population has an indelible memory of Moses coming down from Mount Sinai with the Ten Commandments. Extending the image further, under the fundamentalist concept of biblical inspiration, Moses came down from the mountain with the whole Bible! It is the ultimate erasure of human input in the shaping of the biblical canon. The problem is that this is not how the Bible came to be. A crucial verse in these discussions is 2 Timothy 3:16a: "All Scripture is inspired by God and is useful for teaching, for reproof, for correction, and for training in righteousness" (NRSV). The Living Bible paraphrases this verse, Craig Allert notes, to read: "The whole Bible was given to us by inspiration from God." However, Paul could not have referred to "the whole Bible," Allert rightly notes, since the biblical canon had not been formed yet, and even the document, 2 Timothy, was not part of the canon when those words were written.[92] Consequently, he concludes that "this paraphrase is misleading here and could cause its readers to commit an anachronism by taking this to be a reference to the entire canon of Christian Scriptures, including the New Testament."[93]

Biblical scholars know that the biblical canon, the definitive collection of sacred books for Christians (the result of the canonization process), developed over a period of centuries. It was only in the mid-second century BCE, at the earliest, that such a collection existed for the Hebrew Bible, and the New Testament canon was not initially agreed upon until the late second century CE.[94] Because other documents were circulating at that time, decisions had to be made as to which ones would be included in the canon. Eventually, three criteria seem to have been operative: orthodoxy of content (consistency with the basic doctrines already recognized as normative by churches), apostolicity (the presumption of apostolic authorship), and acceptance (use of these books by the churches and references to them by reliable bishops and theologians).[95] Clearly, human beings made decisions about the shape of the canon. For my purposes, the crucial question is this one—which members of the early churches participated in those decisions? If women had a voice, would the Gospel of Mary be in our canon today?[96] If homosexual men and women had a voice, would we have more developed traditions about "the disciple whom Jesus loved," based on John 19:25–27?[97] These questions are a bit fanciful, to be sure, but my point is simply that, in all likelihood, these groups did not play a large role in the shaping of the canon.

In his work, Allert corrects the usual impression that "the only criterion for canonicity of the New Testament documents was inspiration, and that when the church recognized this inspiration, the New Testament canon was a done deal."[98] Rather, Allert acknowledges that "this was not the way inspiration functioned in the early church," where "inspiration was not seen to be the unique possession of only the documents that came to be part of the New Testament canon." Instead, he argues, "the Spirit was seen as living and active in the entire community of the faithful and therefore inspiring it."[99] My concern is simply whether the Spirit was really thought to inspire "the entire community" or if this is actually a reference to only the privileged heterosexual males of the community.

Opportunities for human input surface, too, in the translation process. In current "cultural wars" over the Bible, there is little attention paid to the fact that English is not the original language of the biblical texts. We forget that the original Hebrew, Greek, and Aramaic had to be translated, and that any translation involves value judgments made by the translators themselves. About 1603, King James of England set out what became the generally accepted conditions for the production of an "authoritative" translation of the Bible in English: "that it should be undertaken by learned scholars from the universities, and that it should be reviewed and approved by the churches, in the form of bishops and their equivalent."[100] Basically, the significance of King James's action is that it ensures the production of biblical meaning by privileged men because they are the ones who exercise leadership in the universities and churches. We should expect, then, to see evidence of their perspectives and attitudes in the King James Version of the Bible, and we do.

As an example, the construction of chapter 1, verse 5 of the Song of Songs is as follows: "I am black [conjunction] beautiful," where the conjunction *waw* can be translated as either "and" or "but."[101] Randall Bailey, an African American biblical scholar, informs us that the Greek translation of the text used "and," but when Jerome subsequently translated the verse into Latin, he could not conceive of someone being "black and beautiful"; therefore, he used the conjunction "but."[102] In the King James Version, Bailey points out, the translators agreed with Jerome and translated the verse as "'dark but comely,' where they could not even admit the possibility of one being 'black.'"[103] Similar differences exist in contemporary English versions of the Bible. The more inclusive ("liberal") New Revised Standard Version (NRSV) reads: "I am black and beautiful," whereas the more exclusive ("conservative") New International Version (NIV) reads: "Dark am I, yet lovely." Obviously, attitudes about color and beauty are communicated in the verse, and these attitudes have more to do with the translators than with God. To complicate matters further, African American churches still favor the King James Version, which intrigues Bailey, "given its status as being the most racist of all English translations," and results in their "adopting another's culture, one which is diametrically opposed to [their] own health and well-being."[104]

Last, but not least, the interpretations of biblical texts are done by human beings. Martin Luther (1483–1546), the founder of the Protestant tradition, was a German Roman Catholic (Augustinian) monk who eventually parted ways with the Roman church. Briefly summarized, "Luther shifted the late medieval focus of attention away from what humans could do to gain favor in God's sight (e.g., by engaging in pious acts of prayer, making pilgrimages, or purchasing indulgences) to what God did in Jesus Christ for humankind."[105] Luther's new understanding stemmed from his reading of the New Testament, especially Romans 1:16–17, with its reference to "the one who is righteous will live by faith," and, as a result, he emphasized salvation (justification) as the result of faith rather than works. In the process, he argued in favor of more literal or plain readings of the Bible (as opposed to the medieval period's more allegorical approaches), and he thought that all authorities, including the (Roman Catholic) church fathers, should be subject to the superior authority of Scripture.[106] Reevaluating church practices accordingly, he found that "the institution of papacy was a human invention, monasticism a fraud, and the sacramental system of the church (though certainly not all sacraments) a medieval accretion."[107]

Luther's method of biblical interpretation put him on a collision course with two religions—Roman Catholicism and Judaism. Luther's attention to the more literal and historical meaning of texts differed from the practices of some in his day and served as the basis for his condemnation of the Roman church. However, his retention of more conventional medieval reading practices allowed him to read the Psalms, for example, as "referring to Jesus both literally and spiritually, as if, indeed Jesus were the literal sense of the *whole* of Scripture."[108] Understandably, then, Luther read Jesus into Old Testament texts and clashed with rabbis who refused to apply a prophetic passage to Jesus.[109] Luther used different tactics to undermine the integrity of these two faith traditions, and what he did informs this discussion about the relationship between human beings and biblical interpretation.

In 1543, Luther wrote "On the Jews and Their Lies," a hateful diatribe that admonishes Christians for "allowing them to live freely in our midst." In the tract, he observes that "we are at fault in not slaying them," and he advises Christians "to set fire to their synagogues or schools."[110] It is chilling how these words took on new meaning much later in Nazi Germany. As William L. Shirer writes in *The Rise and Fall of the Third Reich*:

> [Luther] wanted Germany rid of the Jews and when they were sent away he advised that they be deprived of "all their cash and jewels and silver and gold" and, furthermore, "that their synagogues or schools be set on fire, that their houses be broken up and destroyed . . . and they be put under a roof or stable, like the gypsies . . . in misery and captivity as they incessantly lament and complain to God about us"—advice that was literally followed four centuries later by Hitler, Goering and Himmler.[111]

From Luther's perspective, Jesus Christ is "the literal sense of the *whole* of Scripture," which means that if Jews do not convert and follow Christ, they are simply wrong. In his context, Luther's analysis is problematic but understandable. He wants to emphasize the primacy of Scripture in his fight with the Roman Catholic Church, and one of his assumptions is that a clear, singular, and literal meaning of biblical texts concerning the significance of Jesus exists. The very presence of Jews, then, who have the same texts but a different interpretation, contradicts Luther's basic argument. Are Luther's anti-Jewish polemics understandable in his time and place? Yes, if we acknowledge his need to emphasize Scripture over and against the traditions of the Roman Catholic Church. Are they the expression of eternal, absolute, and unchanging attitudes of the divine? No!

With respect to the Roman Catholic Church, Luther rejected its celibate monasteries as the model Christian life in favor of an ideal heterosexual household. He was able to give that household more value by vilifying Rome, and he did that by labeling it as the alien Other or Outsider (remember, Luther was German) and associating Rome with homosexuality, while assuming that same-sex desire was alien to Germany.[112] There may be some basis, though, for the association that Luther makes between monks and a feminized male (and, therefore, homosexuality). Apparently, "in the Middle Ages, male monks symbolized their renunciation of the world by self-consciously leaving behind their masculine power and adopting a female state of 'lowliness.'"[113] More specifically, in Luther's reading of Genesis 19:4–11 (the siege of Lot's house), "same sex desire marks the anti-society epitomized by Sodom and, for Luther, [is] now incarnate in Rome; thus he delivers a savage condemnation of the Carthusian monks who 'deserve to be hated because they were the first to bring this terrible pollution into Germany . . . from Italy' (LW, 3.252)."[114] In contrast, "the heterosexual society and the heterosexual individual are ordered, disciplined and chaste," as represented by Lot.[115] Taken together, it means that Sodom is the "antisociety," and its status "is marked by its open embrace of same sex desire as normative." Furthermore, the heterosexual household is the Christian model, and "the foundations of the godly society," according to Luther, require condemning homosexuality and keeping same-sex desire suppressed and closeted because, "when these are taken away, society collapses into beastliness, savagery and genocide."[116]

There are some advantages to Luther's focus on the heterosexual household. Luther's shift in emphasis away from the monastic and spiritual world toward "the priesthood of all believers" and the civil society "entailed a major reformation of the previous system . . . with stronger proto-democratic elements that eventually also inclined the West toward a transformation of economic and political life."[117] Luther's challenge went up against more than 1,500 years of tradition. His vilification of the Roman Catholic Church, using homophobia, was a tactic to justify and facilitate that change. Does Luther's reading of Genesis 19 and the use of homophobic rhetoric make sense in his context? Yes, in the sense that he invoked a form of vilification by association to undermine the authority of long-standing traditions. Does it represent the expression of eternal, absolute, and unchanging attitudes of the divine? No!

My last example of the relationship between biblical interpretation and the human context comes from a period closer to our own, and it concerns the fundamentalist movement. According to Margaret Bendroth, "Fundamentalism was born in an era of anxiety over gender roles."[118]

> By the close of the nineteenth century, woman suffragists and social reformers had stretched the traditional boundaries of the feminine sphere to the breaking point. Their "domestic feminism" elevated women as homemakers for the entire nation, responsible for both private and public standards of morality. Middle-class males confronted this challenge to their leadership in the family and public sphere at the same time that the business world was rapidly professionalizing, narrowing the path of individual initiative. Thus, while applauding women's strides toward equality, religious and secular leaders began to worry that the "new woman" was creating an increasingly passive type of manhood. The Protestant churches, already numerically dominated by women, felt the crisis most keenly and responded with urgency.[119]

In the nineteenth century, Bendroth argues, women had taken on significant leadership in missionary and temperance movements, and although they did not necessarily seek ordination, they wanted greater representation within their denominations. They expressed their rights with a nonliteral and more thematic way of reading the Bible, saying that "all the biblical restrictions on feminine leadership were temporary, swept away by the atoning death and resurrection of Christ, when all the world began its final movement toward the perfect consummation."[120] Around that same time, the women's rights activist Elizabeth Cady Stanton brought together a group of feminist scholars, and the two volumes of the *Women's Bible* were published in 1895 and 1898.[121] In this context, Bendroth tells us, "early fundamentalism began to define itself as a theological alternative to evangelical feminism," and it sought a form of Christianity that would be more masculine, in order to bring men back to the church.[122] Some of the following comments were heard at the time from various individuals:

> "The only churches in America that have any considerable number of big hearted brainy men in them ... are those churches that stand ... for biblical doctrines—the great verities of the good Word of God." "It is a mistake to suppose that men like to hear ministers discuss social, economic and political affairs in the pulpit." ... "Men will come only to hear the unvarnished truth, red hot from a courageous heart."[123]

Interestingly, two key doctrines of fundamentalism were helpful in combating evangelical feminism: inerrancy and dispensational premillennialism. The inerrancy doctrine emphasized the literal word of Scripture as well as the divine intent behind it, having determined that female subordination was inherent in the created order.[124] Likewise, dispensational premillennialism contended that men as well as women were "under the curses God instituted after Adam and Eve sinned in the Garden of Eden, waiting for Christ's Second Coming to lift the penalty of sin brought on by the fall; and, in the meantime, dispensationalists argued, attempts to end women's subordination were doomed to failure."[125] The rise of fundamentalism is often explained as a reaction against Darwin's theory of evolution and the development of historical-critical methods in the academy; however, Bendroth's analysis reminds us that issues of masculinity were also at stake. In fact, she mentions that "nearly all of the movement's early leadership was white, male, middle-class, well-educated and Protestant."[126] Once again, does the fundamentalist approach to biblical interpretation make sense in its nineteenth-century context? Yes, if one proceeds from a mind-set committed to male dominance. Does its attitude toward women represent the expression of eternal, absolute, and unchanging attitudes of the divine? No!

Unmasking the Academy

In his recent book, *Sex and the Single Savior*, Dale Martin takes on the academic establishment and its claims of "objectivity" in interpreting biblical texts.[127] He acknowledges that, in his most recent writings, he strives "to undermine a common assumption, common among lay Christians as well as scholars: that the Bible 'speaks' and our job is just to 'listen.'"[128] Such an assumption, he argues, implies "the text of the Bible contains certain, identifiable 'meaning' that it 'communicates' to us, and our task is to be as passive as possible and 'receive' that message without distorting it too much."[129] In contrast, Martin says that his scholarship "has attempted to highlight *the activities of interpretation* by which people 'make meaning' of the biblical texts"; indeed, "texts do not interpret themselves, they must be interpreted by human beings."[130]

Martin identifies three misconceptions scholars have that enable them to perpetuate this common understanding: textual agency, authorial intent, and the value of historical recovery. First, the notion that "the Bible speaks" equates meaning solely with the text, thereby establishing textual agency but denying the human agency that is required for meaning to be derived; "human beings are necessary for meaning to take place, and we can experience no interpretation without human agency."[131] Second, scholars place an undue emphasis on authorial intention and think that the meaning of a text resides in the author's intention. From this perspective, "'meaning' resembles a 'thing' passed from one person to another so if misunderstanding occurs, the 'receiver' should go to the 'source' and check for the 'correct' meaning." As Martin points out, the problem is that we can never retrieve with certainty the author's intention at the time of writing—even if we go back to the author later on—so that "authorial intention is not the answer to the vagaries of interpretation because it is part of interpretation itself."[132] Finally, historical-critical methods are those used in modern biblical studies, and their underlying assumption is that "the primary meaning of the text had to be anchored in its ancient meaning." However, as Martin points out, that would eliminate or at least devalue premodern readings (such as allegorical approaches used during the Middle Ages) and cut us off from earlier church traditions. As a result, he thinks "that any insistence that historical criticism is *necessary* or provides the *ruling or controlling* meaning of the text offends the theological notion of the communion of the saints and is therefore not theologically defensible."[133]

Martin argues that what is involved with these scholarly misconceptions is much more than quibbles over literary theory; at the most fundamental level, it involves an ethical issue:

> I believe that one of the most serious impediments to the ethical use of Scripture, especially with regard to issues of gender and sexuality, has been the myth of textual agency. One regularly comes across a certain tone in debates about Christian ethics, a tone by which one or both parties in the debate seem to say, "Don't blame me! *I'm* not opposed to gay people (or the ordination of women, or name your issue). The *Bible* is. The Bible tells us. . . ." Such people never admit that the Bible doesn't actually talk. They do not acknowledge their own interpretive practices by which they have arrived at what they think the Bible "says." People throughout history, therefore, have committed grave ethical offenses—supporting slavery, oppressing women, fighting unjust wars, killing, torturing, and harming their fellow human beings—under cover of "the Bible says." As long as the text itself is

> thought to provide its own interpretation or to constrain or direct its own meaning, the ethical and political responsibility of interpreters can be masked, denied, or slighted. Immoral interpretations can be—and have been—blamed on the text rather than the interpreter.[134]

Conclusions

Until recently, the leadership circles in both the church and the academy were able to distance themselves from their readings of the Bible by contending that they were merely following divine mandate or scholarly methods. Now, however, there is a sense that the few cannot arrogate to themselves the power to speak for all of humanity—and for God. The particularity of one small segment of humanity—the privileged white, Western, heterosexual male—can no longer masquerade as representing the diversity and fullness of God's creation. Through the tidal wave of publications from "the Other"—those who are different by virtue of race/ethnicity, gender identity, sexual orientation, religion, and hemisphere—God is indeed "troubling the waters." In this context, I am reminded of the words of the Pharisee Gamaliel to the Israelites after the second arrest of the apostles: "So in the present case, I tell you, keep away from these men and let them alone; because if this plan or this undertaking is of human origin, it will fail; but if it is of God, you will not be able to overthrow them—in that case you may even be found fighting against God!" (Acts 5:38–39).

To me, what is eternal, absolute, and unchanging is the divine commitment to justice. I have been forever marked by the words of Martin Luther King Jr.: "The arc of the moral universe is long but it bends towards justice."[135] With an inclusive hermeneutic, the phrase "Sacred Scripture is the word of God" has a meaning much deeper than a simplistic literal one. Instead, it is a root metaphor that functions as "the central and organizing image for the richly complex reality of divine revelation."[136] Under these circumstances, "the Bible is not an archetype, an ideal form that sets an unchanging and timeless pattern, but a prototype that is critically open to the possibility of its own transformation."[137] Because the foundation of an abusive dominant/subordinate paradigm is the privileging of men over women, the starting point of an inclusive critique of a biblical text is to contest any such privileging because it is contrary to God's ongoing work of redemption.[138] From this theological perspective, "whatever diminishes or denies the full humanity of women must be presumed not to reflect the divine or authentic relation to the divine, or to reflect the authentic nature of things, or to be the message or work of an authentic redeemer or a community of redemption."[139]

By hearing the voices of the marginalized, God's work of redemption and reconciliation continues in our midst (2 Cor. 5:16–21). Empowered by the Holy Spirit, those of us who follow in the name of Jesus Christ must work for redemption and reconciliation as well. In fact, the whole meaning of Scripture is rooted in this divine encounter for justice. I readily concede that this is only one way of reading Scripture. But I am convinced that incorporating the realities of the paradoxically marginalized majority is a theological imperative that we must heed.

2

Problematic Biblical Laws

The View from the "Other" Side

For the most part, Christians tend to think that the laws of the Old Testament are irrelevant. The biggest exceptions, of course, would be the Ten Commandments and, to a lesser extent, the laws against homosexuality. The premise of this study, however, is that embedded within these laws are underlying values concerning women, the poor, and non-Israelites that not only are reflected in the biblical narratives but also are captured in subsequent discussions about Old Testament ethics and its requirements for faithful Christian living today. I do not contend that these laws were enforced in ancient Israel as set forth in the Bible; therefore, I am neither using these laws to reconstruct ancient Israelite society nor alleging that any of these groups were actually treated in the ways described in these biblical texts. Similarly, I do not contend that normative Judaism has ever endorsed or currently endorses the kind of marginalization of groups described here. I am well aware that the rabbinic tradition has developed interpretations and rulings that counter some of the problematic aspects of biblical texts identified here.

My interest in developing this analysis is done strictly as a Protestant, with our emphasis on the primacy of Scripture and our resultant tendency toward more literal readings of the Bible. I am also motivated by the need to identify the power of the *mythical norm* in the United States that Audre Lorde describes as "white, male, heterosexual, Christian, and financially secure."[1] Because the leaders who have traditionally interpreted the Bible for the church fit that description, the perspective of that *mythical norm* became synonymous with our faith and has defined what constitutes orthodox (correct) church practices. Such a tendency to posit the economically advantaged (heterosexual) male as the normative experience can be found in the biblical laws themselves. In my book *Women, Ideology, and Violence,* I demonstrated that the laws in the books of Exodus and Deuteronomy construct national and gender identities as they confer relative privileges.[2] Under their provisions, the Israelite (heterosexual) male head of household has the most privileges, and the poor, female, non-Israelite woman has the fewest.[3] My contention here is that the men who fit the *mythical norm* and have the most privileges in their own later historical contexts justify the resulting inequities by arrogating to themselves the same benefits privileged Israelite males have in the biblical texts.

Basically, the privileged position of the economically secure Israelite (heterosexual) male head of household became the privileged position of the economically secure white Christian (heterosexual) male head of household. As a result, there has been no recognition within the faith tradition that those who are "Other," nonwhite, female, homosexual, poor or non-Christian, might have different yet valid experiences of the divine or that they might have different perspectives about the meaning of particular texts. Furthermore, there is little recognition that these groups may be disadvantaged by traditional biblical interpretations simply because they are outside of the *mythical norm*—and not because it is God's will. To the contrary, we could gain a fuller sense of God and who we are to be as the people of God if we would include these experiences and perspectives that are usually excluded.

The following survey of problematic laws concerning women, the poor, and non-Israelites begins with discussions of laws found in the three major law codes—the Book of the Covenant (Exod. 20:23–23:19), the Deuteronomic Law (Deuteronomy 12–26), and the Holiness Code (Lev. 17–26)—and then addresses the Ten Commandments (Exod. 20:2–17).[4]

Women and (Homo)Sexuality

According to Exodus 22:16–18, when a man seduces and lies with a virgin who is not engaged to be married, he must give the bride-price for her and make her his wife. If the father refuses to give his daughter to him, the man must pay to the father an amount equal to the bride-price for virgins. The use of the verb "seduce" here tends to imply that the female consented. However, the female's consent or lack of it is not "a material factor in the case."[5] Indeed, the law assumes that she is incapable of giving consent, and we make the same assumption in contemporary laws on statutory rape with individuals under a certain age. The difference between the contemporary and the ancient treatment of the matter, though, is that in statutory rape, the person's consent is irrelevant because of age, but in this biblical law, the person's consent is irrelevant because she is female.[6]

Under the law, a violation (rape) of a virgin has occurred, and the violation "is not against the woman but against her father."[7] It is the father who receives the monetary compensation. According to Walter Brueggemann, the penalty seems to protect the family's (read father's) honor, and he acknowledges that "the law pays no attention to the violated woman herself."[8] The law implies that the female body should be under the control of a male—whether her father or her husband.[9] The violation, then, was a violation of the father's control. From a female (and liberationist) perspective, the law is problematic because it assumes that females should be under the control of males and that females should not be able to make decisions about their own sexuality. Plus, it minimizes the consequences of the violation, if she had not consented, on the female.

Exodus 22:16–17 provides further that the father may refuse to give his daughter to the man and, if so, the man must pay the bride-price for a virgin. Presumably, the father's refusal to give the man his daughter could come after the daughter has expressed her own preferences. Any opportunity she might have, though, to express her own opinion is taken away in Deuteronomy 22:28–29. In that law, if a man seizes and lies with a virgin who is not engaged and they are caught in the act, the man must pay a specified amount to her father. Furthermore, the law holds that the violator must marry the woman and "because he violated her, he shall not be permitted to divorce her as long as he lives" (Deut. 22:29). Of course, the law is meant to punish the violator and to provide a home for the violated woman, but the final result is that a woman has to marry her rapist. From the female's perspective, she might have preferred to remain within her father's household than to marry the man who raped her—but that is not an option.

In the case of an unmarried virgin who is not engaged, a man who violates her has to pay a fine, and he may have to marry her, as described in Exodus 22:16–17 and Deuteronomy 22:28–29. If she is engaged, however, the man's violation of the woman is a capital offense. Deuteronomy 22:23–27 distinguishes between whether sexual intercourse occurs in the town or in the country:

> If there is a young woman, a virgin already engaged to be married, and a man meets her in the town and lies with her, you shall bring both of

> them to the gate of that town and stone them to death, the young woman because she did not cry for help in the town and the man because he violated his neighbor's wife. So you shall purge the evil from your midst. But if the man meets the engaged woman in the open country, and the man seizes her and lies with her, then only the man who lay with her shall die. You shall do nothing to the young woman; the young woman has not committed an offence punishable by death, because this case is like that of someone who attacks and murders a neighbor. Since he found her in the open country, the engaged woman may have cried for help, but there was no one to rescue her.

The difference in the location matters only in the determination of the woman's culpability. She is deemed guilty if the incident occurred in the town because she is presumed to have consented if she did not cry for help—and, as a female, she is not capable of giving consent. The law, however, overlooks the fact that the male involved might have used force, and that force could have been in the form of a knife or other weapon or in a nonphysical form of force such as a threat or extortion.[10] Clearly, the law does not consider the range of reasons why a woman might not have cried for help. The absence of such considerations has serious implications: "Without an allowance being made for the use of force in these laws, a betrothed female who has intercourse in the city with another man could be executed when her only 'crime' is having been raped."[11]

Notice that the man must die for having intercourse with an engaged woman pursuant to Deuteronomy 22:23–27 whether the incident occurred in the town or the country. The question has to be asked: Why is it that in Deuteronomy 22:28–29, if he has intercourse with a female who is not engaged, he only has to marry her; but in Deuteronomy 22:23–27, with an engaged female, the penalty is death? From the woman's point of view, the injury is the same in both cases; why are the consequences for the violator so different? As Judith Hauptman has surmised, the determinative factor appears to be the injury to the betrothed male; specifically, the rapist has to die because the betrothed male has suffered a loss for which he cannot be compensated, namely, "that he will no longer be the first to have sex with her."[12] Consequently, these laws demonstrate the degree to which the privileged male perspective is upheld and the female perspective is not.

Interestingly, scholars have thought that Deuteronomy "contains some of the most humane regulations in the Old Testament and is especially remarkable for its positive attitude towards women."[13] Such a statement can only be true, as we have seen here, if the male perspective is assumed and the possibility of a different perspective from a female is ignored. In fact, Carolyn Pressler has argued persuasively that the Deuteronomic family laws function primarily to protect the male head of the household's right to control his wife's sexuality and his right to "be certain that his sons were his own."[14] With these protections as the underlying rationale for the Deuteronomic family laws, two laws in that collection are more understandable. First, the law on adultery in Deuteronomy 22:22 states that if a man is caught lying with the wife of another man, both of them shall die. In this way, a man has not committed adultery if he has sexual intercourse with a woman who is neither engaged nor married or, if she is married, if her husband is not a man whom he has to respect, such as another privileged Israelite male. More specifically, he has not committed adultery if he has sexual intercourse with a prostitute, a foreign woman (Deut. 21:10–14), or a female slave (Lev. 19:20–22)—even if these women are betrothed or married. In contrast, under the provisions in Deuteronomy 22:22, a married woman is not to have intercourse with anyone other than her husband. Therefore, adultery limits the extramarital possibilities of wives much more greatly than those of husbands. Moreover, the law on adultery on its face requires that the two are caught in the act, which appears to make it less likely that the man will be apprehended, and it means that the woman could be a rape victim and still suffer the death penalty, if extenuating circumstances are not taken into account. The emphasis in the law of adultery, then, is to highly restrict the sexual activities of married women so that the paternity of the husband's offspring is unquestionable, as Pressler suggests.

Second, in a system that seeks to ensure paternity, marrying a virgin is of crucial importance. Deuteronomy 22:13–21, seemingly reflecting this rationale, indicates that a husband has the right to expect that his wife is a virgin when they marry.[15]

> Suppose a man marries a woman, but after going in to her, he dislikes her and makes up charges against her, slandering her by saying, "I married this woman; but when I lay with her, I did not find evidence of her virginity." The father of the young woman and her mother shall then submit the evidence of the young woman's virginity to the elders of the city at the gate. The father of the young woman shall say to the elders: "I gave my daughter in marriage to this man but he dislikes her; now he has made up charges against her, saying, 'I did not find evidence of your daughter's virginity.' But here is the evidence of my daughter's virginity." Then they shall spread out the cloth before the elders of the town. The elders of that town shall take the man and

> punish him; they shall fine him one hundred shekels of silver (which they shall give to the young woman's father) because he has slandered a virgin of Israel. She shall remain his wife; he shall not be permitted to divorce her as long as he lives.
>
> If, however, this charge is true, that evidence of the young woman's virginity was not found, then they shall bring the young woman out to the entrance of her father's house and the men of her town shall stone her to death, because she committed a disgraceful act in Israel by prostituting herself in her father's house. So you shall purge the evil from your midst.

From the female's perspective, this law is problematic for two reasons. First, the woman is denied protection against a false witness—who in this case is her own husband. Deuteronomy 19:16–21 states that if a malicious witness accuses someone of wrongdoing and it is proved that the person has been falsely accused, then the appropriate authorities are "to do to the false witness just as the false witness had meant to do to the other." In this case, it should have meant that the husband was stoned to death; instead, he only has to pay a fine. Second, if cleared of the charges, the woman has to remain married to this man who has publicly humiliated her.

Generally speaking, then, the laws discussed here value male control over females (gender as male dominance and female subordination) and encourage procreation so that there are descendants, and the paternity of those descendants is clear. The biblical laws on sexuality reflect various aspects of these underlying values. For example, the often-quoted laws against homosexuality are found in Leviticus 18:22 and 20:13:

> You shall not lie with a male as with a woman; it is an abomination. (Lev. 18:22)
>
> If a man lies with a male as with a woman, both of them have committed an abomination; they shall be put to death; their blood is upon them. (Lev. 20:13)

As Danna Fewell and David Gunn convincingly argue, one of the issues in this text (and the ones immediately surrounding it) is the proper use of the male seed, which, presumably, should be procreation.[16] As a result, sex with a menstruating woman is prohibited in Leviticus 18:19 because it was thought to be "a waste of seed, in that the ancients believed that a menstruating woman could not possibly be fertile; it is likely that they thought the seed would simply be washed away by the menstrual flow."[17] Similarly, Leviticus 18:23 prohibits a man or a woman from having sex with an animal (bestiality), based on the understanding that the male seed, whether from a man or an animal, should not be wasted. Likewise, that rationale can explain why there is no prohibition against a woman having sex with another woman here—no male seed is involved.[18] The emphasis on procreation can also explain why there is a law stipulating that no male whose testicles are crushed or whose penis is cut off can be admitted to the assembly of the Lord (Deut. 23:1). In contrast, a later text, Isaiah 56:1–8, announces that eunuchs are able to join the faith community.[19]

Fundamentally, the problem with male-on-male sex acts (referred to for convenience sake as homosexuality) is that it violates the gender paradigm of male dominance and female subordination because men are to be dominant and never subordinate. As articulated by Fewell and Gunn:

> The problem, then, is not so much the man who lies as a man with another man (the inserter—this, of course, is not the only way to envision such sexual relations, as plenty of evidence from the ancient world bears out, but it is, commonly, the patriarchy's stereotypical envisioning). The problem is essentially the man who lies as a woman with another man (the insertee, catamite, *malakos*). The ultimate confusion is for a man, equipped with phallus and the divine seed, to equate himself with a woman, phallus-less and (from the male point of view) seed-less. For patriarchy, that confusion is intolerable, unacceptable, an abomination.[20]

In such a patriarchal hierarchy, sex acts between males *were* condoned if they upheld the male/active and female/passive distinctions: "Thus a relationship between an older man and a youth could be tolerated—as long as the youth was perceived to play the 'woman's' role. Likewise, difference in class could allow an upper class man to take a lower class man as a lover on condition that they affected (at least in public) active and passive roles respectively."[21]

Dale Martin identified the same association between the penetrated man and the subordinate female in the New Testament setting. According to him, *malakos* means "effeminate," but that does not mean only the penetrated man; it refers to "something perceived as 'soft': laziness, degeneracy, decadence, lack of courage, or to sum up all of these vices in one ancient category, the feminine."[22] Therefore, Martin contends that ancient people could use *malakos* as an insult directed against heterosexual men who loved women too much.[23] In this gender ideology of male dominance/female subordination, "women are weak, fearful, vulnerable, tender . . . one might even say that in the ancient male ideology women exist to be penetrated."[24] At the same time, there is a negative association of all things feminine. From this perspective, the problem with the penetrated man is directly related to the prior degrading of the one who is usually penetrated, that is, the woman:

> The ancient condemnation of the penetrated man was possible only because sexist ideology had already inscribed the inferiority of women into heterosexual sex. To be penetrated was to be inferior because women were inferior. . . . People who retain Paul's condemnation of effeminacy as ethical grounding for a condemnation of contemporary gay sex must face the fact that they thereby participate in the hatred of women inherent in the ancient use of the term.[25]

Succinctly phrased, "The ancient condemnation of the penetrated man was possible only because sexist ideology had already inscribed the inferiority of women into heterosexual sex; to be penetrated was to be inferior because women were inferior."[26]

As we know, there is no prohibition against female-to-female sexual activity in the Old Testament, but there is a negative reference to it in the New Testament (Romans 1:24–27). Bernadette Brooten provides a rationale for that negative reference in the Roman world. She mentions that the inhabitants of that world assumed asymmetrical sexual relations as the norm, with one active, superordinate person with a passive subordinate partner, where males could be either active or passive (as when they are boys or slaves), but females were always supposed to be passive.[27] In her analysis of Romans 1:27, then, Brooten finds that ancient authors were suspicious of a woman who had relations with a woman because it is as if she had become like a man—"she was both anomalous and ambiguous by deviating from the norm of a culturally defined femaleness; in other words, her gender was ambiguous."[28] Correspondingly, the problem with male-male intercourse is that it rendered one of the males passive and, therefore, effeminate:

> I suggest that Paul, like Philo and many other Greek-speaking diaspora Jews, considered male-male intercourse a transgression of social roles, which he would understand as dictated by nature. The passive male has allowed himself to play the part of a woman, while the active male has taught his partner effeminacy and participated in his becoming effeminate.[29]

As we saw previously, patriarchal gender constructions dictate that privileged men are to be dominant and never subordinate, and females are to be subordinate and never dominant. We must realize that the biblical laws reviewed here, geared to ensuring male control of a female's body, structure the subordination of women. In other words, they reinforce the notion that women are to be subordinate and never dominant. In the same way, the condemnation of homosexuality reinforces the notion that privileged men are to be dominant and never subordinate. One thing that we can learn from this analysis is that homophobia, the fear and hatred of and discrimination against gays and lesbians, affects more people than just *that* segment of the population. Indeed, homophobia also serves to keep heterosexual men and women locked in their socially defined roles.

The Poor

The prohibitions such as that found in Deuteronomy 24:17–18 against depriving of justice a widow, orphan, or resident alien are well known and associated with notions of a biblical mandate to protect the marginalized. When examined from the perspective of the poor themselves, however, these provisions are not as favorable as they might appear initially. For example, Exodus 21:2–6 limits the indentured servitude of a Hebrew male to six years. He may leave after that time, but if the master has given him a wife and they have children, the wife and children belong to the master, and they will not leave with the man. If the man decides not to leave, he can remain with his family, but he will be his master's slave for life. Obviously, having a limited time for debt servitude is an advantage, but the man's inability to take his wife and children with him (if his wife was given to him by the master) means that it is far more likely that he will remain with the master. From his perspective, a more caring policy would allow him his freedom *and* allow him to keep his family intact. A comparable and more generous provision in Deuteronomy 15:12–18 requires the householder to "provide liberally" to the member of the community when he leaves, and the debt slave may choose to remain there at the end of the six years, but there is no reference to losing his family if he does leave.

The privileged Israelite has advantages in disciplining the household's slaves. A slave owner is liable for striking a male or female slave only if the slave dies immediately (Exod. 21:20). If the slave survives a day or two before dying, "there is no punishment; for the slave is the owner's property" (Exod. 21:21). Whether in that condition temporarily (as a debt slave) or permanently, slaves are human beings and not just "the owner's property." Similarly, if a slave owner destroys the eye or knocks out the tooth of a male or female slave, the slave is able to go free (Exod. 21:26–27). It appears that the purpose of the law about the damaged eye or tooth was to discourage slave owners from disciplining their slaves too harshly. However, a more effective measure from the slave's perspective would be to require the slave owner who injured a slave in this way to provide for that slave in his own household for the rest of the slave's life.

Laws against abusing widows and orphans and allowing the poor to glean from the fields, as a means of providing for them, are found in the major law collections (Exod. 22:22–24; Lev. 19:9–10; and Deut. 24:17–22). These provisions, though, might not have been the most effective way to meet their needs. First, there is no biblical law that allows the widow to inherit her husband's estate; the man's eldest son would inherit it (Deut. 21:15–17). If the man died without a son, the law of levirate marriage requires that his widow marry the man's brother to provide the deceased with an heir (Deut. 25:5–10). Although the widow would get to remain within her husband's household through this marriage, providing for her is not the primary purpose of the law, and if the brother refused to marry her, she and her children would be destitute.[30] From the widow's perspective, the best way to handle the matter is simply to allow her to inherit her husband's estate.

Second, as Harold Bennett rightly contends, the laws on gleaning, among others, would have failed to support the poor adequately.[31] The laws on gleaning, for example, have the marginalized find sustenance from the fruits and vegetables left in the fields; yet, as Bennett notes, it is unlikely that the farmers, knowing that anything left would no longer be theirs, "left huge amounts of vegetables and fruits in the fields and orchards."[32] As a result, Bennett found that the periodic food distribution patterns in these Deuteronomic laws tended to force the poor into debt slavery and prostitution and, in this way, "exacerbated, not rectified, the plight of these types of persons."[33] From the perspective of the poor, a better solution would have been to institute an economic system that treated them more fairly and not just offer amelioration for the hardships caused by an unjust one. As one scholar noted, there is an "absence of laws for the protection of reciprocity, controls on taxes and fines, and protection against oppression and violence."[34]

Nevertheless, Deuteronomy 15: 4–11 exhibits a certain ambivalence about poverty: "On the one hand there is the promise 'there will be no poor among you . . . if you only obey the voice of the Lord your God' and keep his commandments (Deut. 15:4–5), and on the other hand (and implied for most of the time) 'the poor will never cease out of the land' (Deut. 15:11)."[35] Cyril Rodd thinks that this ambivalence results from one biblical tradition that assumes wealth is a reward for goodness, and poverty is a punishment for wickedness, and a different biblical tradition that is a call to treat the poor with compassion.[36] Rodd, however, does not find evidence of a biblical belief that "the presence of the poor in society is somehow 'wrong,' and that society itself must be changed to remove poverty from its midst."[37] To the contrary, though, Leslie Hoppe suggests that Deuteronomy 15: 4–11 reminds us that we can and should end poverty.

> Too often texts like Deut. 15:11, "there will never cease to be some in need on the earth" (see also Matt. 26:11; Mark 14:7; John 12:8), have been read as expressions of fatalism—as though poverty were a part of the natural order of things. When these texts are read against the wider backdrop of the biblical tradition, however, it is not poverty but mutual concern that is to be a normal pattern of the community's life. The Torah makes significant efforts to ensure that justice is done for the poor. The prophets criticize the people of ancient Israel for ignoring their responsibilities to the poor and for making poverty to be a permanent part of ancient Israelite life. "There will never cease to be some in need on the earth" because of people's failure to end poverty. People have created poverty; they ought to be able to end it.[38]

Non-Israelites (Foreigners)

Although the Lord blesses Abram (Abraham) specifically in Genesis 12:1–3, the Lord also says to him "in you all the families of the earth shall be blessed." However, groups that are "Other," because of religious practices, race/ethnicity, or nation of origin, have reason to question any assertion that they have been blessed through Abram (Abraham) and his biblical and spiritual descendants—ancient Israelites and Christians, respectively. In the biblical laws, the prohibition against charging interest on loans applies only to those within the Israelite community; therefore, foreigners can be charged interest (Deut. 25:17–19). Similarly, the limitations on debt servitude protect only Israelites (Exod. 21:2–6 and Deut. 15:1–3); in contrast, those from surrounding nations can be made permanent slaves.

> As for the male and female slaves whom you may have, it is from the nations around you that you may acquire male and female slaves. You may also acquire them from among the aliens residing with you, and from their families that are with you, who have been born in your land; and they may be your property. You may keep them as a possession for your children after you, for them to inherit as property. These you may treat as slaves, but as for your fellow Israelites, no one shall rule over the other with harshness. (Lev. 25:44–46)

Based on these distinctions in the biblical laws, one underlying value is that "Other" groups can be treated differently; another value is that the impact of these differences on the "Other" does not matter. The ban or holy war (*herem*) is the most egregious example of those values at work:

> I will set your borders from the Red Sea to the sea of the Philistines, and from the wilderness to the Euphrates; for I will hand over to you the inhabitants of the land, and you shall drive them out before you. You shall make no covenant with them and their gods. They shall not live in your land, or they will make you sin against me; for if you worship their gods, it will surely be a snare to you. (Exod. 23:31–33)

> When the Lord your God brings you into the land that you are about to enter and occupy, and he clears away many nations before you—the Hittites, the Girgashites, the Amorites, the Canaanites, the Perizzites, the Hivites, and the Jebusites, seven nations mightier and more numerous than you—and when the Lord your God gives them over to you and you defeat them, then you must utterly destroy them. Make no covenant with them and show them no mercy. (Deut. 7:1–2)

> But as for the towns of these peoples that the Lord your God is giving you as an inheritance, you must not let anything that breathes remain alive. You shall annihilate them—the Hittites and the Amorites, the Canaanites and the Perizzites, the Hivites and the Jebusites—just as the Lord your God has commanded, so that they may not teach you to do all the abhorrent things that they do for their gods, and you thus sin against the Lord your God. (Deut. 20:16–18)

From a postcolonial perspective, these texts are deeply problematic. Michael Prior expresses the point well. He thinks they should be seen "in a new light, when one recalls how such texts were used in support of colonialism in several regions and periods, in which the native peoples were the counterparts of the Hittites, the Girgashites, and others.[39] Additionally, Prior recognizes that "on moral grounds, one is forced to question whether the Torah continues to provide divine legitimacy for the occupation of other people's land and the virtual annihilation of the indigenes."[40]

There are, however, factors that distinguish the biblical use of holy war from its use in later imperial and colonial efforts. For example, in Deuteronomy 7:2, there is a specific mention that the nations that are already on the land are mightier and more numerous than the Israelites. These factors concerning the greater strength and number of the indigenous populations, compared with the Israelites, are usually absent in modern colonial endeavors, since colonial powers, unlike the Israelites, have superior military might. Furthermore, I agree with Walter Brueggemann's assessment, based on Norman Gottwald's work, that the entry into Canaan involved a revolutionary cadre of Levites who supported "a peasant uprising against an exploitative [Canaanite] city-state system of economics and politics," and the revolution's goal was to replace that oppressive system with the "Israelite system of covenant."[41]

With this point of departure, "the displacement proposed is not of one ethnic community by another but a hated class of exploiters by those who are too long abused." Thus, as Brueggemann argues, "the destruction to be wrought for the purpose of the revolution, then, is not to kill Canaanites at random but to destroy the 'system,' its practices and symbols, and inevitably its functionaries."[42] Although contemporary colonial efforts may appeal to these texts of holy war to justify their actions, their systems resemble the city-state systems that were rebelled against rather than the Mosaic covenant community to be created by the ancient Israelites. As Brueggemann points out, the conquest did not set up one ethnic community against another. In fact, "the ancient Israelite society . . . was never purely Israelite, for intermixed with free Israelites there were descendants of Canaanite and other Bronze Age town and country folk, landless alien labourers in the countryside, as well as a scattering of foreign craftsmen and traders."[43] More recent colonial efforts, though, tended to position Western nations over nonwhite nations around the world, and thus did set up one racial or ethnic community (white) against the others.

The harshness of these texts about the ban, however, can be mitigated by three factors. First, it is doubtful that such annihilation actually took place because, even though it is described in the book of Joshua, the book of Judges portrays the entry into Canaan in more gradual terms, and there was intermarriage with the Canaanites (Judges 14–16). Second, Susan Niditch, in her work, identified traditions within the Hebrew Bible that are opposed to the atrocities of war (such as Amos 1–2) and "the ideology of expediency," which justifies wars solely undertaken for territorial gain and economic profit.[44] Finally, and most important, Exodus 23:9 enjoins the oppression of a resident alien because "you know the heart of an alien, for you were aliens in the land of Egypt." According to Johanna van Wijk-Bos, this injunction is crucial to the identity of God's covenant community, and she downplays the distinctions usually made among the categories of outsiders in the Israelite community because, for her, they are all outsiders and worthy of inclusion.[45] Specifically, she wants the covenant community "to live a life that emulates God's concern for the creation," and she argues that the faith community cannot do that, with respect to the stranger, unless it remembers its own suffering:

> The stranger will not be excluded from the community insofar as the community is able to name its own experience of exclusion. Rather than pushing this experience away, the call of the text is to

> acknowledge it as a mark of identification, and by implication, the text calls the community to *become* strangers in the land of Egypt. And as the community is called to name and embrace the Egypt experience in the past and present, so it is also exhorted by implication to gain intimate knowledge of the stranger's existence. Without such knowledge, after all, the required posture toward the stranger would not be possible.[46]

Stated alternatively, the faith community cannot consider the suffering of another group unless it remembers its own suffering. It is through their own memory of suffering that the privileged will be able to identify with the stranger, the marginalized, in today's context.

The Ten Commandments (the Decalogue)

The Decalogue "stands at the beginning of all legal material and as such occupies primary place in the divine instruction that comes through the laws of Scripture."[47] Its significance is underscored by the fact that the laws in Exodus 21–23 (the Covenant Code) can be thought of as "a commentary on the Ten Commandments," and the laws in Deuteronomy 12–26 "are structured topically to follow the order of the Ten Commandments."[48] In this way, the Deuteronomic laws "became a veritable commentary on both the Ten Commandments and the entire Exodus Covenant Code as the legal tradition adapted to speak to the changing questions and needs of a developing community."[49] Because the Decalogue expresses foundational values that, to a great extent, are expounded upon in the other law codes, we should not be surprised to see the same exclusions of women, the poor, and non-Israelites there that we saw in the previous law collections.

As Nancy Duff argues, the Decalogue's prologue, "I am the Lord your God who brought you out of the land of Egypt, out of the house of slavery" (Exod. 20:2; Deut 5:6), emphasizes the connection between the commandments and God and our responsibilities given the covenantal relationship with God.[50] Consequently, "the Decalogue is not just a list of rules that moral people everywhere should follow; it is a reminder of who we are as members of the community of faith. . . . The prologue says, in effect, 'I am God; this is what I have done for you. Because of what I have done, you are my people. Remember who you are and act accordingly.'"[51] Because these commandments are addressed to a faith community, they automatically exclude those who are not in that community. In the ancient context, this means that non-Israelites were excluded, and the consequences of that exclusion could be dramatic. For example, the same biblical book, Deuteronomy, that contains the commandment against killing (Deut 5:17) also contains the requirements to annihilate the indigenous peoples of Canaan (Deut. 20:15–18). In our own time period, most English translations of what was the broader (and linguistically more accurate) commandment against killing (Exod. 20:13; Deut. 5:17) have been changed to read more restrictively as "you shall not murder"; this change was done primarily so that churches could support national war efforts.[52] Unfortunately, the common element in these two very different time periods is that killing is condoned, as long as those killed are different from and outside of one's own community.

The commandments in Hebrew use male verb forms, and this has prompted Athalya Brenner to wonder if she, as a female, is addressed and which of the commandments apply to her.[53] Among other things, she notes that "daughters and female slaves at least, are cited as participants in the Sabbath rest together with other inferiors and dependents (Exod. 20:10; Deut. 5:14)" and, because only male envy is discussed in the last commandment (Exod. 20:14; Deut. 5:18), there is no mention of "female envy and its possible outcome."[54] The fact of the matter is that women are not addressed in the commandments, and their absence communicates messages about the appropriate role for women. Brenner concludes with the observation: "Interpretation decrees that women are expected to be silently obedient, bound by the Commandments as implicitly subcategorized addressees," and that if they protest, "feminists are likely to be reprimanded for their uncalled for oversensitivity."[55]

David Clines, however, has identified the Decalogue's intended addressees:

> It is an individual, a male, an Israelite, employed, a house-owner, married, old enough to have working children but young enough to have living parents, living in a "city," wealthy enough to possess an ox and an ass and slaves, important enough to be called to give evidence in a lawsuit. It is a man who is capable of committing, and probably tempted to commit, everything forbidden here—and likely to ignore everything enjoined here, if not commanded to observe it. It is, in short, one might say, a balding Israelite urban male with a mid-life crisis and a weight problem, in danger of losing his faith.[56]

Basically, just as the Decalogue marginalizes non-Israelites and women, it also marginalizes the poor—those who are unable to own animals and slaves. The Decalogue does not address those groups or their realities. Of course, from a liberationist perspective, it is problematic that the Decalogue also condones slavery. As stated earlier, the exclusions found in these laws help us to understand why conservative church traditions exclude the perspectives of these same groups today. After all, it is scriptural, they say—and, on the surface, they are right. At the same time, these exclusions demonstrate more fully why a liberationist approach to biblical interpretation is needed.

Challenging the Principles of Old Testament Ethics

Reading these biblical laws today, it seems obvious that they contain problematic elements that do not provide direct and immutable guidance about how to treat in our own context the poor, females, or anyone who is of a different race, ethnicity, or religious affiliation. Whether we recognize it or not, though, the same underlying attitudes can shape our own attitudes toward comparable groups in the contemporary context. The interpretive impact of these laws does not remain locked away in the ancient Near East because Christian scholars use biblical texts in their discussions of Old Testament ethics that encode the same marginalization. As a result, principles of Old Testament ethics are developed and proposed for contemporary contexts that indirectly condone and perpetuate the silencing of these same marginalized groups.

Examples of the ongoing silencing of marginalized groups can be found in the writings of Waldemar Janzen, Christopher J. H. Wright, and John Barton, as the following critical analysis shows. This discussion is not meant to be an exhaustive treatment of how Christians have used or are to use the Old Testament for ethical guidance. Instead, the writings of these three scholars are analyzed to illustrate how biases encoded in biblical texts can be reinscribed in ethical principles and, if they are not actively challenged, brought into our own context.

Waldemar Janzen: The Familial Paradigm

In his book *Old Testament Ethics: A Paradigmatic Approach*, Waldemar Janzen uses "paradigms," biblical models to discern ethical patterns for the church today.[57] His five major paradigms from the Old Testament are familial, priestly, wisdom, royal, and prophetic. But these are interrelated and not separate understandings of appropriate ways to live out one's faith.[58] To the contrary, the familial paradigm is the "comprehensive ethic," and the other paradigms are subordinate to it and work together to uphold it.[59] For each paradigm, Janzen identifies relevant biblical stories; for the familial paradigm, those stories are Genesis 13, Judges 19, and the book of Ruth. Janzen finds that the significant feature in these three stories is that they model primary commitments to family and the Israelite community. In Genesis 13, Abram divides up the land with his relative, Lot, and Janzen approves of Abram's "nonassertive and peaceful disposition [that] makes him willing to yield the choice to Lot, even at the cost of personal disadvantage."[60] In the book of Ruth, Janzen finds the behavior of Ruth and Boaz to be paradigmatic because they act to preserve "a family that might otherwise have become extinct."[61] In Judges 19, Janzen thinks that the host "holds to the highest ideals of hospitality" because he attempts to protect his guest, the Levite, from the mob and is willing to offer his daughter who "is dearest to him."[62] Janzen does acknowledge initially that "the story is so repulsive and abhorrent to us that we may want to reject it immediately as a text with an ethical message." Yet he goes on to argue that the host and the Levite "outdo each other, as it were, in the greatness of the sacrifice they are ready to offer."[63]

Janzen emphasizes here the importance of commitment and responsibility in communities of faith, but he does so in a way that continues to marginalize the perspectives and circumstances of women, the poor, and non-Israelites. Abram's gift of land to Lot is considered to be exemplary, but the question of how Abram got the land—or, more specifically, from whom Abram took the land (if Joshua and Judges are followed)—is not raised. In their study of Genesis 12–13, Danna Nolan Fewell and David M. Gunn phrase the appropriate question as follows: "The gift of the land collides with the commission to be a blessing to other families of the earth. How can one be a blessing and yet also supplant?"[64] One can only wonder if the "nonassertive and peaceful disposition" for which Janzen admires Abram is exhibited because Abram is giving away land that belonged to another group (the Canaanites) and not to him in any real sense. At any rate, to praise Abram's actions without even acknowledging that the Canaanites were dispossessed ultimately is to imply that the concerns of Canaanites can be safely ignored.

The story of Ruth does allow a family line to continue, as Janzen contends, but it comes at a cost. Ruth 4:17 refers to those who proclaim that "a son has been born to Naomi." As Amy-Jill Levine states, "Ruth, the ostensible heroine of the story, is left an enigma; her continuing relationship to Naomi, her feelings for her son and husband, and her sense of belonging in Israel are never addressed."[65] By implication, Janzen's use of Ruth's story as a paradigmatic model for Old Testament ethics means that the possible concerns and feelings of women are less important than their appropriate behavior. Furthermore, Janzen considers Ruth's story, where a stranger receives an inheritance, to demonstrate that "Israel's familial paradigm goes beyond the general concern for the preservation of life, of a name, of a family line—though those remain prominent—to a special concern for the disadvantaged, the poor, and the needy."[66] The underlying message, though, is that the disadvantaged must leave their own people, culture, and traditions to improve their lot in life. Phrased differently, the book of Ruth implies that being within the Israelite culture is better than being outside of it. Musa Dube, a biblical scholar from Botswana, counters the notion that Ruth, who abandons her culture, is better off than Orpah, who returns to her culture.[67] In Dube's reflections, Orpah is her country's regent queen and a priestess, and she hopes that Ruth will tell her children about her people, the Moabites—"of their origins, of their kindness, of their hospitality and of their struggles for survival."[68]

Overall, Janzen's use of Judges 19 to illustrate hospitality is troubling. First, he does not condemn the violence against the Levite's concubine as strongly as he might. He does mention that the Levite might have offered himself to the mob. However, he writes that to do so "would have exposed him to homosexual practice," which was ranked elsewhere (Lev. 20:13, for example) as "an abomination" that deserved the death penalty.[69] By structuring his argument in this way, Janzen fails to distinguish between "homosexual practice," as he refers to it, and a violent rape, which is what would have occurred if the Levite had gone out to the mob himself. Furthermore, because the Levite's concubine is indeed raped in the story, the clear implication is that the rape of a female is somehow not as egregious an act as the rape of a male would have been.[70]

Second, Janzen mentions only in a footnote, when quoting from Phyllis Trible's *Texts of Terror*, that the hospitality assumed in Judges 19 protected only males.[71] Janzen then writes in a footnote on the next page that "the modern reader wishes with sadness that this ideal of inclusiveness might have embraced the women in the story equally."[72] Nevertheless, for Janzen to use Judges 19 as a paradigmatic model, knowing that women were excluded from the hospitality expressed, simply means that their inclusion is not imperative.

It is worth noting that the three biblical stories used by Janzen for his familial paradigm describe an uncle and his nephew (Genesis 13), a mother-in-law and her daughter-in-law (Ruth), and two male members of the same community (Judges 19)—relationships that are outside of the small nuclear family deemed normative today. Such a difference is not a coincidence. As John Rogerson reports, the family in ancient Israel was "a natural social mechanism that developed initially to meet particular circumstances."[73] In addition, he writes that the biblical family was, among other things, "often polygamous," "the context for rivalry, jealousy, and even fratricide," and "far more advantageous to men than women."[74] He continues: "Anyone who would want to suggest that the Old Testament family as just described should in some sense be a model for the family today could only do so by means of a highly selective and superficial use of the text."[75] Rather than assuming that biblical models apply today, Rogerson calls for new questions to be asked about the effect of family breakups on children, the financial strains that require both parents to work in order to pay the mortgage, and ways to support mothers who also want to have careers, to name a few. He summarizes:

> If the Old Testament says anything to us today, it is that we need to devise theologically driven structures of grace appropriate to our situation that will sustain those aspects of family life which, from a Christian perspective, we deem to be most valuable, and which may be most under threat from the state and powerful interests. This is not something that biblical scholars or theologians can do, without the expertise of lawyers or sociologists.[76]

To answer more justly the questions that our contemporary context raises about responsibilities and commitments in the Christian life, we need to listen to the marginalized voices that have all too often been ignored. In his article "Marriage and Family as Christian Concerns," Stephen Barton proposes that we listen to those whom "we might call the 'outsiders': single people, sexual minorities, the poor, the [physically and sexually] abused, children, and the elderly." For him, the importance of listening to the "outsiders" has been brought to our attention by liberation theology, which is based on "the biblical story where God 'hears' the cry of the slaves in Egypt, and where God-in-Christ responds to the cries for help of the marginalized people of his day." Barton refers to this kind of listening as "an act of love" that calls for a type of attention to these matters that has the potential to transform all relationships, including those within families.[77]

Christopher J. H. Wright: What about the Canaanites?

In his book *Old Testament Ethics for the People of God*, a revised version of *Living as the People of God*, Christopher J. H. Wright covers a range of themes and their implications for contemporary society, including ecology, politics, economics, and the legal system. The preface to that earlier book mentions his understanding that "the Old Testament is absorbed with what it means to be the living people of the living God" and his hope that his insights will be used by Christians who work in these and related fields as "a more coherent and effective application of biblical theology and ethics to the particulars of their own environment."[78] Commenting on the addition of an appendix to the 2004 version of his book entitled "What about the Canaanites?" Wright admits in the new preface that he did so "simply because I get asked that question so often. Invariably, it seems, hearing or reading the phrase, 'Old Testament ethics' arouses in people's minds what they regard precisely as the *unethical* dimensions of these texts. This book, however, was never intended as a book about the ethical *problems* of the Old Testament (as we perceive them)."[79]

Wright argues in his appendix that there is no contradiction between Israel's election as a "blessing to the nations" and "God's use of them [Israel] to bring such suffering on the Canaanites." As he explains it, God's eschatological purpose is to bless the nations, but "God remains the moral judge of all human action, and it is an equally essential part of the biblical testimony that God acts within history in judgment upon the wicked." In other words, Wright views Israel's actions in Joshua to be an instance of God's use of human agents as "the vehicle of his moral judgment."[80]

He finds further support for his position in texts that attest to the "wickedness of Canaanite society in moral and social terms" (citing specifically Lev. 18:24–25; 20:22–24; Deut. 9:5; 12:29–31) and the fact that "the same YHWH who acted in moral judgment on Israel's enemies would act in precisely the same way on Israel itself."

> So the consistent biblical affirmation that the conquest constituted an act of God's punishment on a wicked society, using Israel as the human agent, must be taken seriously (by those who wish to take the Bible's own testimony seriously) and not be dismissed as self-serving disinfectant for the poison of Israel's own aggression.[81]

By including a discussion about the Canaanites, Wright has not ignored their treatment altogether, but he has clearly made that treatment a marginal issue by addressing it in an appendix, away from the rest of his analysis. But the harsh treatment of the Canaanites and other indigenous groups is not found just in the book of Judges; it is also mandated by laws such as Deuteronomy 20:17–18 that require their annihilation. Most important, Wright has not considered the possible reactions or perspectives of the Canaanites, undoubtedly none of whom would want to perish under such conditions. Wright can bracket out the ethical questions raised by the Canaanites because he is not one of those against whom the conquest narrative has been invoked.

Robert Allen Warrior, on the other hand, is a Native American who identifies with the Canaanites in the text. In an influential essay, he points out that as the Exodus story is usually read, indigenous populations are asked to believe in a "liberationist picture of Yahweh" who has become "Yahweh the conqueror."[82] Just the same, Wright considers the story of Rahab, "set in the midst of the conquest narrative," to demonstrate "the power of 'repentance' and faith and God's willingness to spare his enemies when they choose to identify with God's people."[83] For Warrior, the emphasis on the liberative message of the Exodus has meant that, even if the annihilation actually did not take place, the indigenous people who followed this new god were betrayed. In his words, "They [the Canaanites] were assimilated into another people's identity and the history of their ancestors came to be regarded as suspect and a danger to the safety of Israel."[84]

Obviously, Wright fails to consider the ways in which the Exodus story has been used by European Christians to separate indigenous (nonprivileged) populations from both their cultures and their lands.[85] As Warrior suggests, "We need to be more aware of the way ideas such as those in the Conquest narratives have made their way into Americans' consciousness and ideology." He specifically recalls how Puritan preachers would refer to "Native Americans as Amalekites and Canaanites—in other words, people who, if they would not be converted, were worthy of annihilation."[86] Warrior's words remind us that any notion that God can order the annihilation of a population creates an ethical slippery slope. It becomes far too easy for subsequent groups with adequate force to say, "God has annihilated populations as in Joshua and, since God is on our side, we are acting on God's behalf, which means we can do the same thing in our own time and place."

Wright insists that the annihilation of the Canaanites was prompted by God's interests alone (divine punishment) and not those of the Israelites (land acquisition). However, other scholars who also take the Bible seriously have identified the role of human interest or ideology in the biblical texts. For example, Walter Brueggemann describes the biblical text in general terms as "an act of imaginative remembering" that has been shaped by "real people who live real lives in socioeconomic circumstances where they worried about, yearned for, and protected social advantage and property."[87] Consequently, biblical traditions have been influenced by human interests, and those interests have involved gender, race, class, and ethnic distinctions.

More specifically, Israelite interests are identifiable in the biblical depictions of the Canaanites as sexually deviant. Wright notes that the Canaanites are deemed wicked and worthy of punishment due to their "sexual promiscuity and perversion particularly associated with fertility cults."[88] Yet Robert Oden has written that such accusations do not mean that the Canaanites behaved in such a manner. Instead, he submits that such depictions may have had a role in "defining Israel and Israelite religion as something distinctive."[89] Similarly, Randall Bailey, an African American biblical scholar, points out that to label non-Israelites as sexually deviant is to dehumanize them, and "once this is done, other acts of Israelite oppression or devaluation of these people are readily sanctioned, condoned, and accepted by the reader, both ancient and modern."[90] Furthermore, Bailey argues that the same sexualization of African Americans through negative stereotypes has been used to justify racist oppression in the United States.[91] It would seem that ignoring the human interest or ideology in biblical texts, as Wright does, makes it more likely that the same dehumanizing dynamic can be used to marginalize another group in a different historical period.

Rather than accepting marginalization, Warrior has two suggestions at the end of his essay that are worth noting in the context of this discussion. First, Warrior thinks that "the Canaanites should be at the center of Christian theological reflection and political action" because of the violence and injustice their portrayal has condoned and engendered.[92] Accordingly, the treatment of the Canaanites should not be covered in an appendix to a lengthy treatise. The characterizations of the Canaanites raise fundamental issues about the construction of a national identity and intergroup relationships that are as vital today as they were in ancient Israel, if not more so, and they need to be engaged. Second, Warrior suggests that Christians, whether Native American or not, must learn to participate in a struggle for justice "without making their story the whole story."[93] In other words, Christians need to hear other voices and consider the existence of and need for their different realities.

John Barton: The Basis of Old Testament Ethics

Barton has identified three basic models for ethics in the Old Testament: obedience to God's declared will, natural law, and the imitation of God. Each of these models, however, is problematic when considered from the perspective of women, the poor, and non-Israelites, and the biblical laws that affect them. Obedience to God's declared will, according to Barton, reflects the assumption held by "ordinary Israelites as well as those who wrote the biblical books that 'the good' [is] that way of life which God enjoined."[94] Although Barton acknowledges that such obedience is not meant to be blind, difficulties remain. If biblical laws concerning these marginalized groups are considered to express the divine will, then questions about their treatment are discouraged and their marginalization remains unchallenged. For example, there are laws requiring a raped woman to marry her rapist (Deut. 22:28–29), and, as mentioned earlier, a bride's family has to show proof of her virginity if demanded by the groom (Deut. 22:13–21). Challenging such laws in the contemporary context becomes more difficult if they are thought to express the divine will. A more liberative reading becomes possible when the human interest underlying the law is pinpointed, that is, the male interest in ensuring the legitimate paternity of descendants.[95]

Divine guidance is discernible in other parts of the canon, too, but Bruce Birch cautions, "Although it is through Israel that God's word and will are mediated, Israel is not the perfect embodiment of the living out of that divine moral vision." Birch submits that "Israel's unexamined participation in widespread social practices" such as the subordination of women and slavery and "the stories of Israel's sin such as its excesses of nationalism" indicate that "Israel's story is not intended to model normative moral behavior in all of its particulars." Therefore, obedience to the divine will must involve a discernment process that distinguishes between divine concern and human interest. As stated by Birch and referred to in the previous chapter, "Any adequate approach to the Old Testament as moral resource must seek not only to *retrieve* moral perspectives that inform our ethics but in some instances to *reclaim* the biblical text from elements that distort or limit its moral witness."[96]

Another basis for Old Testament ethics, according to Barton, is natural law, which he defines as the principles that exist in the biblical text itself. Consequently, Barton's use of the term is distinguishable from both Western natural law traditions and "positive law" as found in contemporary law codes.[97] Yet Barton considers natural law and positive law in the Bible to be "two ways by which ethics flows from God: they are not to be opposed as respectively human and divine."[98] Barton sees natural law in two ways: (1) the ethical principles that are inherent to all humankind as alluded to in the oracles against the nations in Amos 1–2, and (2) the ethical concepts that are built into the nature of things, the structure of the world, as evidenced by Isaiah's distress at the state of affairs in Isaiah 3.[99]

Nevertheless, Barton's concept of natural law would not be an adequate basis on which to radically change the circumstances of the nonprivileged today. For example, he thinks of the Decalogue as "natural law in practice."[100] However, the Decalogue condones the subordination of women as well as slavery, and its protections apply only to those within the covenant community, not outsiders. Likewise, Barton finds a commitment to justice ("poetic justice") in the prophets, as in Isaiah 5:8–9, that promises judgment against those who have exploited the poor.[101] While it is true that just reducing oppression is beneficial to those who suffer, it would not result in the end of oppression. Cyril Rodd has concluded that "what is not found [in the Old Testament] is a belief that the presence of the poor in society is somehow 'wrong,' and that society itself must be changed to remove poverty from its midst."[102] Today, when capitalism has contributed to greater disparities between the rich and the poor around the globe, very fundamental and systemic changes are needed.

Barton's third basis for Old Testament ethics is the imitation of God. For Israelites, it means "to take God's character as the pattern of their character and

God's deeds as the model for theirs."[103] This basis is derived from laws such as Deuteronomy 10:17–19 ("The LORD your God is God of gods and Lord of lords . . . who is not partial and takes no bribe . . . and loves the strangers, providing them with food and clothing. You shall also love the stranger") and Leviticus 19:2 ("You shall be holy, for I the LORD your God am holy").[104] Barton suggests that the moral life here "is envisaged as a cooperative venture between God and humanity. Its commonest image is that of a path, leading to the place where it will converge with the highway trodden by God."[105]

Rodd thinks that such a basis for Old Testament ethics is questionable. He argues that "if the idea of actively *imitating* God and not just living a life which is *similar* in some respects to that of God underlies so much of the Old Testament," it would have been found more often and not just in Deuteronomy 10:17–19 and Leviticus 19:2.[106] Furthermore, Rodd contends that "the divine life and the human life run parallel," and the moral actions required of each may differ. Therefore, Rodd argues that although Israel and God are to be holy, such divine holiness and human holiness may call for different kinds of moral actions.[107] Following Rodd's logic, then, the convergence of divine and human holiness proposed by Barton is not inevitable. Rodd ends his critique of the imitation of God concept by admonishing those who "read into the Old Testament modern ideas and virtues that are attractive to us," and by underscoring the need to recognize the distance between the world of the Old Testament and our own: "It is a foreign country on which we gaze."[108] Recognizing the historical and cultural differences between the biblical world and our own, as Rodd suggests, might make it easier to determine which norms concerning the treatment of women, the poor, and others are applicable today and which are not. However, Barton's articulation of the basis of Old Testament ethics continues the marginalization of females, the poor, and those who are presumably ethnic outsiders. Moreover, the resultant silencing of those voices is not contested, and so appears to be an ethical occurrence. The lack of attention paid to the perspectives of these groups in the biblical texts and the ethical principles as articulated by Jantzen, Wright, and Barton must surely be related to the lack of attention most Christians pay to the perspectives of these same groups today.

The Bible, Ethics, and the Margins

In general, traditional biblical interpretation and ethical constructions ignore the realities of the marginalized; in contrast, a liberationist approach uses the realities of the marginalized as its point of departure. As Miguel De La Torre rightly concludes, such a radically different approach to ethics is needed because "the dominant culture's ethics has historically been and, some would argue, continues to be, a moral theorizing geared to protect the self-interest of those who are privileged."[109] The theological premise of a liberationist approach is that, given "the God of Exodus who can hear the cries for freedom from the marginalized and enters history to lead them toward liberation, any ethics arising from that faith that wishes to remain faithful to that religious tradition must remain rooted in the praxis of liberation."[110]

> The church of Jesus Christ is called to identify and stand in solidarity with the oppressed. The act of solidarity becomes the litmus test of biblical fidelity and the paradigm used to analyze and judge how social structures contribute to or efface the exploitation of the marginalized. To be apart from the marginalized community of faith is to exile oneself from the possibility of hearing and discerning the gospel message of salvation—a salvation from the ideologies that mask power and privilege and the social structures responsible for their maintenance.[111]

Engaging biblical texts and discerning ethical principles are markedly different enterprises when the perspectives of the marginalized groups are taken into account, that is, when they are dealt with as human subjects rather than subordinate objects. It means that conventional interpretations of biblical laws will be challenged, and a fuller sense develops of what the community of faith can be for all its members. One example will have to suffice, and it is from the Ten Commandments. The Eighth Commandment, the commandment against stealing, is usually interpreted from the perspective of the privileged. As a result, it is used primarily to condemn the stealing of property, and so it tends to protect the property of the "haves" from stealing by the "have-nots."[112] Nevertheless, Walter Harrelson suggests that the commandment has a different meaning if thought of from additional perspectives:

> When workers fail to render a day's work for a day's pay, they steal from their employers. When employers fail to provide fair payment and fair benefits for workers, they steal from their employees. When teachers fail to provide students with their best instruction, they steal from those students. When lobbyists unduly influence legislators or others to support damaging policies, they and their employees steal from the public. "You shall not steal" is a commandment that applies over the entire sweep of a society's social, economic, and cultural activities.[113]

Likewise, Harrelson notes, unfair and disproportionate use of the earth's goods is a form of stealing because it robs of resources not only the current generation but also generations to come. With this more comprehensive analysis, stealing can be defined as "any activity that damages or destroys a person's or a community's opportunity for a tolerable life in community—consisting at least of adequate food, clothing, shelter, work, and hope for the future."[114]

Essentially, any reassessment of biblical laws is part of the ongoing work of creation. As Terence Fretheim suggests, "The laws that God gives Israel are understood basically in terms of creation and vocation." His argument is that the law is fundamentally creational because it is "in the service of life and well-being," and it is vocational because "God gives the law not only for the sake of the life of those who receive it but also for the sake of the life of the neighbor, indeed all of creation, whom they are called to serve."[115] On this basis, Fretheim appropriately sees the revision of where the wife is mentioned in the commandment against coveting [Exod. 20:17 (she is within the list of household property) and Deut. 5:21 (she is listed separately from the household property], for example, as a sign that an earlier tradition was reshaped for a different setting.

Fretheim finds it remarkable that these different traditions remain in the same Bible and were not "smoothed over." For him, the presence of different traditions means that there is "an ongoing witness to the changing character of life and the changing character of the will of God as it relates to that life," so that "*development in the law* is just as canonical as individual laws or the various collections of law."[116] Furthermore, "for God's will to be linked to life in such a central way makes the law an even more gracious gift than it would be if understood as immutable."[117]

In this context, Fretheim notes that the New Testament community, like the Old Testament one, "doesn't simply accept every Old Testament law as binding law; it works through the laws in a variety of ways in view of the new situations in which it finds itself."[118] Using the ambiguous traditions regarding clean and unclean food as his example (Mark 7:1–23 and Acts 10:1–16), he finds that these laws continue to have paradigmatic value as Christian communities today, just like ancient ones, must ask questions about particular laws and their ongoing relevance in changed circumstances.[119] Fretheim's discussion of inner-biblical development of the law creates exciting possibilities for a biblically based inclusive biblical hermeneutic and its ability to affirm, reinterpret, or reject biblical laws, as current conditions and consequences warrant. As he expresses it, "interpreters should not make a blanket statement about all biblical laws, as if they were equally applicable or obsolete; we are called to study each and every law seeking to discern whether it continues to serve the life and health of the community, indeed the larger created order, and see what might come of that conversation."[120] The inclusive biblical approach advocated here is consistent with Fretheim's call for creative conversation in contemporary faith communities as they determine the applicability of biblical laws today. It insists, though, that the voices of women, the poor, and the ethnically or religiously "Other" also be part of that conversation.

3

Ruth and Esther as Models for the Formation of God's People

Engaging Liberationist Critiques

It is safe to say that the biblical narratives of Ruth and Esther are known in most, if not all, Christian faith communities. The stories about these two female characters are presented early, in children's Sunday school classes, and they are presented regularly in sermons and Christian education classes for adults. The books of the Bible that bear their names are readily recognized as part of the Christian canon and, as such, offer guidance for our faith and serve as "a measuring stick" to evaluate our lives in accordance with that faith.[1] We know Ruth and Esther to be exemplary models of loyalty, faithfulness, and commitment to the people of God, and we are told to act likewise.

However, we tend not to know (or, if we know, we tend not to consider) the critiques of that dominant portrayal of Ruth and Esther offered by feminist/womanist, queer, and postcolonial readings, referred to here collectively as "liberationist critiques." The goals of this chapter are to engage these critiques by presenting the challenges they pose to conventional readings of these texts and, after discussing these critiques, to identify themes yet within these texts that avoid the problematic implications. Finally, an interpretive approach will be proposed that allows Ruth and Esther to be read as models of Christian formation that are inclusive and mutually enriching.

In general, the books of Ruth and Esther have much in common. Not only are they both found in the Writings of the Hebrew Bible, they are in the *megillot*, or five scrolls, and, as such, they are each associated with a specific Jewish festival: Ruth (Pentecost) and Esther (Purim).[2]

More specifically, though, the female character after whom each book is named acts within a foreign environment. Ruth is a Moabite in Judah, and Esther is a Jewish woman in Persia. Their respective narrative contexts express a concern with the formation of Jewish identity in the Second Temple period (538 BCE to 70 CE).[3] The underlying questions are the following: Should we include foreigners in our Jewish community (Ruth)? And, correspondingly, when we are in the midst of foreigners, how can we maintain our Jewish identity (Esther)? Even though these questions about community identity and its preservation were posed in another time and place, they remain of critical importance for people of faith today—both Jewish and Christian. The easy answers to these questions would be to exclude all who are different or simply assimilate by adopting the dominant religious and cultural identity, but the books of Ruth and Esther resist such easy answers. Nevertheless, such answers have been given to or have been adopted by certain marginalized groups. It is therefore as a form of resistance that liberationist readings have developed and their critiques are considered in the following sections of this chapter.

Ruth: A Woman, a Daughter-in-Law, and a Moabite

Feminist/Womanist Critiques: Empowering the Marginalized

The story of Ruth can be a positive one for women. For example, the black South African biblical scholar Madipoane Masenya reads the book in the context of postapartheid South Africa, with its legacy of white superiority that severely damaged African self-identity.[4] In that context, she argues, the story of Ruth the Moabite is one that reminds "all of us, particularly the powerful, that God is not partial to any person." Therefore, Masenya continues, God does not define us on the basis of race or gender but on the basis of our availability "as agents of God's transforming *hesed* in the lives of our neighbors," where the Hebrew word *hesed* means "kindness, lovingkindness, faithfulness, or loyalty."[5] Similarly, for the Taiwanese biblical scholar Julie Chu, Ruth is the story of a woman whom a man, Boaz, describes as "worthy"; hence, she is an equal partner to some extent (3:11) who is valued "more than seven sons" (4:15).[6] Furthermore, Chu finds in Ruth a demonstration that a mother and her daughter-in-law can cooperate rather than compete, as is sometimes the case in her cultural context.[7] For women of color, who are in contexts where issues of race as well as gender are constantly before them, Ruth's story is one of "a subversive character in that she subverts gender and ethnic boundaries in her actions."[8] In her South African Indian womanist reading of Ruth, Sarojini Nadar articulates the power of Ruth's story in the following way: "At the beginning, Ruth is portrayed as oppressed in every sphere. She is a woman, a foreigner, a widow, and childless. By the end, we see that Ruth, through dexterity and intelligent action, has managed to cast aside all oppressive roles assigned to her."[9]

In contrast, some feminist scholars in the United States find certain aspects of the Ruth narrative to be deeply problematic. Summarizing the work of biblical scholars Katherine Sakenfeld, Amy-Jill Levine, and others, the theologian Kwok Pui Lan writes that it "does not challenge patriarchal and heterosexual familial structures."[10] More specifically, "a widow can only find economic security through remarriage; marrying a man with some means (no matter the age difference) guarantees financial gains; giving birth to a son is the greatest responsibility of women; a male child is more valuable than a female child; and the authority of the mother-in-law is over the daughter-in-law."[11]

Similarly, Masenya, who otherwise sees Ruth as a positive text for women, acknowledges that the suggestion of a sexual encounter between Ruth and Boaz on the threshing floor (3:6–15) implies that in a patriarchal society (both Israelite and African) "women would even risk to avail their bodies for male abuse as a coping strategy."[12] She notes, furthermore, that "in a world where women are not expected to have control over their bodies, it is commonplace to find women availing their bodies, whether willingly or not, as a coping mechanism to survive through marriage."[13] Likewise, Anna May Say Pa, in her Asian (Burmese) woman's reading of Ruth 3:1–5, sees the text as reinforcing cultural notions of submission, self-sacrifice, and obedience that often work to the detriment of Asian women.[14]

Just the same, Kwok acknowledges that "feminist scholars want to retrieve liberating moments in the story, since it is rare to find women with such major roles in a book in the Bible."[15] As Masenya identified, one of those "liberating moments" is that, in spite of the constraints of patriarchal hierarchies and ethnic boundaries, Ruth is not defeated by her circumstances but takes action to change her dire situation and, as such, is a model for impoverished and marginalized women in southern Africa—and elsewhere.[16]

Queer Critiques: Challenging the Exclusive Focus on Males

Another of the "liberating moments" offered in the book of Ruth is that, contrary to earlier notions of Ruth as a woman committed to her deceased husband, she can be seen as "a woman-identified woman who is forced into the patriarchal institution of levirate marriage in order to survive."[17] From this perspective, other elements of "a woman-identified" world are evident. Naomi tells her daughters-in-law to return to "your mother's house," rather than the usual reference to the father's house (1:8), and both Naomi and Boaz recommend that Ruth stay among the women in the fields (2:8, 22–23), indicating that "it is in the company of women that Ruth, like Naomi, will find safety."[18] Finally, when Ruth's son is born, the women of the neighborhood name him, and he is referred to as Naomi's son rather than that of her deceased husband or sons (4:17).

The clearest statement by Ruth as "a woman-identified woman," of course, is found in the first chapter (Ruth 1:16–17):

> "Do not press me to leave you
> or to turn back from following you!
> Where you go, I will go;
> where you lodge, I will lodge;
> your people shall be my people,
> and your God my God.
> Where you die, I will die—
> there will I be buried.
> May the Lord do thus and so to me,
> and more as well,
> if even death parts me from you!"

As Rebecca Alpert writes in her lesbian (or queer) reading of the text, if the speakers here were of opposite sexes, such a statement would certainly be read as "a poetic statement of (sexual) love," and its affirmation and commitment of and to a woman results in its widespread use in lesbian ceremonies—both Jewish and Christian.[19] Alpert rightly contends that "without romantic love and sexuality, the story of Ruth and Naomi loses much of its power as a model for Jewish lesbian relationships," and adding such elements is a form of midrash, "reading between the lines," that is supported by "literary, historical, and logical possibilities."[20] For example, a literary possibility is based on the statement in 1:12 that Ruth "clung" to Naomi because the Hebrew verb there (*dabaq*) is the same as used in Genesis 2:24 to describe the model heterosexual relationship: "Therefore a man leaves his father and his mother and clings to his wife, and they become one flesh."[21]

Alternatively, the story of Ruth and Naomi portrays a nonsexual affirmation of women as friends, in other words, female bonding, that develops across various differences. As expressed by womanist biblical scholar Renita Weems, "Ruth and Naomi's legacy is that of a seasoned friendship between two women that survives the test of time despite the odds against women as individuals, as friends, as women living without men."[22] Weems then suggests that, from this narrative, we should "take seriously the quality of our relationships with the women and men in our lives" and "refuse to be forced to choose between two good relationships—a romantic partnership with a man and a sustaining friendship with a woman."[23]

Postcolonial Critiques: Struggling against the Colonial Empire

Ruth is a Moabite, a tribe descended from an incestuous relationship between Lot and his daughters (Gen. 19:30–38) and barred from membership in the ancient Israelite community by law (Deut. 23:3–6). In the narrative, Ruth ignores the possibility of exclusion and goes to Judah with Naomi, but in so doing, she loses her land, her people, and her own gods. In other words, the price of inclusion is relinquishing who she is and all that she has known. Some scholars from groups that have experienced forms of Western colonialism notice the striking similarity between their stories and that of Ruth. Indeed, their encounter with a colonial or the global empire has meant the loss of land and of indigenous traditions, and specific comparisons can be made to the African American and Native American historical contexts.

First, as African American biblical scholar Randall Bailey has written, the same association of deviant sexuality with the Moabites and Ammonites has been made with African Americans to justify our social oppression and our devaluation as a people.[24] In the very same way, Andrea Smith (Cherokee) notes that the early colonizers in this country marked Native Americans as a sexually perverse group to justify their actions.[25] Moreover, the pattern is to associate deviant practices particularly with the women in the targeted community, whether it is "the wanton Jezebel" of the black community or "the exotic hooker Suzie Wong"[26] of the Asian community, to give just two examples. From this perspective, Ruth the Moabite's behavior with Boaz on the threshing floor (chapter 3) illustrates such associations of "foreign" women with deviant sexuality. Consequently, Ruth's brazen actions may only be acceptable in the narrative because she is a foreigner. In that case, Levine argues, "It is the reader's task to determine whether the book affirms Ruth or ultimately erases her, whether she serves as a moral exemplar or as a warning against sexually forward Gentile women."[27]

Second, Ruth's apparent assimilation into the Israelite community marks her erasure as a Moabite, and comparable cultural erasure was attempted with Native Americans. By the end of chapter 4 in the biblical narrative, Ruth's voice is not heard at all, and the emphasis shifts to the genealogy of the Davidic line. Ruth has been absorbed into the community, even if not fully accepted as a member. By all appearances, the same strategy of assimilation helped colonizing powers conquer indigenous populations in the Americas. As Laura Donaldson points out, Thomas Jefferson's solution to "the Indian problem" was intermingling between whites and certain Indian groups, and severe disruption of cultural patterns, land loss, and the elimination of leadership roles for Native women resulted.[28] In this context, postcolonial readings of Ruth have been proposed that seek to counter the cultural erasure that comes about from assimilation. Correspondingly, Orpah, the other Moabite daughter-in-law in the narrative, the one who does return to her mother's house, as Naomi suggests (1:6–14), becomes more important as a model for colonized populations. Because Orpah, unlike Ruth, symbolizes the preservation of indigenous cultures, Donaldson feels that, for Native women, Orpah becomes "the story's central character." [29] Accordingly, Donaldson writes that "to Cherokee women . . . Orpah connotes hope rather than perversity, because she is the one who does not reject her traditions or her sacred ancestors. Like Cherokee women have done for hundreds if not thousands of years, Orpah chooses the house of her clan and spiritual mother over the desire for another culture."[30]

From this perspective, one postcolonial reading of the book of Ruth is to emphasize Orpah as a biblical character. Another postcolonial reading, done by Musa Dube, is to imagine that Ruth never forgot her heritage and that, after returning home, Orpah became the regent queen and a priestess.[31] Then, according to Dube, in the last of a series of "unpublished letters from Orpah to Ruth," Orpah asks that Ruth instill in her children a respect for her native people (and theirs), the Moabites. In this imagined correspondence, Orpah writes to Ruth that she should tell her children the stories of the Moabites: "of their origins, of their kindness, of their hospitality, and of their struggles for survival."[32] In other words, the harmful effects of cultural absorption can be reduced if those in the midst of a colonial power remember who they are and inform those in power of the humanity and dignity of their people. The positive but usually limited view of Ruth's acceptance as an individual must be expanded to mean that a deeper understanding and respect results for her group—and other traditionally excluded and despised groups.

Dube, in a more recent article, sees in Ruth and Naomi's relationship the same unequal relationship that exists between nations in today's international setting.[33] Specifically, Dube determines that the relationship between Ruth and Naomi is an unequal one, since Ruth pledges herself to Naomi, but Naomi does not reciprocate. Consequently, "Ruth's pledge to Naomi has the tones of a slave-to-master relationship rather than an expression of mutual love between women or two friends," and this human relationship "connotes the relationship between Judah and Moab."[34] In the narrative, she argues, Moab, the subordinate nation, is associated with death (most notably, Elimelech and both sons die there), but the resources of Moab (Ruth's fertility) can be used for the benefit of Judah, the dominant one. Consequently, for Dube, Ruth's story is "unusable as a model of liberating interdependence between nations," but creating and maintaining mutually beneficial relationships is "indispensable" to healing our world today.[35]

The preceding discussion shows that interpretations of Ruth vary widely, even within liberationist circles. Such lack of uniformity, of course, is related to the variety of social contexts in which the text is interpreted. At the same time, though, some of the diversity is due to the text itself. In Carolyn Pressler's opinion, the range of readings is attributable, to some degree, to the storyteller and the artful way in which various themes are woven into the book: "Ruth is about economic survival *and* about loyalty *and* about accepting foreigners *and* about the loyalty of one woman to another." Pressler is aware that "the storyteller has put a number of ideas in conversation with one another"; therefore, "the conversation continues through centuries of interpretation."[36] Clearly those conversations continue in our own day and time. As we will see in the next section, such a range of interpretations also exists for the book of Esther.

Esther: A Woman, a Queen, and a Minority

Feminist/Womanist Critiques: Who Really Wins?

At first glance, Esther is a biblical character who has three strikes against her: she is female, an orphan, and, as a Jew in the Persian empire, a member of a marginalized group. In spite of the odds against her, she marries the king, making her the queen, and she uses her influence with the king to save her people when their lives are threatened. All of this should make her the obvious hero/ine of the story, but her role has not always been given its due. As Sidnie Ann White Crawford tells us, "The tendency among scholars was to exalt Mordecai as the true hero of the tale and to downplay or even vilify the role of Esther."[37] For example, one commentator wrote that "between Mordecai and Esther the greater hero is Mordecai, who supplied the brains while Esther simply followed his directions";[38] another one questioned her sexual ethics, accusing her of having sought to join the king's harem "for the chance of winning wealth and power."[39] An early stage of feminist critique, then, was to simply acknowledge Esther's efforts in the unfolding of the story.[40]

It did not take long, though, before questions were raised about Esther's appropriateness as a feminist model. Essentially, the concern was that "the book of Esther is about the status quo, maintenance of it, and finding a proper place within it."[41] Addressing the gender messages in the story, Susan Niditch shows that "its heroine is a woman who offers a particular model for success, one with which oppressors would be especially comfortable. Opposition is to be subtle, behind the scenes, and ultimately strengthening for the power structure."[42]

According to South African biblical scholar Itumeleng Mosala, patriarchal gender roles are not challenged in the text: "Esther struggles, but Mordecai reaps the fruit of the struggle."[43] Not only is Mordecai the one who ends up with the deceased Haman's house and royal position (8:1–2), but the text clearly indicates that gender struggles are less important than the struggle for national survival.[44] In an immediate crisis, it might be true that national survival is the most pressing issue, but all too often, marginalized groups are *always* in a struggle for survival, and so the issue of gender equality is infinitely deferred. Instead, gender equality must be seen as an integral part of national survival here and now. Nevertheless, the status quo is not maintained uniformly in the text because a reversal does take place in the book of Esther—a threat against the Jews becomes a threat against the Persians. Yet as Nicole Duran surmises, "What has not reversed is the relative positions of men and women" because Esther accomplishes what she does "by using the gender role assigned to her, not by opposing it."[45] So who really wins in the narrative? Not Esther!

At this point, the female character in the book that takes on new importance is Vashti, the first queen mentioned in the book, whom King Ahasuerus deposes. While he was enjoying a banquet, attended by all of his top (male) officials, he commanded that Queen Vashti be brought before him "wearing the royal crown, in order to show the peoples and the officials her beauty; for she was fair to behold," but she refuses to go (1:11–12). As could be expected, the king is furious, and his advisers warn him that word of Vashti's actions will spread to all women, and when that happens, the women will "look with contempt on their husbands" (1:13–17). To head off that crisis, Vashti is sent away, a new queen is to take her place, and a royal decree is sent out that "every man should be master in his own house" so that "all women will give honor to their husbands, high and low alike" (1:17–22). After this incident, any doubt about the patriarchal nature of the culture described here is eliminated. As Linda Day observes, "Men are the acting subjects, gaining their power by means of the objectification of women"; "the degree of their worthiness is the degree to which women are able to, or choose to, please men"; and "female worth is measured by male assessment, adjudicated in the eyes of a man."[46]

In such a context, Vashti's refusal is truly a massive act of disobedience, and her banishment functions as a warning to other women who might consider acting in this way. Vashti's apparent strength and willingness to speak her mind when the odds are against her make her an attractive role model for feminists. Often, though, too strong a contrast is made between a supposedly independent and rebellious Vashti and a relatively passive and obedient Esther. It must be pointed out that both women are "guilty of disobedience in terms of approaching the king, hence of taking control over her relationship with her husband."[47] Vashti refuses to appear before the king when invited, but Esther appears before the king without being invited, an act that was punishable by death (4:9–17). Furthermore, although the two females are presented as oppositional characters, Esther may have owed Vashti a debt of gratitude because Esther benefited from a lesson Vashti taught the king. As Weems has concluded: "King Ahasuerus might not have been so predisposed to forgive Queen Esther her brazen disobedience had not his first wife taught him that, like it or not, some women make their own decisions. At least with Esther, the king was willing to hear her out."[48]

Even if this book offers somewhat positive images of women in Vashti and Esther, there is still a problem with the sexual exploitation of young girls in the text. In chapter 2, the king chooses his next queen by having "all of the beautiful young virgins" from all the provinces brought to him, and "the girl who pleases the king [will] be queen instead of Vashti" (2:1–4). Each girl is brought to the king for a night. The obvious implication is that the king had intercourse with each of these females (probably teenage girls), because they were returned to a different harem, the harem of the concubines, the next morning (2:12–14).[49] For the females who are forced to participate in this competition, there are dramatic consequences "in a society where virginity is a girl's only ticket to respectable adulthood."[50] The selection scheme described is an abuse of power that denotes "an all-powerful monarch, whose every need, including sexual ones, had to be taken care of, irrespective of the women he violated in the process."[51]

Given the plot's development, Sarojini Nadar contends, little attention is paid to King Ahasuerus's selection process—the narrative quickly shifts from Vashti to Esther—and the result is to "erase" from our awareness the sexual violence against females that occurs.[52] The problem is that when such texts are read today in contexts with a high incidence of rape, whether South Africa or, I would add, the United States, they tend to desensitize us to that ongoing violence as well, similarly erasing it from our awareness. To reverse that tendency, if we become more aware of the inherent violence of such biblical texts and start to contest it, we will be better able, as people of faith, to confront and contest sexual violence today.[53] Going beyond the hyperbole and humor in the book of Esther, Nicole Duran is left with two key questions: "What *really* happens to a woman who disobeys her husband, in a society that gives the husband complete authority over his wife?" and "What *really* happens to the girls whom the man in power considers unworthy?"[54] So who really wins in the narrative? Not females.

Queer Critiques: To "Pass" or Not to "Pass" Is the Question

When Esther is presented to the king, she does not divulge that she is Jewish (2:10). Interestingly, Mordecai had told her not to tell, even though Mordecai had identified himself as a Jew (3:4). His warning Esther not to inform anyone of "her people or her kindred" means that Mordecai either sensed or knew from experience that being non-Jewish brings about privileges and opportunities that being Jewish in the Persian court forecloses. In the same way, African Americans have known that to be non–African American in a racist society would confer advantages. As a survival strategy, some light-skinned people of African descent would "pass" for white, that is, they would not divulge that they were African American, thereby enabling them to have access to education, housing, and employment that would be denied otherwise. In our post–civil rights era, the need for "passing" to avoid lawful restrictions by race is less likely to occur.[55] Nevertheless, the need to "pass" due to sexual orientation continues. A homophobic environment means that if gays and lesbians divulge who they truly are, they confront the general population's prejudices and discrimination by law. Previously, heterosexual African Americans were discriminated against solely due to their race while some other racial/ethnic groups were exempt. Now, negative impacts are experienced by gays and lesbians, whether they are African American or members of other racial/ethnic groups. To avoid that effect, some gays and lesbians "pass" as heterosexual and do not divulge their full identity.[56] Under these circumstances, Esther's lack of candor feels very familiar, and her strategy comes across as a viable model of survival.

On the one hand, therefore, a queer critique recognizes that Esther's way of dealing with prejudice, by "passing," may be needed. On the other hand, there is the recognition that Vashti's defiance is instructive and necessary. As Gary Comstock writes in his book *Gay Theology without Apology*, "Vashti's refusal, not Esther's behind-the-scenes manipulations," can be encouraging and empowering.[57] Although recognizing that her story was meant to intimidate women (and others) by demonstrating the cost of refusal and resistance, Comstock argues that "we can turn that story around." In so doing, we can change her story from one of unacceptable behavior as usually thought into one which shows "that Vashti's actions were righteous and her punishment was unjust." [58]

Referring to the significance of Vashti in liberationist theologies, both feminist and queer (referring specifically to Comstock's work), Linda Day elaborates on the continuing message of Vashti's story for any group that has been marginalized and silenced.[59] Pragmatism may point to Esther's model as the better one, she agrees, but sometimes personal integrity requires following in Vashti's footsteps:

> Yet in certain situations persons need to stand up against what they perceive to be immoral or unjust, to speak for righteousness without regard for the consequences. Freedom can prove to be expensive. But there are moments in life when enduring enslavement, in whatever guise it presents itself, is no longer an option, and one becomes willing to pay that price. At such turning points, one can only maintain personal integrity by standing up and taking the risk.[60]

In summary, a queer critique of Esther utilizes both Esther and Vashti as viable models. The message is clear: sometimes you have to "go along to get along"; at other times you have to "act up." To pass or not to pass is the question.

Postcolonial Critiques: Imperial/Colonial Powers, Marginalization, and Violence

Whether it was actually written during the Persian or the Hellenistic period, the book of Esther is set in a time when a foreign imperial power ruled Judea. In that context, Jews were a marginalized community and relatively powerless. Sidnie Ann White Crawford has argued consistently that, for these reasons, Esther becomes the model of success for Jews. Her argument is that, because Esther is basically powerless as a woman (and an orphan), her situation is comparable to that of dispersed Jews who are also powerless with respect to the imperial dominance: "Because she was successful in attaining power within the structure of society, she served as a role model of diaspora Jews seeking to attain a comfortable and successful life in a foreign society."[61]

In today's context, a postcolonial critique examines how groups or nations survive their marginalization, whether that marginalization occurs politically, militarily, or economically, and how the Bible has been used to support such marginalization.[62] From this postcolonial perspective, the book of Esther is problematic.

In Esther, a royal decree has gone out, at Haman's urging, that all Jews are to be destroyed (chapter 3), but Esther prevents its implementation, and thousands who were "enemies of the Jews" (non-Jews), in addition to the ten sons of Haman, are killed instead (chapter 9). In the narrative, Esther is a "trickster" because "she ultimately succeeds in reversing the evil that was supposed to befall her own people by 'tricking' the king to join her side."[63]

Using a postcolonial critique, this does indeed demonstrate one of the survival strategies of the powerless, as Masenya contends.[64] Unfortunately, though, groups that are forced to survive as tricksters in this way are also forced to support the maintenance of the oppressive system, since they dare not challenge that system itself.

Another problematic aspect of the narrative is the obvious retaliatory violence involved. In the past, anti-Jewish Christian interpreters have interpreted the text in ways that condemned Judaism by "treating the story's violence as normative and essential to Judaism rather than as a defensive response to mortal danger."[65] Given the reality of the Shoah (the more appropriate term for the "Holocaust"), where the annihilation of Jews was attempted and partially successful, Christians must reconsider such interpretations.[66] More specifically, Christians should reflect on the damaging ways in which Christianity has been constructed unfairly in opposition to Judaism and negatively influenced the interpretation of biblical texts such as Esther.[67]

Rather than being laudatory, though, the violence in the book of Esther shows the harm caused by volatile mixtures of colonialism and racial/ethnic/religious differences. More specifically, the book portrays the cycle of violence instigated when one group exercises power over another one: "Esther reminds modern readers of the ties between colonialism and violence and of how tension and hostility, when built up among different peoples brought together by imperialist powers, result in cycles of reciprocal revenge and persecution."[68] Referring to the tragedy of September 11, 2001, and the subsequent global "war on terrorism" declared by the U.S. government, Wong Wai Ching Angela writes that it shows the massive damage caused when, in a "spirit of revenge," there is "a sweeping resolve from all sides to use violence for violence."[69] The book of Esther, therefore, glorifies a national identity that "promotes the establishment of an exclusive community by a victory over ethnic rivals gained through revenge and destruction."[70] Wong, disheartened by the interreligious/racial/ethnic struggles around the world today, must conclude that the book of Esther does not model ways for different groups to respect and accept one another. Instead, Wong contends that Esther must invite us to work toward creating a multicultural sense of community that includes "many ethnicities, languages, religions, and cultures."[71] I could not agree with her more.

Conclusions

In traditional interpretations of their narratives, Ruth and Esther are unquestionable paragons of virtue and exemplary models for the life of faith, yet the preceding discussion shows the range of challenges to those interpretations offered by feminist, queer, and postcolonial readings. Having considered these challenges, we can no longer ignore them. We have to ask ourselves: How can we now use these texts as models for the formation of God's people, but avoid the negative consequences that the liberationist critiques have identified? An answer to this question requires a reading strategy that opens up these texts in new ways. For example, new questions must be allowed for the book of Ruth (concerning Orpah after she returned home and Ruth after her baby was born) and for the book of Esther (concerning the fate of Vashti and the slaughtered "Other"). Such a strategy cannot be simplistic, literal, or one that reads biblical passages in isolation. To the contrary, the reading strategy proposed here is a process that looks at texts thematically, intertextually, and contextually.

Thematically, there is a strong continuity between Ruth and Esther because they both engage in the work of redemption. As Johanna van Wijk-Bos defines redemption, it is "the responsibility people have for one another"; therefore, "redeemers are people who are appointed to take care of people who cannot take care of themselves."[72] Accordingly, Ruth is a redeemer because she makes herself responsible for Naomi's well-being and provides her with a son.[73] Similarly, Esther is a redeemer because she makes herself responsible for her people's well-being and removes the threat against their continued existence. Although there are specific biblical laws that refer to the responsibilities of a redeemer, those responsibilities can be thought of more expansively.[74] Following van Wijk-Bos's lead, the role of the redeemer is to carry out acts that maintain the overall welfare of the community (Esther) and reintegrate into the community those that would otherwise be separated from it (Naomi and Ruth).

Furthermore, the contours of the redeemed community itself are discernible in Ruth 4. Sakenfeld suggests that, although it is different from the more commonly accepted eschatological texts, Ruth 4 provides a vision of hope, "an extended metaphor for God's New Creation that we must find ways to re-express in language appropriate to God's continuing work in our midst."[75] In her analysis, she identifies the following features of this vision:

> a community that is characterized by reciprocal movement from margin to center and from center to margin, by racial/ethnic inclusiveness, and by adequate physical sustenance for all; a community of upright individuals together creating and affirming justice and mercy; a community in which weeping turns to joy and tears are wiped away; a community in which children are valued and old people are well cared for; a community in which a daughter is greatly valued.[76]

Sakenfeld admits that it is this vision that must be culled from the text rather than the expressions of the ancient Israelite culture identified there or the questionable means of achieving the vision in the narrative.[77] In other words, perceiving the story of Ruth as the story of a new vision of community toward which we should all work does not mean that the cultural biases of an ancient time and place have to carry over into our own contexts. Plus, reading Ruth 4 as an eschatological text emphasizes the role that human beings must play in bringing about that vision. Sakenfeld notes that more conventional eschatological texts, such as Jeremiah 31 and Ezekiel 47, offer divine promises and indicate that human actions are not needed because "all is in God's hands."[78] In contrast, neither the book of Ruth nor that of Esther includes a report of direct intervention by God; and in Esther, there is no mention of God at all.[79]

Next, reading these texts intertextually means that Ruth and Esther are read in conjunction with at least one other biblical text. Notably, van Wijk-Bos has observed, as have others, that there are similarities between Esther and the Exodus story.[80] She thinks of these books as two poles of the Exodus experience, where Esther represents the pole of oppression and the Exodus story represents liberation. An intertextual reading of Ruth and Esther, therefore, indicates that redemption is associated with liberation and that to redeem (or liberate from oppression) is the work of the people of God. The relative absence of God in both books indicates that human beings are called to act and not rely solely on divine intervention. As described by Fewell and Gunn, in spite of appearances to the contrary, God is in the book of Ruth because "God can be found somewhere in the mixed motives, somewhere in the complicated relationships, somewhere in the struggle for survival, anywhere there is redemption, however compromised."[81] Correspondingly, to do acts of redemption is to do God's work in the world.

Furthermore, in her work on Ruth, Jacqueline Lapsley identifies a pattern of blessing, where Boaz invokes a divine blessing on Ruth (2:12), Naomi on Boaz (2:19 and 2:20), and Boaz on Ruth (3:10), and the women bless YHWH for not leaving Naomi without kin (4:14).[82] Lapsley finds that "the centrality of their relationship to God empowers them to seek blessings for others, and to act out blessings for others through their own acts of *hesed*."[83] A liberationist reading of Ruth and Esther, consequently, demands that the people of God create a new kind of community, one that blesses, and we are to do that by redeeming/liberating/freeing those who are usually excluded because of marginalization, exploitation, or other types of oppression.

Any community must confront the various differences that exist among human beings (and other communities) based on gender, class, race/ethnicity, sexual orientation, religion, and national origin. All too often, though, a determination that a group is different based on one or more of these criteria means that the group becomes "less than" or unacceptable to some degree, and it then becomes acceptable to mistreat that other group. The contemporary notion of "liberating interdependence" accepts these differences and affirms the interconnections between (and within) cultures, sexes, races, religions, and nations while it seeks connections that are not oppressive and exploitative.[84] In other words, liberating interdependence "defines the interconnectedness of relationships that recognize and affirm the dignity of all things and people involved."[85]

Such considerations are crucial because, all too often, the freedom of one group has occurred at the expense of another. Historically, those who have experienced oppression have gone on to become perpetrators of oppression.[86] Hopefully, a commitment to liberating interdependence may help to break the cycle of violence. Conventional readings of Ruth and Esther describe the creation of a community, but that community continues to be marked by exclusion, exploitation, and violence, as the feminist/womanist, queer, and postcolonial critiques contend. However, the vision of community offered in Ruth 4, as Sakenfeld suggests, is inclusive, sustaining, and affirming. As people of faith, we are called not just to create a community but to create a certain kind of community, one of liberating interdependence—a redeemed community in which the negative consequences of exclusion and exploitation have disappeared.

Finally, the strategy presented here requires contextual readings. As stated earlier, feminist/womanist, queer, and postcolonial readings of Ruth and Esther tell us that conventional barriers to community membership and participation must be removed. For that to happen, though, marginalized groups have to be aware that they are excluded and "to cry out on account of their taskmasters" (Exod. 3:7). To develop this awareness, they must read biblical texts contextually, that is, the group must consider their own historical memories and their cultural/political/economic circumstances to determine if their experience is closer to that of Ruth or Orpah or to Esther or Vashti, and so forth. In other words, today's groups must resist the tendency to immediately identify with the privileged "chosen" group in these narratives, when their realities more closely resemble those of the excluded groups. Such resistance is difficult to muster because these same marginalized groups are usually told that the traditional reading, the reading of "the chosen people," is the only valid one. Yet, as mentioned earlier, if they ignore the marginalization occurring in the text, they are more likely to ignore the marginalization occurring in their own lives. Developing such an awareness is a complex task, though, because within any one group are individuals with differing relative privileges. Consequently, some in the group may experience privileges based on race or class, but others within the same group may experience disadvantages based on sexual orientation or gender. Allowances for diverse experiences must be made, therefore, within groups and between groups.

Basically, the objective of a liberationist reading is to reconsider each of these categories that are traditionally used to exclude—such as gender, sexual orientation, and national/cultural identity—and then ask new questions. Because the responsibility as a person of faith is to redeem, those with privileges according to these criteria must ask themselves: How have I/we excluded some groups, and how should I/we act to incorporate them fully in the community? Correspondingly, those who are currently excluded or denied full participation based on these criteria must ask themselves: How can my/our voices be heard, and what kind of redemption/inclusion do I/we seek? Given these elements, a liberationist reading of Ruth and Esther, or any other biblical text for that matter, is thematic, intertextual, and contextual. Finally, it is a dynamic process that requires the critical reflection and participation of all alike, incorporating the dominant and the subordinate characters in the text and the current winners and past victims in our world today.

Ruth and Esther were marginalized women who were disadvantaged in three different ways in their contexts as female, widow, and foreigner (Ruth) and female, orphan, and foreigner (Esther). They are remarkable figures in a cultural setting and a biblical canon in which women are most often unnamed and are acted upon rather than able to act in their own right. From this perspective, Ruth and Esther serve as models of hope and inspiration for marginalized groups today. They also serve, though, as a reminder that marginalized groups, those who experience the trauma of exclusion and violence, must speak out. Simultaneously, Ruth and Esther prod the privileged into doing acts of redemption that serve the well-being of the full community, and redemption can be achieved only by including those once excluded. God calls us to form redeemed communities, but we can only do that if we heed the voices we usually prefer to ignore. The choice is up to us.

Reading Ruth and Esther in the Real World: A First World Response

In the preceding discussion of feminist criticism and the book of Ruth, I could not help but notice a difference in the evaluations the book received. Scholars from the so-called Two-Thirds World (South Africa and Taiwan) thought that the book offered positive images for women, but the First World scholars (based primarily in the United States) thought that the book merely reinforced traditional patriarchal (heterosexual) family structures. I could not help but wonder about that difference. How can women from these two different geographic and political regions engage one another when there are very different starting points? I also had to notice that, in this context, I am in the First World camp. As an African American, I usually think of myself as among "the Other," but in this context, my social location changes. I am among the privileged.

Mary Ann Tolbert, a white New Testament scholar, has reflected on the encounter between North American and Two-Thirds World feminist scholars, and she offers some significant insights. At an international gathering of scholars that took place at Vanderbilt University in 1993, she had to acknowledge her inherent privileges—the location of the conference in the United States, English as the language of communication, and the hegemonic influence of the Western academy on all scholarly discussions.[87] Tolbert also recognized that the international participants spoke from the perspective of the colonized. She, however, represented the colonizer, the one who had justified much of that expansion on the basis of spreading the gospel and who benefits from unfair economic systems today that "continue the economic plundering of other countries."[88] After this realization, she proposed that First World scholars engage Two-Thirds World scholars in a three-step process of listening, reflecting/analyzing, and acting."[89]

For Tolbert, listening was a "crucial step in constructing appropriate forms of cooperation with those whose oppressive treatment falls in some way, no matter how distantly, under one's own charge or with those whose marginalization is somewhat symbolically linked to one's own dominant position." Listening is a difficult step to take, she knows, because it means that the listener must admit ignorance, and "the denial of ignorance is an essential part of the ideology of dominance."[90] As a result, equal doses of humility and caution, including listening before judging, help.[91] Reaching similar conclusions in her own reflection on such encounters, Sharon Ringe writes that such qualities of humility and caution are crucial for authentic conversations to occur because, given the dominant role of the United States globally, scholars from the United States can have "a hermeneutics of authority and control" about everything and everyone:

> The economic, political, and military dominance of the United States over other parts of the world, and with that power also the cultural

> hegemony of the European heritage of the majority of our people (especially powerful people), often translate on our part into a hermeneutics of authority and control. We are accustomed to talking while others listen and to being granted the right to name the world. Our experience becomes the norm by which we judge others' lives and commitments, rather than simply the base on which we stand.[92]

In a comparable reflection, Phyllis Bird noted the impact of the colonizer/colonized divide in those international gatherings and recognized that she represents "a Euro-American colonial history—including an intellectual history" that participants could "rightly see as an enemy."[93] She hoped that signaling the problem might help them ultimately negotiate the boundaries: "We must try to avoid setting up those on either side of the cultural divide as antagonists or naively assuming that we can be 'partners' or 'share insights' when our interpretations are rooted in political and cultural realities that have been deeply detrimental to genuine partnership."[94]

While listening to the scholars from the Two-Thirds World, these European American women found that they learned things that could help them become more fully aware of their own social locations and negotiate more critically. Antoinette Clark Wire heard a call to First World feminists "to be led through our concerns with gender oppression to do postcolonial readings that unmask the full range of racial, economic, political and religious oppression, rather than collaborating in silence whenever our own privilege allows us this advantage."[95] Similarly, Ringe found instructive the Asian women's concept of "relational hermeneutics," which assumes the legitimacy of divergent voices and readings and seeks to understand and explore these differences.[96] She thought it would help North American women negotiate their own "culture wars":

> Women who find in the Bible support for our quest to participate fully in the institutions and activities of the society, secular and religious alike, and persons who find in the Bible grounds for still keeping us in our traditional "place" will never agree, and will probably never really understand each other. But with a relational instead of an over-against hermeneutics, each grants the other a place to stand and the right to speak, and each respects the other's basic human dignity.[97]

Tolbert, like Ringe, thought that the First World scholar's difficulty in listening was the legacy of imperialism and had to be the first step of engagement. The second step, which followed from it, is reflecting and analyzing the resultant status of privilege. Because of that privilege, Tolbert noted First World scholars use metatheories that failed to take into account the particularities of the Two-Thirds World, primarily because they have not realized that "methods are no less ideologically shaped than any other cultural tools."[98] To counter that tendency, she proposes that First World scholars use their analytical methods to address their *own* contexts and circumstances, having noted that "the analysis of what it means to live as a more privileged person in relation to other people in the world is in general strikingly absent from most First World scholarship."[99]

In the final step of engagement, Tolbert wants First World scholars to act, by decentering and empowering. Using the Gospel of John as her text, she notices how John the Baptist "uses the power he controls to promote the influence and value of someone else."[100] With John the Baptist as her model, she thinks that First World scholars should inform themselves about the writings of Two-Thirds World scholars, make a commitment to stay engaged in dialogue and "employ the power one has, however limited one may believe it to be, to level the playing field of world society in search of a more just social order."[101] From this perspective, Tolbert has identified a dialogue process that works well in any situation of privilege/nonprivilege. It can even serve as a model for encounters between traditional privileged male scholars here in North America as they deal with their feminist, queer, and postcolonial counterparts at home.

4

Jesus, Paul, the Law, and Inclusive Biblical Interpretation

Focusing on Jesus

As seen in chapter 2, there are some problematic Old Testament laws from the perspectives of women, the poor, and non-Israelites (with references to "non-Israelites" applied today against those of non-Christian religious as well as nonwhite racial/ethnic backgrounds). These problems stem from the negative impact that their underlying values continue to have on these or similar groups in more contemporary historical settings. Yet some Protestants, many of whom support literal interpretations of the Bible and would otherwise argue against "picking and choosing" which portions of the Bible are relevant today, assume that most of these laws have no relevance for Christians. Some others might be aware of the church tradition that considers only the moral law of the Old Testament to have continuing validity for Christians. It is on that basis, then, that they would explain the continuing validity of the Ten Commandments for Christians, but not the laws thought to pertain to ancient cultic practices. On the whole, though, when confronted with the questionable laws discussed earlier, an expected response is as follows: "Didn't the New Testament get rid of those laws?"

In other words, there is a common perception that most, if not all, Old Testament laws are abandoned in the New Testament. As will be shown here, this is not the case. Furthermore, such a misperception of biblical laws is related to popular notions that Jesus himself rejected "Judaism," thereby becoming "Christian" and so was no longer "Jewish." If it is thought that Jesus rejected "Judaism" and, correspondingly, its laws, then it stands to reason that the followers of Jesus would do the same. However, the seemingly logical argument, that Christians can abandon the law since Jesus did is based on several faulty premises.

From an inclusive perspective, one faulty premise is that Jesus was antinomian, that is, he was against the Law. To the contrary, there is every indication that he was an observant Jew. As required in Deuteronomy 22:12 and Numbers 15:37–40, his garment had fringes, or "tassels," as mentioned in Matthew 9:20, 13:36, and 23:5, Mark 6:56, and Luke 8:44. In Matthew 17:24–27, we are told that Jesus paid the Temple-tax—half a shekel—which is based on a comparable payment to the sanctuary specified in Exodus 30:13. Furthermore, Jesus upholds the sacrificial rites prescribed in Leviticus 14:1–7 in that, after curing a leper, he instructs the healed person to report to a priest "and offer for your cleansing what Moses commanded" (Mark 1:44; Matt. 8:4; Luke 5:14).[1] Jesus probably observed the Sabbath.[2] Furthermore, it is the disciples who apparently violated the Sabbath by harvesting corn (plucking the corn, rubbing it in their hands, and then eating it)—and not Jesus (Mark 2:23–28; Matt. 12:1–8; Luke 6:1–5).[3] In the same way, it is the disciples who set aside traditional rules regarding the washing of hands before meals—and not Jesus (Mark 7:1–8; Matt. 15:1–9).[4]

It might appear, though, that Jesus rejects the law concerning the dietary restrictions. Notably, in Mark 7:19, Jesus "declares all foods clean," contrary to the laws in Leviticus that distinguish between "clean" and "unclean" foods, but not all early Christian communities were aware of that declaration. Therefore, some Christians, like Peter, were observing these dietary laws after Jesus' death and resurrection (Acts 10), and the restrictions were an issue for the community in Galatia (Gal. 2:11–14).[5] Contrary to denying the traditions of ancient Israel, Jesus says in Matthew 10:17–20 that he has not come to "abolish the law or the prophets" but "to fulfill" them, and he asserts that the one who does the commandments and teaches them "will be called great in the kingdom of heaven":

> "Do not think that I have come to abolish the law or the prophets; I have come not to abolish but to fulfill. For truly I tell you, until heaven and earth pass away, not one letter, not one stroke of a letter, will pass from the law until all is accomplished. Therefore, whoever breaks one of the least of these commandments, and teaches others to do the same, will be called least in the kingdom of heaven; but whoever does them and teaches them will be called great in the kingdom of heaven. For I tell you, unless your righteousness exceeds

> that of the scribes and Pharisees, you will never enter the kingdom of heaven."

Jesus against the Pharisees and Their Great Tradition

If Jesus was an observant Jew and he upheld the law and the prophets, what was the nature of his dispute with "the Jews" and with "the Pharisees"? To answer these questions, several other current (but very faulty) premises need to be addressed. To begin, Christians today often mistakenly equate New Testament references to "the Jews" with contemporary Judaism. With this understanding, it follows that, if Jesus had been outside of that community of faith, he is separate and distinct from it, thereby reinforcing the notion that Jesus was not Jewish. However, the translated word "Jews" for the Greek term actually used in the New Testament can be misleading:

> Bible translators and interpreters are essentially anachronistic when they assert that the New Testament Greek word "*Ioudaios*" means Jew, and that "*Ioudaismos*" means Judaism in the sense of Jewishness. Actually, "*Ioudaios*" means of or pertaining to Judea; "*Ioudaismos*" means the behavior typical of and particular to those from Judea.[6]

Consequently, biblical references to "the Jews" literally mean "the Judeans" and can be merely an ancient geopolitical designation. Instead, contemporary Judaism traces its roots to the Babylonian Talmud and the rabbinic tradition starting in the fourth and fifth centuries CE.[7] Given the deep familiarity with the term "the Jews" in the church, it will be retained in this discussion. Nevertheless, it is important to remember that the "Jewish" religious beliefs and practices described as objectionable in the New Testament are not attributable to contemporary Jews, and that Jesus' issues were with the leadership at that time and not with the people.

From this linguistic and historical clarification, two more important points emerge. First, since "the distinctively 'Jewish' tradition did not emerge until at least the late fourth century CE," Jesus could not have rejected "normative Judaism" because it did not exist in his day in the forms in which it exists today.[8] Second, Christians often mistakenly think that the same Judaism of today existed in Jesus' time so that any differences between the Jewish leaders and Jesus are thought to indicate a "breaking away" from the earlier tradition. Instead, normative Christianity *and* Judaism developed about the same time; therefore, both traditions are "fifth-century outcomes rooted in the postexilic Israelite world of first-century Palestine."[9] Consequently, interpretive stances that Jesus takes on the laws can also be found in the formative Judaism of his day.[10]

If Jesus followed the laws and was within the Jewish community, who were the Pharisees, and why did Jesus have problems with them? Basically, the Pharisees were a separatist group that sought "the scrupulous observance of the Torah according to the interpretive traditions they claimed to have received from their ancestors."[11] Key elements of their observances were "the proper sanctifying of the Sabbath, full tithing, and the application of the priestly laws of purity to the preparation and consumption of the ordinary food that they ate every day." The key feature of Pharisaic observances, therefore, is that although the Pharisees were laity, they felt that they were called to the same degree of holiness practiced by the priesthood.[12] Because of their insistence on strictly observing these priestly food laws, the Pharisees were defined by "the exclusiveness of their communal table fellowship."[13]

The Pharisees sought to follow the laws of Moses to the fullest extent possible, but sometimes the laws are ambiguous. For example, the Sabbath day is to be kept holy, but the Torah does not indicate precisely how that is to be done, so the Pharisees devised rules and regulations that assisted them in keeping this and other Mosaic laws.[14] The following examples of ambiguity are instructive:

> When it was eventually determined that a faithful Jew should not go on a long journey on the Sabbath, it had to be decided what a "long" journey was, and consequently what distance a Jew could travel on this day without violating its holiness. Likewise, a worker who believed that he or she should not labor on the Sabbath had to know what constituted "work" and what therefore could and could not be done.[15]

This tradition that the Pharisees developed in interpreting these laws eventually had a status of its own and became the "oral" Law that was set alongside the "written" Law of Moses.[16] This oral tradition "continued to grow and to be invested with greater authority"; around the year 200 CE it was written down, and "today it is known as the Mishnah, the heart of the Jewish sacred collection of texts, the Talmud."[17] With this explanation, the difference between Jesus and the Pharisees becomes more understandable. Jesus, like the Pharisees, affirmed the importance of the laws of Moses and the need to observe them. However, Jesus "did not think that scrupulous and detailed adherence to the laws of Torah was the most important aspect of a Jew's relationship with God, especially as these laws were interpreted by the Pharisees."[18] In this way, we can see how Jesus could reject the Pharisees' interpretations of laws, but not the laws themselves. Jesus' encounter with the Pharisees in Mark 7:1–8 now takes on new meaning. When the Pharisees challenge the disciples of Jesus for eating with "defiled hands," Jesus accuses them of having abandoned the commandment of God and holding to human tradition instead (Mark 7:6–8). The "human tradition" to which Jesus refers is the interpretation of the purity laws reached by the Pharisees based on their understanding of the requirements of a holy life. Jesus therefore rejects the Pharisaic application of the law and not the concept of purity itself:

> Then he called the crowd again and said to them, "Listen to me, all of you, and understand: there is nothing outside a person that by going in can defile, but the things that come out are what defile." When he had left the crowd and entered the house, his disciples asked him about the parable. He said to them, "Then do you also fail to understand? Do you not see that whatever goes into a person from outside cannot defile, since it enters, not the heart but the stomach, and goes out into the sewer?" (Thus he declared all foods clean.) And he said, "It is what comes out of a person that defiles. For it is from within, from the human heart, that evil intentions come: fornication, theft, murder, adultery, avarice, wickedness, deceit, licentiousness, envy, slander, pride, folly. All these evil things come from within, and they defile a person." (Mark 7:14–23)

According to modern anthropology, the disagreement between Jesus and the Pharisees in Mark 7:1–23 can be traced to the difference between the "Great Tradition" and the "Little Tradition." The Great Tradition, or the "tradition of the elders," as the Pharisees refer to it in Mark, "was largely maintained, defined, and practiced by small, elite groups in towns, notably by the Pharisees and their scholars (called 'scribes')."[19] Most important, "these minority groups expected and demanded that every Israelite please God in the way these groups believed they must; hence, they viewed unwashed Galilean peasants and fishermen as outside the law (see John 7:48–52)."[20] However, maintaining the purity laws according to the standards set by the keepers of the Great Tradition was difficult for those peasants and fishermen:

> Keeping such purity laws was a near impossibility for peasant farmers, who may not have [had] the required water for ritual baths or been able to postpone plowing/planting after rain fell because of ritual requirements. Like fishermen, they also came in constant contact with dead fish, dead animals, and the like. It was also very difficult for people who traveled about, such as Jesus and his disciples, to maintain ritual purity. As a result, the "Little Tradition" of rural peasants had adapted itself in significant measure to the realities of peasant life.[21]

As a definition, then, the Little Tradition reflects the perspectives and realities of the peasants in the rural villages who are the majority of the population but who do not have the ability to oppose the minority and their Great Tradition directly.[22] Jesus redefines the purity laws by arguing that it is not what goes into a person that defiles, but the evil intentions and actions that come out of a person's heart (Mark 7:17–23). In this way, Jesus affirms that the laws should govern daily life, yet his interpretation takes into account the affect on nonelite groups, and he changes the requirements so that peasants and fishermen—as well as the elite—can observe them. Jesus did not reject the purity laws—he expanded them. Jesus' understanding of purity takes the realities of those otherwise excluded into account, and he offers a new interpretation of purity laws that is inclusive.

Jesus: Elements of Inclusive Biblical Interpretation

As mentioned earlier, the scribes and Pharisees were the small group in ancient Judea who "expected and demanded that every Israelite please God in the way these groups believed they must."[23] The Pharisees were essentially arguing that failing to follow their interpretations of the laws was tantamount to rejecting the laws, but Jesus was only rejecting *their* interpretations of the laws. In our own context, recognized church leaders have established a conservative tradition, today's "tradition of the elders," that they feel everyone else should follow in order to be a good Christian. The similarities are striking. The traditional leaders of the church—a relatively small group of white, heterosexual, Western, and privileged males—are our own Pharisees. It is only to be expected, then, that those of us who do not accept those traditional interpretations are accused of rejecting the law and violating scriptural authority. Instead of rejecting the laws, though, we are affirming their authority and merely seek to consider the realities of those groups that are "Other," just as Jesus does for the peasants and fishermen in Mark 7 and for other marginalized groups elsewhere in the Gospels. The Pharisees are the ones who exclude, and Jesus is the one who seeks to include. In this way, Jesus' exchanges with the Pharisees about the Law are instructive because they provide the elements of inclusive biblical interpretation.

There is a clear advantage to drawing the parallels between Jesus and the Pharisees of the biblical era and the progressives and the conservatives in our own time. Such parallels underscore the fact that Jesus and the Pharisees were within the same faith community. Contrary to what Christians often think, Jesus was not speaking against Judaism as an outsider. Jesus and the Pharisees were engaged in an inner-group struggle. In the same way, conservatives and progressives within Christianity are involved in an inner-group struggle. A word of caution is warranted, however. Drawing these parallels should not imply that the Pharisees are accurately portrayed in the Gospels. After all, "we possess no primary text that unquestionably comes from the hand of a Pharisee."[24] Moreover, the developing rabbinic tradition and normative Judaism did and do in fact have interpretations similar to those Jesus advocated.[25] Correspondingly, no conclusion can or should be made that contemporary Judaism still holds the positions of the Pharisees on these matters.

Actually, there is reason to believe that the encounters between Jesus and the Pharisees are exaggerated. If historical accuracy is a concern, you need to know that the Pharisees "were not numerous in the days of Jesus"; "they were not influential in the politics of Palestine at that time"; and "they were not concerned that everybody else (i.e., non-Pharisaic Jews) conform to their own rules and regulations for purity."[26] It is only after the death of Jesus and especially after the destruction of the Jerusalem in 70 CE, when the Romans gave them the authority to handle the civil matters of Palestinian Jews, that there were more frequent interactions between the Pharisees and Christian churches.[27] After acknowledging these historical facts, we are forced to ask a question: "Is it possible that the opposition leveled against the church by Pharisees after Jesus' death affected the ways that Christians told stories about his life?"[28] In other words, it is worth wondering if "because of their own clashes with the Pharisees, could Christians have narrated stories in which Jesus himself disputed with them (usually putting them to shame), even though such disputes would have happened only rarely during his own lifetime?"[29] The analysis done here is not relying on the historical accuracy of the encounters described or the usual depiction of these exchanges as ones between the Jewish Pharisees ("bad") and the Christian Jesus ("good"). Instead, these texts are read thematically and theologically to discern how Jesus developed a more inclusive way of interpreting biblical laws and rejected the exclusive table fellowship of the Pharisees. As Christians who follow in his name, we should "go and do likewise" by creating inclusive communities.

JESUS CONSIDERS THE IMPACT OF AN INTERPRETATION ON THE MARGINALIZED

> Then he said to them, "You have a fine way of rejecting the commandment of God in order to keep your tradition! For Moses said, 'Honor your father and your mother'; and, 'Whoever speaks evil of father or mother must surely die.' But you say that if anyone tells father or mother, 'Whatever support you might have had from me is Corban' (that is, an offering to God)—then you no longer permit doing

> anything for a father or mother, thus making void the word of God through your tradition that you have handed on. And you do many things like this." (Mark 7:9–13)

In Mark 7:9–13, Jesus addresses the issue of the Corban. "Corban" was a type of offering of goods made to the Temple, but the term "appears to have taken on the status of a vow attached to goods, which meant that those goods could not be used for any other purpose."[30] Jesus questioned the practice because, once the vow was offered, it deprived the faithful of resources that could be used to support their parents, as required in the Ten Commandments. Jesus' objection here appears to be that the official policy of preventing the retraction of the vow was tantamount to "the elders teaching people to disregard the commandment of God."[31] The argument Jesus presents here makes the most sense in a context where people have limited financial resources—and that is exactly the context of the agrarian peasants of Jesus' day. In an essentially hierarchical system, peasants (who constituted about 70 to 80 percent of the population) bore the brunt of taxation and tithing requirements by both the Roman colonial presence and the priestly aristocracy in Jerusalem.[32] Under these circumstances, the Temple's demands of tithes and offerings from peasants forced them to choose between their religious duties and their families' livelihood:[33] Therefore "peasants could support their parents and other elders in the village or pay their tithes and offerings," but "when they chose to support their families, they were vilified as unclean and Torah disobedient."[34]

Jesus' objection to the Corban is directly related to its impact on the peasants and demonstrates that he was aware of his social setting and the circumstances of those around him. Such an awareness of social conditions makes Jesus, in today's academic terminology, a contextual theologian.[35] In fact, based on his study of the parables, William Herzog has concluded that political and economic issues were at the heart of Jesus' ministry.[36]

> It is a conceit of the North American church that Jesus was not involved in politics and economics but limited himself to spiritual matters. Although this view may allow some the luxury of limiting ministry to so-called spiritual needs, it violates the fundamental practice of Jesus. To put it a bit differently, . . . Jesus' proclamation of the reign of God, including its attendant theology and ethics, grew out of his social analysis. He did not proclaim the reign of God in a vacuum or teach theology and ethics devoid of social context.[37]

As discussed in the first chapter, contextual theologians and biblical scholars are now advancing understandings of God and interpretations of biblical texts that are different from traditional ones. Yet they are different only because they reflect the political and economic realities of women, the poor, and the foreigner and consider the impact that traditional interpretations have on these groups. Although those who uphold the traditional Christian interpretations, today's Pharisees, vilify the contextual approach, it is exactly the kind of approach that Jesus used.

JESUS' NEW INTERPRETATION IS GROUNDED IN THE BIBLICAL TRADITION

> So the Pharisees and the scribes asked him, "Why do your disciples not live according to the tradition of the elders, but eat with defiled hands?" He said to them, "Isaiah prophesied rightly about you hypocrites, as it is written,
> 'This people honors me with their lips,
> but their hearts are far from me;
> in vain do they worship me,
> teaching human precepts as doctrines.'
> You abandon the commandment of God and hold to human tradition." (Mark 7:5–8)

When Jesus responds to the Pharisees in Mark 7, he quotes the prophet Isaiah (Isa. 29:13 in the Septuagint). In Isaiah, the people are being castigated because they have substituted human teaching for true devotion to God, and the prophet "introduces the distinction between outward piety and devotion to God in one's heart."[38] The same distinction is being made in the Gospel according to Matthew. There, Jesus condemns the hypocrisy of the scribes and Pharisees who focus on relatively minor matters while ignoring the "weightier matters of the law":

> Woe to you, scribes and Pharisees, hypocrites! For you tithe mint, dill, and cummin, and have neglected the weightier matters of the law: justice and mercy and faith. It is these you ought to have practiced without neglecting the others. You blind guides! You strain out a gnat but swallow a camel!
>
> Woe to you, scribes and Pharisees, hypocrites! For you clean the outside of the cup and of the plate, but inside they are full of greed and self-indulgence. You blind Pharisee! First clean the inside of the cup, so that the outside also may become clean.
>
> Woe to you, scribes and Pharisees, hypocrites! For you are like whitewashed tombs, which on the outside look beautiful, but inside

they are full of the bones of the dead and of all kinds of filth. So you also on the outside look righteous to others, but inside you are full of hypocrisy and lawlessness. (Matt. 23:23–28)

By leveling such charges against the scribes and Pharisees, Jesus is invoking the tradition of the eighth-century prophets who railed against the excesses and economic exploitation of the marginalized. Two well-known passages from the prophet Amos are worth considering at this juncture:

Thus says the Lord:
For three transgressions of Israel,
and for four, I will not revoke the punishment;
because they sell the righteous for silver,
and the needy for a pair of sandals—
they who trample the head of the poor into the dust of the earth,
and push the afflicted out of theway;
father and son go in to the same girl,
so that my holy name is profaned;
they lay themselves down beside every altar
on garments taken in pledge;
and in the house of their God they drink
wine bought with fines they imposed. (Amos 2:6–8)

I hate, I despise your festivals,
and I take no delight in your solemn assemblies.
Even though you offer me your burnt-offerings and grain-offerings,
I will not accept them;
and the offerings of well-being of your fatted animals
I will not look upon.
Take away from me the noise of your songs;
I will not listen to the melody of your harps.
But let justice roll down like waters,
and righteousness like an ever-flowing stream. (Amos 5:21–24)

Without a doubt, the scribes and the Pharisees were striving to follow the Torah according to their understanding, but it was just that—their understanding. Jesus' words and their resonance with themes from earlier prophets, though, simply underscored the fact that their concept of holiness based on following the purity laws had to be expanded to include doing justice. Most important, Jesus' words from the prophetic tradition as well as the justice-oriented themes within the Torah would have resonated with peasants who struggled for survival. For them, these scriptural traditions would have evoked images of God's justice that directly contradicted the patterns of exploitation and oppression that were found in their own time.[39] In contrast to those exploitative patterns, "the Torah may have called for tithes and offerings, but it also called for a sabbatical and jubilee pattern of debt cancellation, redistribution of land, and freedom from debt-servitude," therefore the following question is warranted: "How could one appeal to the Torah for support of tithes and ignore the call for justice found in the sabbatical-jubilee traditions?"[40]

Representing the Great Tradition, the scribes and Pharisees based their interpretations on the Torah. But it is not that they relied on Scripture and Jesus did not. Jesus, representing the Little Tradition, is reminding them of biblical mandates about justice that might be conveniently forgotten otherwise. In our own time, those who are committed to Christianity *and* to justice are reminding the keepers of orthodox Christianity that there are additional mandates to fulfill. Inclusive interpretations that require us to listen to voices that we usually ignore may seem new, but they are not. They are thoroughly grounded in the biblical tradition.

JESUS IDENTIFIES THE ABSOLUTE REQUIREMENT OF GOD

> When the Pharisees heard that he had silenced the Sadducees, they gathered together, and one of them, a lawyer, asked him a question to test him. "Teacher, which commandment in the law is the greatest?" He said to him, "You shall love the Lord your God with all your heart, and with all your soul, and with all your mind." This is the greatest and first commandment. And a second is like it: "You shall love your neighbor as yourself." On these two commandments hang all the law and the prophets.' (Matt. 22:34–40)

In this scene from the Gospel according to Matthew, Jesus is asked for only one commandment—the greatest commandment, but Jesus responds with two commandments. In so doing, Jesus shows that the commandment to love God is inseparable from the commandment to love one's neighbor.[41] Expressed in a slightly different way, "one cannot first love God and then, as a second task, love one's neighbor. To love God is to love one's neighbor, and vice versa" (Matt. 25:31–46).[42] It should not be forgotten that the love (*agape*) called for here "is not a matter of feeling, which cannot be commanded in any case, but of commitment and action, and it is related to the Old Testament word for 'covenant love' or 'steadfast love' (*hesed*)."[43] In essence, then, the foundational requirement of our covenantal relationship with God is to love God, and we do that by loving our neighbor, and that love is to be expressed through concrete actions.

Interestingly, that same covenantal requirement is expressed in Matthew as "having mercy towards another." In Matthew 15:21–28, a Canaanite woman approaches Jesus to request that he heal her daughter. Her first words to him are: "Have mercy on me, Lord, Son of David; my daughter is tormented by a demon" (verse 22). In that cultural context, mercy means both the willingness to pay back and the act of paying back an obligation to God and other human beings; "to have mercy means to pay one's interpersonal obligations."[44] In other words, she is asking, as a Canaanite and therefore an outsider, to be included in the same circle of care that would be owed to her if she were Jewish—and Jesus does so. Overall, Jesus justifies violating the Pharisees' rules and regulations concerning the Sabbath when a human need is being met—whether that need is for food (see Mark 2:23–28) or for healing (see Mark 3:1–6).

In fact, Jesus' emphasis on covenantal obligation under the Torah may explain why he does not directly address the Roman colonial presence around him but focuses on the scribes and Pharisees instead. Unlike the Jewish leaders, the Roman authorities were simply not subject to the same covenant and its responsibilities:

> One possible reason that Jesus focused on internal elites and virtually ignored the Roman colonial presence was the fact that Jewish leaders were honor bound to follow the Torah, and prophets from Amos to Jeremiah had used the appeal to Torah as leverage to launch their prophetic critiques of abusive ruling elites and institutions like the temple. Rome had no counterpart to the Torah, at least not one that would resonate in Galilee and Judea.[45]

At the same time, Jesus clearly recognizes that laws may not fully express the covenantal obligation to one another and so may have to be violated. In Matthew's version of the incident of plucking grain on the Sabbath, Jesus says the following words: "Have you not read in the law that on the sabbath the priests in the temple break the sabbath and yet are guiltless? I tell you, something greater than the temple is here. But if you had known what this means, "I desire mercy and not sacrifice," you would not have condemned the guiltless" (Matt. 12:5–7). In this pericope, Jesus again turns to the prophetic tradition, quoting from Hosea 6:6: "I desire steadfast love [*hesed*], not sacrifice." In the early Greek version of the Hebrew Bible (the Septuagint), the Hebrew word for covenant loyalty (*hesed*) was translated as "mercy" (*eleos*).[46] Because "mercy" is the word that appears in English translations today, as seen in the New Revised Standard Version quoted here, we must remember that, for us, "mercy" connotes a voluntary action whereas "mercy" in the biblical sense implies an obligation to act for the benefit of another. Stated alternatively, mercy refers to fulfilling a covenantal obligation to another.[47] When Jesus says, then, in Matthew 12:5–7 that "something greater than the temple is here," he is referring to God's steadfast love that we are to express. Jesus recognizes that our expressions of this love may require going beyond the traditional temple practices and its related sacrificial system, while knowing that these practices were originally intended to fulfill that obligation.[48] Changing circumstances may require that our covenantal love be expressed in a different way.

Jesus does not assume that biblical laws necessarily express the divine intention eternally for humanity, as seen in his critique of the biblical law concerning divorce (Mark 10:1–9). There, he says that allowances were made for certificates of dismissal because of human "hardness of heart," but that allowance was not God's intent. Likewise, Jesus recognizes that following the letter of the law is not always sufficient, as seen in his encounter with the rich man who had observed the commandments since his youth (Mark 10:17–22). Jesus told him that he needed to do more—to sell what he owned and give the money to the poor. In today's controversies, the traditionalists seem to think that citing a specific biblical text can silence or condemn the perspectives (when voiced) of the marginalized groups discussed here. However, this closer examination of Jesus' treatment of the Law shows that our obligation to love goes beyond the letter of the Law. In this context, Jesus' encounter with the affluent man in Mark 10:17–22, as well as the parallels in Matthew 19:16–30 and Luke 18:18–30, demonstrate how inadequate it may be to merely follow biblical laws with respect to only some groups in the community. The man asks what he must do to inherit eternal life. When Jesus quotes several of the Ten Commandments to him, the man responds by saying, "Teacher, I have kept all these since my youth" (Mark 10:20), but clearly Jesus does not think he had done enough. As Herzog describes the encounter, the rich man has not shown mercy to the marginalized, that is, he has not carried out his interpersonal obligation to them:

> Perhaps it has not occurred to the rich ruler that, while he has never killed a man face to face, he has most likely degraded peasant farmers to the status of day laborers . . . It may never have occurred to the rich man that, while he has not borne false witness in a court, he has defrauded the people of the land. Every time he has blamed his victims for the plight that he and his class have visited upon them, he is bearing false witness against them. It probably has not occurred to the rich man that, while he has never mugged anyone on the street and taken their money, he has used the system to rob the poor blind. He

> could not achieve his prominence and his wealth except at the expense of others, but he does not see this as stealing. It is called getting ahead and climbing the ladder of power and prestige.[49]

JESUS INCLUDES THE EXCLUDED The "Great Tradition" or the "tradition of the elders" as upheld by the Pharisees, whether those Pharisees were in an ancient Roman colony or are in the United States today, create outsiders—those who do not meet the established standards. In his time, Jesus violated those standards to reincorporate those who had been excluded and, therefore, every report of healing or exorcism was in fact "a gathering of the exiles."[50] Most obviously, Jesus incorporated the outsiders by eating with them:

> At table with outcasts and outlaws, Jesus was acting out an alternative political vision for the renewal of Israel that includes the ingathering of those who were made outcasts by the propagation of the great tradition of the elders. What is at stake is who will be welcomed to the table and who will be included in the meal . . . If Jesus gathers with toll collectors and sinners, he would seem to be announcing by means of this enacted parable that the purity codes of Torah, so important for the great tradition, are irrelevant at best and an obstruction at worst to the work of God's covenant renewal.[51]

The inclusive table fellowship of Jesus stands in stark contrast to the exclusive table fellowship of the Pharisees. Yet, today, marginalized groups who want to be part of Christian fellowship still struggle to be seated at the table.

Their continuing struggle may be explained at least in part by the fact that the Gospels themselves differ as to which groups are to be within the fellowship and therefore owed the covenantal obligation of love. For instance, liberation theologians are attracted to the Sermon on the Plain in Luke 6:20 and its blessing on those who are poor; but the Sermon on the Mount in Matthew would be preferred by traditionalists, since its blessings are on "the poor in spirit" (Matthew 5:3) and could refer to rich and poor alike. Similarly, there is a commandment to love one another, but the orthodox and the liberationists can disagree on which groups are to benefit from that love. In Matthew, the commandment to love extends to even the enemy (see Matt. 5:43 and 25:31–46), but the Johannine love commandment is restricted to the "Christian insider"—"the brothers and sisters" (John 13:34; 1 John 2:9–10; 3:15).[52] A necessary step in dealing with these scriptural differences, then, is to consider the different time periods and circumstances under which these Gospel narratives were written. It is worth noting, for example, that the Gospel of John was the last one written, probably between 90 and 110 CE, and its audience consisted of Christians who had previously worshiped in synagogues but had now been expelled; consequently, relations between the two groups were strained.[53] It stands to reason, then, that they would not have been in any mood to love those from whom they had recently separated, whether voluntarily or involuntarily! However, that underlying historical context should not restrict our ability to live out a more comprehensive love commandment today that includes our enemies. It is therefore incumbent upon contemporary followers of Jesus Christ to understand the sociohistorical settings behind our biblical texts and their interpretation. More important, we must interrogate any particular biblical interpretation by asking questions such as these: "Whose interest is served by the traditional interpretation of that text?"; "What is the impact of that interpretation on *all* segments of the community?"; and "Does that interpretation help to create a more inclusive table fellowship in today's world?"

In Luke 14:16–24, there is the parable of the great dinner that reads as follows:

> then Jesus said to him, "Someone gave a great dinner and invited many. At the time for the dinner he sent his slave to say to those who had been invited, 'Come; for everything is ready now.' But they all alike began to make excuses. The first said to him, 'I have bought a piece of land, and I must go out and see it; please accept my apologies.' Another said, 'I have bought five yoke of oxen, and I am going to try them out; please accept my apologies.' Another said, 'I have just been married, and therefore I cannot come.' So the slave returned and reported this to his master. Then the owner of the house became angry and said to his slave, 'Go out at once into the streets and lanes of the town and bring in the poor, the crippled, the blind, and the lame.' And the slave said, 'Sir, what you ordered has been done, and there is still room.' Then the master said to the slave, 'Go out into the roads and lanes, and compel people to come in, so that my house may be filled. For I tell you, none of those who were invited will taste my dinner.'"

Commenting on this parable, Jack Nelson-Pallmeyer notes that "some of the invited guests 'will not taste' the dinner because they reject the invitation; they miss abundant life because they are preoccupied with other things of their own choosing."[54] Therefore, Nelson-Pallmeyer continues,"Jesus invites all to live and experience abundant life here and now in the presence of God's invitational Spirit, but our choices determine whether or not abundant life is experienced."[55]

Likewise, the interpretations we choose determine if abundant life is experienced not only by all who call themselves Christians but by those others around us with whom we live in our nation and our world. Although there are texts elsewhere in the Gospels with a more apocalyptic emphasis, the following text, as interpreted by Nelson-Pallmeyer, offers an open invitation to all to experience the abundant life here and now, if we only follow the nudge of God's bidding:

> God's Spirit can and does bid us to be loving, generous, and to work for equity and justice, but divine threats and God's "power" cannot force us to be just. The result of my bad choices is that I miss out on abundant life and hurt others. The result of collective refusal of the Spirit's invitation can be catastrophic, not because of God's punishing violence but because our choices lead to war and not peace, inequality and not shared gifts, environmental stress and not the health of the earth. The spiral of violence is unchallenged and unbroken.[56]

Focusing on Paul

The same elements of inclusive biblical interpretation found in the Gospels are found in the Pauline writings. As we will see, Paul identified the absolute requirement of God, he grounded his interpretations in Scripture, he considered the impact of interpretations on the excluded and marginalized, and he extended community boundaries to include those formerly excluded.

Before beginning to cover the specific elements of Paul's inclusive biblical interpretation, though, I need to explain how I can even mention Paul and an inclusive/liberationist approach to biblical interpretation in the same sentence. Isn't Paul antiwomen, antigay, and pro-slavery? Consequently, before developing his inclusive approach, I have to review the traditional interpretations and show how more liberative interpretations of these same texts are possible. Stated alternatively, I need to "liberate Paul" from the dominant readings that have protected privileges and upheld the marginalization of women, people of color, and homosexuals.[57] For this reason, I have to address the common misconceptions about Paul and the New Testament writings that can be attributed to him.

At first glance, there are thirteen New Testament writings that were written by Paul. However, biblical scholars, noting differences in writing style, vocabulary, and theology, divide these writings into three categories. There are the seven undisputed Pauline epistles: Romans, 1 Corinthians, 2 Corinthians,

Galatians, Philippians, 1 Thessalonians, and Philemon. These epistles have stylistic and thematic similarities, and "the issues they address can plausibly be situated in the early Christian movement of the 40s and 50s of the Common Era, when Paul was active as an apostle and missionary."[58]

The Deutero-Pauline epistles are next (Ephesians, Colossians, and 2 Thessalonians); scholars think they may possibly have been written pseudonymously, that is, by authors who were writing under a false name. In this case, these pseudonymous documents are referred to as Deutero-Pauline because they are "thought by many scholars to have been written by a 'second Paul,' a later author (or rather three later authors) who was (or were) heavily influenced by Paul's teachings (the term 'Deutero-' means 'second').[59] Although the debates are ongoing, "most scholars continue to think that Paul did not write Ephesians and probably not Colossians and the case for 2 Thessalonians has proved somewhat more difficult to resolve."[60] The three Pastoral Epistles (1 Timothy, 2 Timothy, and Titus) were written after the Deutero-Pauline texts and provide instruction to pastors engaged in pastoral duties. It is thought that these letters were written by a later member of one of Paul's churches who wanted to appeal to his authority in dealing with situations that had arisen after his death.[61]

These distinctions about the Pauline writings are important to this study because, since we want to know about Paul's theology and ethics, our analysis has to focus primarily on the seven undisputed writings. Moreover, the existence of the Pastoral Epistles in Scripture demonstrates how a tradition, the Pauline tradition, is adapted to a later time and place to fit the needs of a subsequent generation. Some Christians might mistakenly feel disappointed after learning that the Deutero-Pauline texts and the Pastoral Epistles were, in all likelihood, not written by Paul. Instead, there should be a sense of assurance because these texts show us how Paul's tradition became a living tradition. Paul's influence did not end with his death but continued afterward because those who followed in his name extrapolated Pauline themes from his writings and used them to address the concerns of these later faith communities. Accordingly, we should feel divinely empowered to adapt comparable Pauline traditions to the concerns of our faith communities today. Having covered these distinctions among the Pauline writings, we now have a better background for discussing Paul's thoughts on women, sexuality, and slavery.

Women

The restrictive language concerning women in the Pauline corpus is well known: "Wives, be subject to your husbands" (Eph. 5:22; Col. 3:18), and "I permit no woman to teach or to have authority over a man; she is to keep silent" (1 Timothy 2:12). Obviously, the first point to make is that these texts, Ephesians, Colossians, and 1 Timothy, were probably not written by Paul. Instead, they reflect the concerns of later generations, one of which was the need to emphasize the paterfamilias, the (heterosexual) male-headed family unit, as "the appropriate ordering of the household."[62]

> It was generally accepted that wives, children, and slaves should submit fully to the rule of the husband-father-master and practice his religion. The household was believed to be an economically independent, self-sufficient unit that was the basis of the state. Several households constituted a village, and several villages a city-state or *politeia*.[63]

Scholars have proposed different reasons for why the paterfamilias needed to be emphasized in those subsequent generations. As summarized by Clarice Martin, these include "minimizing the perception that the Christians were a threat to the Greco-Roman social order"; and, after they had benefited initially from a more egalitarian ethos in those early Christian communities, the "enthusiasm of women and slaves" was being restricted so that order could be restored to the patriarchal household.[64] For the purposes of this study, what is most significant is that the paterfamilias was the social pattern of the day, and (heterosexual male) Christian leaders were making sure that their families functioned in the same way. However, in the United States today, the civil society allows for more egalitarian roles between women and men, yet traditional Christians cling to the paterfamilias model as biblically mandated. We tend to forget that the biblical mandate was an accommodation to the Greco-Roman world made, in all likelihood, to avoid accusations of being disruptive or threatening social conventions. Since our faith is a living tradition, though, Christians can now adopt more inclusive and empowering models that are consistent with our early history and the contemporary culture in which we live.

There is, however, 1 Timothy 2, which implies a universal rationale for women's subordination, rather than a contextual one, based on Genesis 2–3. As mentioned earlier, though, 1 Timothy is one of the pseudonymous writings and, as such, was not written by Paul. In fact, on at least two points 1 Timothy contradicts statements from the undisputed Pauline writings. For example, in 1 Timothy, Eve is blamed for the transgression in the garden, but "according to Paul, Adam, the first human, committed the first sin—disobedience (Rom. 5:12–21)."[65] Similarly, according to 1 Timothy 2:15, women are to achieve salvation through childbearing, but "Paul advocates celibacy rather than marriage and motherhood for women, although he also considers marriage fully legitimate (1 Cor. 7:1–40)."[66]

Nevertheless, there are two negative passages toward women in the undisputed Pauline corpus that must be considered, both of which are in 1 Corinthians. First Corinthians 14:33b–36 mandates that "women should be silent in the churches. For they are not permitted to speak, but should be subordinate, as the law also says." However, such "an outright ban on women speaking in church contradicts Paul's earlier instructions in 1 Corinthians 11:5."[67] Furthermore, J. Paul Sampley states emphatically that "in the six undisputed letters apart from 1 Corinthians, *no passage suggests any limitation on the roles or functions of women in the Pauline churches.*"[68] Because this limitation is similar to that found in Ephesians and Colossians and the later Pastoral Epistles, Sampley thinks that the language in 1 Corinthians is an interpolation, that is, language that was added at a later point in time:

> If Paul's letters were collected around the turn of the first and second centuries, as is a reasonable assumption, a time sometimes also argued for the writing of the Pastoral Epistles, then the redactor could readily have inserted 1 Cor 14:34–36 to bring the picture of Corinth's worship practices in line with what he thought appropriate in his own time. The result: Women should be silent in church and submissive to their husbands, despite the fact that neither of these positions is sustained by the rest of 1 Corinthians nor by the six other undisputed Pauline letters that we can be sure came from the hand of Paul.[69]

In 1 Corinthians 11:2–16, Paul is disturbed that some of the women in the congregation are not wearing head coverings. Based on his research, Richard Burridge concludes that the crux of the matter was decorum in worship rather than gender relationships in general, given the extensive references in the undisputed Pauline writings to the women who helped him in his ministry.[70] Moreover, a discernible theological principle in Paul's writings is that the death and resurrection of Jesus shattered creation's boundaries and also shattered traditional human boundaries such as those of gender.[71] Accordingly, Brian Blount sees in Pauline theology a basic affirmation that "all people, regardless of gender, ethnicity, race, status, or stature are equally acceptable in God's sight and therefore must be equally treated in human living."[72]

Slavery

The *Haustafeln* (Household Codes), which mandated that wives were to be subject to their husbands, also mandated that slaves were to obey their masters (Eph. 6:5–8; Col. 3:22–25). As Clarice Martin documents in her article on these codes, the American slavery system was justified by directly appealing to these codes as representing "the infinite intelligence of a personal God, whose will, because of his infinite excellence, is necessarily the ultimate ground and rule for all moral obligation."[73]

At the same time, those who sought to abolish slavery also appealed to biblical texts, but naturally ones that are different from those used by slave-holders and their supporters:

> A favorite New Testament narrative used in the argument against slavery was Acts 17:26: God "made from one [ancestor] every nation of men to live on all the face of the earth, having determined allotted periods and the boundaries of their habitation." First Corinthians 12:13 was also a favorite text: "For by one Spirit we were all baptized into one body—Jews or Greeks, slaves or free—and all were made to drink of one Spirit." The unmistakable emphasis on the "universal parenthood of God" and the "kinship of humankind" was a persistent theme in abolitionist rhetoric.[74]

Martin asserts that before, during, and after the Civil War, "African Americans rejected the proslavery, literalist interpretations used to sanction involuntary servitude, proclaiming, to the contrary, that the Bible witnessed to an all-powerful, liberating God who in Jesus Christ was concerned for the ultimate and holistic liberation of all of humanity."[75] For our purposes, it is noteworthy that African Americans appealed to First Corinthians, an undisputed Pauline text, whereas the slave owners appealed to the Household Codes, which are Deutero-Pauline, at best. In this contest, the antislavery position was a better representation of the foundational Pauline tradition.

Nevertheless, problematic texts concerning slavery do exist in the undisputed Pauline corpus. First Corinthians 7:21–24 reads as follows:

> Were you a slave when called? Do not be concerned about it. Even if you can gain your freedom, make use of your present condition now more than ever. For whoever was called in the Lord as a slave is a freed person belonging to the Lord, just as whoever was free when called is a slave of Christ. You were bought with a price; do not become slaves of human masters. In whatever condition you were called, brothers and sisters, there remain with God.

As Neil Elliott points out, verse 21 can be translated as "Even if you have the opportunity to become free, make use of your slavery instead" (as reflected in the NRSV), but it can also be translated with an opposite meaning: "If you have the opportunity to become free, by all means take it!"[76] After his extensive analysis of this verse, Elliott argues that the former interpretation is the one more widely used simply because translators read the Household Codes into this passage. In this way, he sees "the pseudo-Pauline writings contaminating the interpretation of 1 Corinthians 7:21–24."[77]

Similarly, Paul's epistle to Philemon is disappointing from a liberationist perspective because he returns Onesimus to Philemon, his owner. Nevertheless, Burridge thinks that there is "subversive rhetoric" that underlies Paul's letter:[78]

> On the surface level, Paul keeps the law and returns Onesimus, Philemon's runaway slave, to him (v. 12). He even offers to take responsibility for any losses or amounts owing (vv. 18–19). He goes out of his way not to command Philemon "to do your duty," yet instead he delivers lots of rhetorical appeals to how much Philemon owes Paul (vv. 8–9, 14, 19–21). The reason for all this is that Onesimus has been converted by Paul in prison; he is no longer just a slave but Paul's "child" and "a beloved brother" (vv. 10, 16). Paul appeals to his central ethical value of love (v. 9) that Philemon should "welcome him as you would welcome me" (v. 17).[79]

Lloyd Lewis, in his African American appraisal of this epistle, notes the same emphasis on familial language in Philemon and combines it with the imagery of the family of God in Galatians 3:1–4:7.[80] Taking both texts into account, Lewis thinks that "Paul has brought to light the implications of [Philemon] being his child and the child of God in a church and community where equal status under the gospel, as shown in Galatians, is a virtue and where an apostle, a runaway slave, and a slaveholder can be interchanged."[81]

It is in the setting of this new family of God that Philemon is to determine Onesimus's fate. On the whole, the Pauline tradition has been interpreted in ways that are not helpful to any liberationist struggle. Nevertheless, we have seen that alternative interpretations of these texts are possible, and there are theological elements underlying these texts that can be used by inclusive Christian communities.

Sexuality

In 1 Corinthians 7:1–24, Paul does recommend a degree of mutuality between husbands and wives:

> The husband should give to his wife her conjugal rights, and likewise the wife to her husband. For the wife does not have authority over her own body, but the husband does; likewise the husband does not have authority over his own body, but the wife does. Do not deprive one

> another except perhaps by agreement for a set time, to devote yourselves to prayer, and then come together again, so that Satan may not tempt you because of your lack of self-control.

However, as Jouette Bassler observes, "Paul's insistence on sexual relations within marriage, however mutual they might have been, is predicated on a concern for self-control" and he defines sex within marriage "in rather joyless terms."[82] She continues by writing: "He seems to view marriage exclusively and negatively as a means of sexual containment, and there are no references to love or procreation."[83] Dale Martin makes the same point, but more bluntly:

> Paul was apparently not a very romantic fellow. While most modern Christians consider marriage the proper sphere for the expression of desire (perhaps we should specify *heterosexual* desire), Paul considered marriage a mechanism by which desire could be extinguished. In Paul's view, unlike that of some other ascetic-oriented writers of his day, sex was not so much the problem as desire. And sexual intercourse within the bounds of marriage functioned to keep desire from happening. Sex within marriage was not the expression of desire, proper or improper; rather it was the prophylaxis against desire.[84]

As a related issue, Martin argues that moralists in the Greco-Roman world (including most Jewish moralists of Paul's day) "generally believed that homosexual behavior sprang from the same desire that motivated heterosexual sex."[85]

> According to these moralists, some people, due to unrestrained sexual desire, grew bored with "basic" sexual activity and went cruising for new and untried pleasures. Women, no longer satisfied by sex with their husbands, would be led in their lasciviousness to experiment with bestiality. Men were so enslaved to their lusts that they were eager to try activities out of the ordinary, such as sex with one another. The problem had to do not with *disoriented* desire, but with *inordinate* desire. Degree of passion, rather than object choice, was the defining factor of desire.[86]

Correspondingly, Martin contends that references to "unnatural acts" in this ancient context do not refer to desire but to acts that violate the presumed male dominance/female subordinate gender paradigm.[87] That gender paradigm presumes that the man is dominant, the penetrator, and that the female is subordinate, the penetrated. Male homosexuality is therefore thought to be "unnatural" because it connotes a male who is penetrated and therefore subordinate.

Although the amount of literature on homosexuality, the Bible, and the church has increased tremendously,[88] Paul's negative view of *heterosexuality* is usually not considered along with his negative view of *homosexuality.* If we consider both simultaneously and are trying to adopt Paul's attitudes as our own, we must exercise great caution. We need to realize that Paul does not have an adequate view of heterosexuality, so it should not be surprising that his view of homosexuality is not adequate either. At the very least, we should be puzzled, as Burridge is, over "why being against homosexuality, about which Jesus and the gospels have nothing to say and Paul has only these passing references alongside many other sins equally common to heterosexuals (1 Cor. 6:9–11, 1 Tim. 1:10, and Rom. 1:24–27) should have become the acid test of what it means to be truly 'biblical' in a number of quarters in recent years."[89]

The goal of the preceding discussion on women, slavery, and sexuality was to undermine the apparently ironclad association of Paul with antiwomen, antigay, and pro-slavery sentiments. These texts have traditionally been interpreted in ways that work against the interests of the "Other." As we have seen, though, the texts can be read differently. Hopefully, we will be able to read Paul now in a more contextual and liberationist manner.

Paul: Elements of Inclusive Biblical Interpretation

PAUL INCLUDES THE EXCLUDED AND HE BASES IT ON THE BIBLICAL TRADITION

In Galatians 1:13–17, Paul describes himself as having advanced in his faith beyond many among his people because he was far more zealous for the traditions of his ancestors. During this time, he "was violently persecuting the church of God and was trying to destroy it." That persecution of the early Christians ended with Paul's Damascus Road experience (Acts 9:1–30; 22:1–21; 26:1–18). As a result of that experience, Paul knew that Christians (particularly Gentiles) were also the people of God, and he expanded his notion of the faith community to include them. Contrary to popular (Christian) belief, Paul was an observant Jew and remained so (see, e.g., Acts 21:17–26). Consequently, some scholars have indicated that references to Paul's "conversion" have been misleading and that it is more accurate to describe his experience as a "calling" to the Gentiles.[90] Paul's encounter with Jesus on the Damascus Road, as reported in Acts, reshapes his theology, and from that time onward, Jesus' life, death, and resurrection have fundamental implications for the new life in Christ that directly impact Paul's understanding of the basic relationship between God and human beings.[91]

From this theological perspective, Paul envisions a new community that is shaped by two primary rites: baptism (Rom. 6:1–14; 1 Cor. 12:12–13; Gal. 2:26–29) and the Lord's Supper (1 Cor. 10:16–17 and 11:17–34).[92] In this way, "Paul redraws the boundary around the people of God, those 'inside' the group, such that it includes all who are in Christ, both Jews and Gentiles."[93] Therefore, merely "being in Christ is the basis for the solidarity of this new community."[94] Paul finds the biblical basis for his new theological insight in his rereading of Scripture. In Galatians 3:15–20, Paul distinguishes between the promise of blessings God gave Abraham and his offspring, and the giving of the law that occurred 400 years later. He concludes that the law could not annul that previous covenantal promise. Furthermore, those blessings were meant to include Gentiles ["all the nations"] through Abraham; therefore, Gentiles can be heirs of the promise and participants in that tradition—even though they do not follow the law.[95] In this way, Paul is basing his radically inclusive ministry on the biblical tradition itself.

On the whole, Paul's view of the law is quite negative in Galatians. In that epistle, Paul is responding to Christian missionaries (formerly referred to as Judaizers) active within the congregation who required circumcision as a necessary means of entering into covenantal relationship with God.[96]

> Paul equates being under the law (3:23) to being under sin (3:22), under a yoke of slavery (5:1) and in prison (3:23). He even equates the Galatians' desire to be under the law with a return to their previous idolatry: "Now, however, that you have come to know God, or rather to be known by God, how can you turn back again [by submitting to circumcision] to the weak and beggarly elemental spirits? How can you want to be enslaved to them *again*?" (4:9)[97]

In addition, Paul insists that the law, among other things, "could not and did not have the function of justifying or making righteous (2:21; 3:11) . . . it had a more limited, temporary, but nevertheless important role of the *paidagōgos*, the slave charged with training, disciplining, and protecting the master's sons until they came of age (3:23–26)."[98]

Paul's vehement opposition to mandatory circumcision was because of its connotation that Gentiles are not entirely acceptable to God as they were:

> Paul's response was dictated by his opponents' insistence that Gentile believers were *required* to come under the law, that is, to become Jews, in order to be full members of God's people. To Paul that meant that Gentiles *as Gentiles* were not acceptable to God, yet the workings of the Spirit among the men and women in Galatia provided compelling

> evidence, to Paul, at least, that Gentiles *were* acceptable—as Gentiles—to God. Therefore Gentiles must not come "under the law"—that is, become Jews—for to do so would deny the reality of the grace they had all experienced.[99]

Paul includes the formerly excluded, the Gentiles, as they were and without requiring that they be changed through circumcision. His acceptance of them into the full fellowship of God, though, is done on the basis of his understanding of preceding theological and biblical traditions.

PAUL CONSIDERS THE IMPACT OF AN INTERPRETATION OR POLICY ON THE MARGINALIZED In 1 Corinthians 8:1–13, one of the issues dividing the congregation was the use of meat that had been offered to idols (sacrificed meat). As explained by Ehrman:

> Meat that was sold at the pagan temples could be purchased at a discount . . . Some of the Corinthian Christians (those who were less educated, in the lower classes?) thought that to eat such meat was tantamount to sharing in idolatry; they would not touch it on any condition. Others (more highly educated, in the upper classes?) claimed superior knowledge, in this case, pointing out that idols had no real existence since there were no gods other than the one true God. Eating such meat could therefore do no harm and actually save much needed resources.[100]

Obviously, Paul knows that other gods do not exist, but he advises against eating the meat because "those who see a ('knowledgeable/strong') Christian eating such meat (the 'weak') may be encouraged to do so themselves, even while thinking that the gods do exist" and so harm their conscience (8:7–10).[101] The lesson Paul teaches in this pericope is that "believers must factor into their moral deliberation not only how the contemplated action fits them and their relation to God but also how such an action might affect another."[102] Considering 1 Corinthians 8–10 as a unit means that Paul allows those who honor the restrictions to continue (but they are not to enforce those restrictions on others (see Gal. 2:11–14). At the same time, those who would not ordinarily be concerned about the restrictions must be sensitive to those who are concerned about them and exercise some restraint (thereby restricting their freedom) by not forcing the other group to abandon their food laws.

In David Horrell's analysis of Pauline ethics, this pericope demonstrates the importance of one's regard for the other in Christian community and constitutes a norm that he refers to as "other-regard." As he describes it, "The basis for discerning what is good and acceptable is not what one knows to be the case ('there is no idol in the world') and what is therefore justifiable—ethics based on theological knowledge—but rather a generous regard for the other, a self-giving love as embodied in Christ."[103] Paul's Christological model is made more explicit in 1 Corinthians 10:31–11:1: "So, whether you eat or drink, or whatever you do, do everything for the glory of God. Give no offence to Jews or to Greeks or to the church of God, just as I try to please everyone in everything I do, not seeking my own advantage, but that of many, so that they may be saved. Be imitators of me, as I am of Christ."

Paul discusses a comparable issue about food in Romans 14–15. There, however, the issue is about unclean food according to Jewish law, rather than sacrificed meat as in 1 Corinthians. In the Roman setting, there are essentially two groups that are at opposite ends of a spectrum: "one abstains entirely from meat and wine to avoid breaking the law and contamination; the other regards all food and drink as clean and acceptable."[104]

> Welcome those who are weak in faith, but not for the purpose of quarrelling over opinions.Some believe in eating anything, while the weak eat only vegetables. Those who eat must not despise those who abstain, and those who abstain must not pass judgment on those who eat; for God has welcomed them. Who are you to pass judgment on servants of another? It is before their own lord that they stand or fall. And they will be upheld, for the Lord is able to make them stand. (Romans 14:1–3)

Consequently, Horrell sees Paul legitimating here different patterns of ethical conduct within the same community and removing from those differences a basis for judgment or criticism. For Horrell, such accommodation to difference exemplifies Paul's ethic of "other-regard" because it shows that "the basis for ethical action is not one's own convictions and judgments in regard to a substantive issue but rather one's responsibilities towards others."[105]

> The Pauline Christian cannot do ethics monologically, reflecting in isolation on what is right and wrong, but can only make that discernment as a situated participant, in the context of human relationships: what is right or wrong in terms of one's conduct cannot be specified in the abstract, but only in terms of a particular community setting, in relation to the others with whom one is placed.[106]

A responsibility to others also includes those of a different socioeconomic level, since class divisions are implied in 1 Corinthians 8–10 and are made more explicit in 1 Corinthians 11:17–22:

> Now in the following instructions I do not commend you, because when you come together it is not for the better but for the worse. For, to begin with, when you come together as a church, I hear that there are divisions among you; and to some extent I believe it. Indeed, there have to be factions among you, for only so will it become clear who among you are genuine. When you come together, it is not really to eat the Lord's supper. For when the time comes to eat, each of you goes ahead with your own supper, and one goes hungry and another becomes drunk. What! Do you not have homes to eat and drink in? Or do you show contempt for the church of God and humiliate those who have nothing? What should I say to you? Should I commend you? In this matter I do not commend you!

Apparently, during community gatherings for the Lord's Supper, some members who were more affluent were able to arrive early and have food and drink; whereas those who arrived later were poorer, and they "found, along with tipsy coworshippers, leftover food at best."[107] Paul's chastising of the affluent in these texts has led Elliott to conclude that Paul is setting out a critique of the ideology of privilege.[108] Developing more fully the notion of Paul's mission as a form of resistance, Richard Horsley suggests that Paul is proposing an alternative society, and he wants each congregation "to maintain their solidarity as an exclusive community that stands against the larger (imperial) society."[109]

PAUL IDENTIFIES THE ABSOLUTE REQUIREMENT OF GOD As covered earlier, the essence of Jesus' ethics was the double commandment to love God and neighbor.[110] Although Paul does not quote the double command as such, love features prominently in his writings, and it is motivated by his Christology because he "describes love in the same terms he uses for Christ."[111]

> Love does not seek its own (1 Cor. 13:5), even as Christ did not please himself (Rom. 15:3; Phil. 2:3–5). To "walk," or live, "in accord with love" (Rom. 14:15), is to live "in accord with Christ Jesus," . . . (Rom. 15:5). To be "rooted in love" is another way of being "rooted in Christ" (compare Eph. 3:17 with Col. 2:7). Paul was supremely motivated by Christ, "who loved me and gave himself for me" (Gal. 2:20). God's love is shown by the death of Christ "while we were yet sinners," and "poured into our hearts through the Holy Spirit" (Rom. 5:5, 8).[112]

After his review of the relevant literature, Burridge concludes that "love is a central theme for both Paul's theology and his ethics, arising from his own personal experience of the love of God in Christ: 'The life I now live in the flesh I live by faith in the Son of God, who loved me and gave himself for me' (Gal. 2:20)."[113] Paul's emphasis on love influences his understanding of the Law, as seen in Galatians 5:14 and Romans 13:8–10. Basically, loving your neighbor fulfills the law.

> For the whole law is summed up in a single commandment, "You shall love your neighbor as yourself." (Gal. 5:14)
>
> Owe no one anything, except to love one another; for the one who loves another has fulfilled the law. The commandments, "You shall not commit adultery; You shall not murder; You shall not steal; You shall not covet"; and any other commandment, are summed up in this word, "Love your neighbor as yourself." Love does no wrong to a neighbor; therefore, love is the fulfilling of the law. (Rom. 13:8–10)

Therefore, Paul can assert that "Christ is the end of the law" (Romans 10:4), which, it is important to point out, "probably means that Christ is the *goal*, not the termination of the law."[114] In other words, Christ is the goal of the law because of the love he exhibits for others; in turn, our exhibiting that love is the goal of the law, too. Similarly, James Dunn suggests that, for Paul, the law can only be fulfilled through the love command, and "it is epitomized supremely in the life of Jesus himself."[115] Burridge describes Paul's Christological emphasis on love in the following way:

> Once again, Christology is central in that the law is fulfilled in what the love of God has done in Christ. Accordingly, such love, as exemplified in the life and teaching of Jesus, is the supreme commandment, which is to be lived out in the ethical behaviour of Christians. While they have been set free from the demands of the law, they are not lawless or immoral antinomians—for the Spirit of Christ provides both the power and the desire to live a holy life.[116]

Conclusions

In brief, both Jesus and Paul were aware of the realities of the excluded and the hardships caused by those exclusions, and they expanded the boundaries of their faith communities to include those groups. Jesus included primarily the peasants who had been marginalized but were ostensibly within the community already. Paul included the Gentiles who had been explicitly excluded from the community as outsiders. In both cases, the motivation for these expanded community boundaries was theological. The central message of Jesus' ethical teaching was that "the kingdom of God is at hand" (Mark 1:15; Luke 10:9).[117] Correspondingly, Paul's emphasis was Christological because he affirmed that God was inaugurating the divine reign in Jesus, and, as people of faith, we were to respond to what God has done in Christ.[118] Most important, both of them emphasized the life of faith as one lived in a new community of those who had similarly responded to God's call.[119] The traditional categories of gender, religious heritage, ethnicity, and class no longer restricted participation in that new realm.

It is clear from the structure of this chapter, though, that Jesus and Paul did not just consider the realities of the excluded and the impact traditional interpretations had on them. They also rejected and reinterpreted laws and policies that continued the exclusion and marginalization. In so doing, they grounded their expanded understandings of the laws and policies in the biblical tradition and the absolute requirement of God. As for biblical traditions, Jesus referred to the prophetic tradition (Mark 7:5–8), and Paul found the basis for an inclusive community in his reading of the divine promises to Abraham and his descendants (Gal. 3:15–20). In the same way, both of them found the law of loving God and neighbor to be the absolute requirement of God (Matthew 22:34–40; Galatians 5:14; Romans 13:8–10). Stated alternatively, the law of love overrides and transcends traditional boundaries and is the theological basis for their inclusive biblical understandings.

From a liberationist perspective, Matthew 22:40 and its expression of the double love commandment expresses the purpose and unity of Scripture and constitutes a norm that can be used to critically evaluate biblical interpretations and church policies.[120] Precedent for the rule of love can also be found in the writings of Augustine, who "identifies the purpose of scripture as love for God and neighbor," as well as in one of the foundational documents of the Reformed tradition, the Second Helvetic Confession of 1566, which "holds as 'orthodox and genuine' those interpretations of scripture that 'agree with the rule of faith and love, and contribute much to the glory of God and man's salvation.'"[121]

However, not all New Testament scholars would agree that a rule of love is sufficient as a guide. For example, Richard Hays does not think that love is a unifying theme of New Testament ethics.[122] And as Dale Martin points out, Hauerwas contends that "love" is "an abstraction" and its application is too often "sentimental."[123] Yet Martin strongly feels that the Christian community that both Hauerwas and Hays posit will be deficient if they have not grappled sufficiently with the concept of loving the excluded. He writes that "the invocation of Christian 'community' may appeal to those who have experienced Christian groups as open-minded, loving, and benevolent; but to many of us—most lesbian, gay, and other 'nonstraight' Christians—Christian communities have just as often been a source of hatred and sin."[124] Martin finishes his critique of their concept of community by stating that these communities still need to practice love toward those now marginalized. As described by Martin, "the recent popular appeal to Christian community, therefore, is not only less than satisfactory for most of us lesbian and gay Christians. We find the easy appeal to 'community' not only too facile but even threatening without more emphasis on a demand that those communities practice, *toward us*, love."[125]

In this regard, it is important to combine the double love command of Jesus with his exhortations to love one's enemies. As Richard Burridge explains, "The centrality of love in Jesus' ethics even extends to the love of enemies," and Burridge cites, among other passages, the parable of the Good Samaritan (Luke 10:29–37), where the community's concept of neighbor is "widened beyond national boundaries, even to those who are despised."[126] It seems to me that a rule of love can take on new meaning if the focus shifts toward loving the groups that have been systematically marginalized, that is, those that are outside of the *mythical norm*. In today's Christian communities, the rule of love would stretch us toward inclusion, where inclusion is defined by Eric Law as follows: "Inclusion is a discipline of extending our boundary to take into consideration another's needs, interests, experience, and perspective, which will lead to clearer understanding of ourselves and others, fuller description of the issue at hand, and possibly a newly negotiated boundary of the community to which we belong."[127] As mentioned previously, the privileged elite tend to ignore the perspectives of the "Other" and the consequences of their traditions and rulings on those groups. A true act of love would be to listen, to learn of their struggles, and then be open to transformation. One crucial thing that the privileged elite could learn through this process is that *their* concept of love is not the same as that of the subordinate groups. To the contrary, the elite group's concept of love has contributed to their marginalization. Here are some representative statements about love from the privileged perspective that have shaped human history: "We love our [white] women so we want to protect them and keep them in the home"; "We love dark-skinned peoples so we will colonize them and bring them civilization"; "We love Jews so we will convert them all to Christianity."

What constitutes a loving act is defined and evaluated by the privileged elite and, as the preceding examples demonstrate, the violent consequences to the subordinate groups are ignored. Under a dominant/subordinate paradigm, the subordinate are rendered objects and their full humanity is not recognized. The subordinate groups are spoken to; they do not speak. A redefined rule of love, therefore, should prompt encounters between those in the dominant group and those of the nondominant groups, where the dominant will listen and the subordinate will speak. In that way, we can all work toward a fuller expression of God's love in our midst and the corresponding development of radically inclusive communities.[128]

5

The Protestant Reformers and Inclusive Biblical Interpretation

I contend, among other things, that the "official" Christian tradition is usually defined by the exclusion of certain perspectives, including those of women, people of color, and gays and lesbians. Accordingly, groups that uphold those exclusions today are considered to be more consistent with Christian principles ("the conservatives") than those groups that try to include these different persons and their perspectives ("the liberals"). In this chapter, I will show that inclusive approaches to theology and biblical interpretation are entirely consistent with the Protestant tradition—and that may come as a surprise to some! Initially, I will discuss the ongoing validity of biblical law as acknowledged by the major Protestant reformers, Martin Luther, John Calvin, and John Wesley. The next section of this chapter outlines how each of these reformers took into account both his historical context and his theological understanding when reading the Bible—hence the heading, "Thinking Contextually/Thinking Theologically. That section is followed by one that addresses the related issues of the reformers' concept of biblical authority and its influence on how they interpreted the Bible. The final section presents a more focused discussion of just one aspect of each reformer's thought that supports inclusive biblical interpretation. As will be seen, the Protestant heritage is one that is based on biblical readings that are both contextual and theological, and these readings can result in interpretations that go against the received tradition. Contemporary interpreters, then, who recognize the harm caused by exclusion and read the Bible in ways that affirm the inclusive love of Jesus Christ, are today's standard-bearers of that heritage.

Concerning the laws of the Old Testament, many Protestants assume that they were nullified by the Christ event and the texts of the New Testament. However, the major Protestant reformers, Luther, Calvin, and Wesley, considered biblical laws to have ongoing validity in Christian life. As the founders of substantial branches of the Protestant tradition, their attitudes toward these laws are important to people of faith in our own time. Generally speaking, all Protestants trace their spiritual lineage back to Luther, but the denominations related to the Lutheran tradition do so more directly. Likewise, Calvin and his writings are significant to those denominations in the Reformed tradition such as the Presbyterians, and Wesley is the spiritual father of the Methodist tradition and its related denominations.[1]

For Luther, biblical laws (referred to collectively as the law) served two purposes. In other words, there is "a double use of the law."[2] One of these is the civic use, which functions to "restrain transgressions." Luther describes it as follows in his comments on Galatians 3: "When I refrain from killing or from committing adultery or from stealing, or when I abstain from other sins, I do not do this voluntarily or from the love of virtue but because I am afraid of the sword and of the executioner."[3] In this way, Luther sees a divine purpose in the role of parents, teachers, and judges, as well as in the existence of civic ordinances to "restrain the wicked."[4] The second use of the law is "the theological or spiritual one," which reveals to human beings their sinful nature, when they arrogantly presume their own righteousness, and so makes them aware of their need for God.[5] As Luther expressed it, "the true function and the chief and proper use of the Law is to reveal to man his sin, blindness, misery, wickedness, ignorance, hate and contempt of God, death, hell, judgment, and the well-deserved wrath of God."[6]

Similarly, Calvin sees the law as having a role that "displays the justice of God" and so reveals to those who had convinced themselves of their own righteousness just "how far they were distant from true righteousness."[7] Consequently, this use of the law is pedagogical because "it warns, informs, convicts, and lastly condemns, every man of his own unrighteousness," and, after having "convict[ed] man of his infirmity," it then moves "him to call upon the remedy of grace which is in Christ."[8] Furthermore, just as Luther did, Calvin sees a political use of both biblical and civic laws that serve "by fear of punishment to restrain certain men who are untouched by any care for what is just and right unless compelled by hearing the dire threats in the law."[9] However, unlike Luther, Calvin also identified a third use of the law in the life of the faithful Christian. For him, this third use is the law's principle purpose and more closely reflects the correct purpose of the law as it "finds its place among believers in whose hearts the Sprit of God already lives and reigns."[10] In this way, Calvin thought the law helped to make stronger and more obedient Christians: "because we need not only teaching but also exhortation, the servant of God will also avail himself of this benefit of the law: by frequent meditation upon it to be aroused to obedience, be strengthened in it, and be drawn back from the slippery path of transgression.[11]

For Luther and the Lutheran tradition, a third use of the law risks creating a new form of legalism in which it is thought that one's acts according to the law result in salvation; yet for Calvin and Calvinism, the law has a positive role for believers as it conveys images of "order and structure" that are indicative of God's love in creation and the offer of redemption.[12]

For Wesley, too, the law's use does not end with one's justifying faith in Jesus Christ, as was argued by the Moravians of his day; Wesley was well aware of the ways in which believers still struggled against sin:[13]

> For it is still of unspeakable use, first, in convincing us of the sin that yet remains both in our hearts and lives, and thereby keeping us close to Christ, that his blood may cleanse us every moment; secondly, in deriving strength from our Head into his living members, whereby he empowers them to do what his law commands; and thirdly, in confirming our hope of whatsoever it commands and we have not yet attained, of receiving grace upon grace, till we are in actual possession of the fullness of his promises.[14]

Summarizing the uses of the law, Wesley finds that they convince individuals of their sinful nature (which is the work of the Holy Spirit); they bring the sinner to Christ; and they help to "keep . . . alive" persons of faith.[15] To help persons of faith who were progressing in their spiritual journey, Wesley recommended preaching the law "not only as a command but a privilege also, as a branch of the glorious liberty of the sons of God," but if the faithful were "drawing back," then the preacher should preach the law as done "before they were convinced of sin."[16] As seen in Wesley's statement, a basic Protestant understanding is that sinful human beings had not been able to live according to the dictates of the law, but after the Christ event and receiving the gifts of the Holy Spirit and a justifying faith in God, they have internalized the law and are now able to do what they could not have done previously. Correspondingly, Calvin recognizes, as did Wesley, the same positive role of the law in the life of believers: "To be Christians under the law of grace does not mean to wander unbridled outside the law, but to be engrafted in Christ, by whose grace we are free of the curse of the law, and by whose Spirit we have the law engraved upon our hearts" (Jer. 31:33).[17]

Having established that biblical law in general has uses in the lives of Christians, it is worth investigating which laws in particular were upheld by the Protestant reformers. On the one hand, they considered to be obsolete the ceremonial laws pertaining to ancient Israelite religious practices (including those of the Temple) and laws relating to the judicial system of that ancient community. On the other hand, they thought that the moral law had continuing relevance, and the epitome of moral law was the Decalogue (Ten Commandments). However, for each of the Protestant reformers, the dictates of the Decalogue were augmented by their understandings of Jesus Christ. Luther's concept of the Decalogue was broader than the biblical one because he envisioned additional requirements given through Christ with new insights about God's will and new powers to live accordingly. Specifically, Luther's expanded concept of the Decalogue recognizes that Christ called for "an extreme expression of love, namely, suffering."[18] Similarly, Calvin thought that the commandments not only contained prohibitions but "enjoin[ed] positive obligations as well."[19] From his perspective, the prohibition against murder goes beyond a requirement that they not kill one another to become a requirement that "they are to go out of their way to enhance the physical and spiritual well-being of their neighbors."[20] As Calvin writes: "Scripture notes that this commandment rests upon a twofold basis: man is both the image of God and our flesh. Now, if we do not wish to violate the image of God, we ought to hold our neighbor sacred. And if we do not wish to renounce all humanity, we ought to cherish his as our own flesh."[21]

Moreover, for Calvin, Christ's two great commandments (Matt. 22:37–40) summarize the Ten Commandments and "express God's unchanging will for God's people."[22] Wesley, too, thought of the law in more expansive terms than just the Decalogue. To him, Jesus represents the law of God because he is "a copy of the eternal mind" and, consequently, the guide for the ethical Christian life is Jesus' Sermon on the Mount.[23] In fact, thirteen of Wesley's published sermons are on the Sermon on the Mount, and "it was in the radical teachings of Jesus that Wesley found the understanding of righteousness that brought sinners to repentance and prodded the Christian to ever more diligent efforts."[24]

Apparently, the Protestant reformers affirmed the validity of the Ten Commandments, but they knew that the true Christian life required more of believers. Rather than just following the negative dictates of the Decalogue, a Christian had additional responsibilities. Stated in a different way, the Protestant reformers did not think that the Ten Commandments were a full and complete expression of Christian responsibilities. Such a nuanced view of the Decalogue is helpful because, as argued in an earlier chapter, it is problematic from the perspective of women, slaves, and those who are different because of race/ethnicity or religion. Under its provisions, wives are subordinated within the husband's household, slavery is condoned, and its benefits inure only to those who are members of the ancient Israelite community and not to those of other groups. From the liberationist perspective of those who are traditionally marginalized, we can conclude that the Decalogue is not the full and complete expression of Christian responsibilities, just as the reformers did. Furthermore, as will be seen in the following section, the Protestant reformers engaged in readings of the Bible that were theological as well as contextual. As a result, contrary to what conservatives might contend, the Protestant tradition itself provides precedent for the kinds of theological and contextual readings that liberationists encourage.

Thinking Contextually/Thinking Theologically

The relationship between the historical contexts of the Protestant reformers and their theological concepts is not routinely considered; yet, such a relationship exists. For example, Martin Luther (1483–1546) asserted that "we are saved by grace alone through faith alone," which provided a sense of security to those in the late medieval period who were traumatized by death due to plagues and experiencing spiritual insecurity about their relationship to God.[25] The dominant theology of the day held that a person became righteous before God as righteous acts or good works were done, but then the question arose: "How do I know if I have done my best?"[26] Referred to as "covenantal theology," the medieval understanding was that doing one's best was related to the grace one received from God.

> Medieval theology and pastoral care had attempted to provide religious security by what we may call a covenantal theology which said that if we do our best then God will not deny us grace. Although theologians employed numerous and subtle qualifications, the gist of the universal theme *facere quod in se est* ("do your best") was that people could at least initiate their salvation. That is, if you strive to love God to the best of your ability, weak as it may be, God will reward you with the grace to do even better.[27]

Covenantal theology assumed that, given the relationship between God and the people of God, their work, their efforts toward salvation, would be rewarded. In this way, there was to have been "an avenue of security through participation in the process of salvation," but "the consequence of this theology...was to enhance insecurity and uncertainty because it threw individuals back on their own resources."[28] Given the anxieties of the age, the popularity of the indulgences then offered by the Roman Catholic Church makes more sense. Initially, indulgences were related to the sacrament of penance and referred to payments that could be made to the church to atone for sins committed instead of having to complete various acts such as fasting or making a pilgrimage.[29] However, with aggressive selling techniques, purchasing indulgences became a sure way to heaven.[30] Luther, a parish priest at the time, "was appalled" when members of his flock told him that "they no longer needed confession, penance, and the mass because now they had tickets to heaven."[31] Luther felt that he was responsible to God for his parishioners and that he "had to warn them against spiritual pitfalls."[32] Although he had criticized the practice of indulgences as early as 1514, it was on October 31, 1517, that Luther posted his famous Ninety-five Theses.[33]

Luther, an Augustinian monk and a Bible professor, had determined through his study of the Bible that "the crisis of human life is not overcome by striving to achieve security by what we do, but by the certainty of God's acceptance of us in spite of what we do."[34] Luther's approach was a complete reversal of the prevalent theological understanding: "We do not do good works in order to become acceptable to God; rather, because God accepts us we do good works."[35] Clearly, Luther's assurances would have been as comforting to some as they were controversial to others. Nevertheless, he conveys a message of God's love at a time when that message was sorely needed. As a result, there is a convergence of God's loving assurance and its expression in a particular historical context. In order to bring that spiritual message, though, Luther had to oppose the commonly accepted theology of his day.

There was a similar convergence of context and theological message in the work of John Calvin (1509–1564). Calvin, who was twenty-six years younger than Luther, was a second-generation reformer.[36] As a result, he confronted issues that arose as the Protestant movement matured. One of these issues, once again, was the role of good works in the life of a Christian. The severing of the relationship between good works and salvation, although liberating at first, seemed to be a hardship on those it was to have helped. In the secular world, people measured their lives by what they had achieved, and it seemed unrealistic and unnatural to expect them not to do that in their religious lives; as a result, salvation by faith alone became for some "more burdensome to the conscious than the religious introspection and good works it was designed to replace."[37] It seems that disconnecting good works from salvation posed new and different problems but problems nonetheless:

> Although Luther's theology demanded constant good works from the Christian, it also severed every conceivable connection between good works and salvation. Luther observed that people found it exceedingly unnatural to do good works simply out of thanksgiving to God and love of their neighbor, with no expectation of divine reward.[38]

Under these changed circumstances, Calvin modified the Lutheran affirmation of salvation by grace alone, by reinterpreting the role of good works:

> When we rule out reliance upon works, we mean only this: that the Christian mind may not be turned back to the merit of works as to a help toward salvation but should rely wholly on the free promise of righteousness. But we do not forbid [the Christian] from undergirding and strengthening this faith by signs of the divine benevolence toward him.[39]

As explained by a church historian, these "signs of divine benevolence" to which Calvin refers are the believer's own good works.

> The Calvinist saint is saved by faith undergirded and strengthened by works that attest divine presence and grace. He may not say that he is saved by these works, yet regular good works are clear signs of present divine favor and assure him that he is on the path to glory. Religious confidence is thus "formed" by the fruits of self-discipline as well as by the promises of God; in actual practice, good works are presumptive evidence that one is among the elect.[40]

Consequently, even though good works do not have the salvific role that they had in medieval theology, Calvin's teaching "once again made good works and moral behavior the center of religious life."[41] My point here is that, based on the uneasy reaction of some Protestants to the classical Lutheran stance on good works, Calvin's theology offered a welcomed alternative. In other words, since God's people needed to remain assured of God's love, a different context prompted a different theology.

It is worth noting that the same convergence of context and theology occurs with Calvin's doctrine of predestination. Essentially, predestination follows from the notion of salvation by God's grace alone and underscores the fact that salvation is God's act and God's alone. The doctrine is based on Calvin's reading of Christ's statement to his disciples found in John 15:16: "You did not choose me, but I chose you."[42] In effect, the doctrine was reassuring to Protestant individuals and communities alike:

> The doctrine of predestination therefore is not an effort to probe and map the mind of God, but an expression of pastoral care. On the personal level it is the proclamation that salvation is God's gift and choice of the person in spite of his or her doubts, unbelief, and external circumstances. On the communal ecclesiastical level it is the proclamation that in spite of conditions and events, God's church will prevail.[43]

According to Carter Lindberg, these communal assurances were of crucial importance "to the early Reformation churches suffering persecution [in France]; and it was precisely to them that Calvin addressed the comfort of predestination."[44] Once again, there is a connection between the context and the theology developed.

John Wesley (1703–1791) and his era are about 200 years later than that of Calvin. Wesley lived in eighteenth-century England at the beginning of the Industrial Revolution and deepening disparities between the rich and the poor. Two examples of those disparities are worth mentioning here. First, at a time when England was proud of its "unmatched Constitution," men, women, and even children could be hanged for numerous minor offences, such as picking a pocket for more than one shilling or shoplifting the value of five shillings.[45] Second, in one of his tracts, Wesley himself asked, "Why are thousands of people starving, perishing for want, in every part of the nation?" and he went on to write "I have seen it with my own eyes, in every corner of the land. I have known those who could only afford to eat a little coarse food once every other day."[46] Wesley's theology developed in this context and, correspondingly, differs from that of Calvin in two important ways. First, he rejected the concept of predestination. To Wesley, "the idea that God would elect people without regard to their willingness, and especially that God would elect some for damnation, was abominable."[47] To the contrary, Wesley supported the ideas of Jacob Arminius, a person who had articulated a theology of universal salvation, and Wesley started to publish a magazine, the *Arminian*, which proclaimed "the universal love of God and His willingness to save all men from all sin."[48] Second, unlike the Calvinist tradition, Wesley placed only a secondary emphasis on the fruits of faith. John Cobb Jr. describes the Calvinist understanding as follows: "Whether one had authentic faith, and was therefore justified, was to be decided by whether the fruits of faith were manifest in one's life. These fruits are the evidence of one's faith. If they are clearly present, one may be assured that one is a Christian. Thus assurance was a rational deduction from the evidence."[49]

In contrast, Wesley's primary emphasis was on the direct witness of the Holy Spirit, which must come before the fruits are observable. Cobb thinks that Wesley's different emphasis is attributable to Wesley's own direct experience at Aldersgate of which he wrote: "I felt I did trust in Christ, Christ alone for my salvation; and an assurance was given me that He had taken away *my* sins, even *mine*, and saved *me* from the law of sin and death."[50] Combining these theological elements allowed for the development of a renewal movement which held that salvation was available to all and that inner holiness to improve oneself was primary but directly related to acts of outer holiness, social righteousness, to better the circumstances of others. Manfred Marquardt, in his assessment of Wesley's ethics, concluded that Wesley awakened an ethical power "firmly founded in connection with Christ" that overcame the fatalism of the predestinarians and "enabled many to bring about social change in their vicinity."[51] It is the combination of these elements that helps to explain the popularity of Methodism in eighteenth-century England. It helped to meet both the spiritual and physical needs of those who were otherwise overlooked:

> To begin with, Methodism gained its victories in the middle and lower classes, among the miners and in the industrial towns. To the middle and lower classes it brought a new sense of the sacredness of personality; it appealed to the popular imagination, and awakened a devotion which found expression in a most self-sacrificing charity. . . . It had brought the impulse of personality and individuality into the life of the masses, who were being brutalized by the industrial system, and with its charity it helped them in their distress.[52]

By now, some patterns should be evident. Each of the major Protestant reformers provided new insights about God to their faith community, and those insights met the community's spiritual needs. In other words, each of the reformers was aware of the everyday realities of Christian believers and their corresponding experiences and doubts. Clearly, Luther, Calvin, and Wesley did not write their theologies in a vacuum, unaware of the cultural conditions around them. To the contrary, through them and their awareness, God's voice arose in a new way that was suited to each particular context. In other words, the awareness that the reformers had of their contexts as well as the corresponding plight of believers allowed God's tailored communication to emerge, just as God is using those who articulate contextual theologies today.

Even though those messages of the Protestant reformers varied from and even contradicted one another, each reformer is communicating a message of God's love to the people of God. The form of that message of love varied among the different historical settings, but the content remained the same. Such a contextual message of love affirmed them as children of God and provided hope and a sense of direction in a hurting, complex, and often confusing world. Most significantly, in order to express the appropriate form of that contextual theological message, each of them had to challenge some aspect of the prevailing Christian traditions of their day. Luther challenged aspects of the Roman Catholic tradition, Calvin challenged aspects of the Lutheran tradition, and Wesley challenged aspects of the Calvinist tradition. With such a pattern in the Protestant tradition itself, support for contextual biblical interpretation is found. Our current context is one in which we are aware of the physical harm and psychological anxiety caused by exclusionary church doctrines and practices that marginalize those who are different primarily because of gender, sexual orientation, or race. That awareness opens up an opportunity to hear God's message of love for all of God's people in a different way. In turn, our call to express that constant message of God's inclusive love means that we have to challenge the prevailing Christian traditions of our own day, just as Luther, Calvin, and Wesley did before us.

The Protestant Reformers, Biblical Authority, and Biblical Interpretation

Without a doubt, Luther, Calvin, and Wesley affirmed the notion of biblical authority. It is therefore instructive to explore what the "Bible" meant to them and how they were able to interpret the Bible in ways that went against long-standing traditions. For Luther, the Bible was where "you will find the swaddling cloths and the manger in which Christ lies, and to which the angel points the shepherds," and, although "simple and lowly are those swaddling cloths," they hold a precious treasure because Christ is wrapped in them.[53] With this point of departure, Luther saw Christ in both the Old and the New Testaments, and he felt that passages had only one meaning—and it was the Christological one.[54] Therefore, for example, he "unhesitatingly called Moses and the patriarchs Christians whenever he spoke of their faith in the promise of the future Redeemer."[55] Luther's approach would obviously contradict Jewish interpretations of these texts, but it also contradicts the dominant mode of biblical interpretation in the late Middle Ages.

In that era, it was accepted that a passage of Scripture could have four possible meanings: the letter, the allegory, the moral teaching, and the anagogy, with the differences between them summarized as follows:

> The letter shows us what God and our fathers did;
> The allegory shows us where our faith is hid;

The moral meaning gives us rules of daily life;
The anagogy shows us where we end our strife.[56]

Luther disagreed with allegorical readings as done by the Scholastics of his day, and he preferred the more literal meaning—but what Luther thought that literal meaning was is not what is ordinarily thought. For example, the first verse of Psalm 76, which reads, "In Judah God is known, his name is great in Israel," can be used to illustrate the difference between the "letter" or a literal reading and an allegorical one.[57] The "letter" or the literal reading refers to Judah and Israel, which were the southern and northern kingdoms of ancient Israel, respectively. However, a medieval allegorical reading allows the verse to take on specific meaning for Christians and is understood to refer "to the church and Jesus where God is known through his revelation and saving act of redemption [in Jesus Christ]."[58] In general terms, Luther understood the "literal" meaning or "the letter" of the Bible to speak only of Christ, rather than the more historically accurate meaning.[59] Basically, then, scholars have described the kind of meaning Luther found in biblical texts to be "literal-prophetic;" but the term "literal" here is not the historical, factual meaning of passages that we normally have in mind. In fact, Luther was not at all interested in the kinds of historical-critical questions that have fascinated biblical scholars since the Enlightenment concerning who wrote which texts or when and under which circumstances the texts were written.[60] Instead, the "literal-prophetic" term refers to interpretation that "speak[s] out of the spirit of the prophets which pointed to the coming Christ."[61] A better term for Luther's interpretive approach, then, is probably "prophetic-Christological" because it retains both the Christological emphasis and the prophetic way he reads Christ in both the Old and New Testaments.[62]

It is worth noting that Luther's Christological emphasis shaped his view of the canon along with his reading of biblical texts. As stated by David Steinmetz, Luther had one basic question that determined whether he thought a book of the Bible should be in the canon: "Does this book teach well the notion that we are justified by Christ freely by faith alone through God's grace?"[63] If a book did, then Luther felt it should be in the canon; if it did not, then he felt that it should probably be removed (although he did not actually remove any books from the canon).[64] Correspondingly, he felt that Romans, Galatians, Ephesians, and 1 Peter contained "the kernel and marrow of the gospel," but Hebrews, James, 2 Peter, Jude, and Revelation "[do] not preach Christ in his fullness, or else they proclaim[ed] doctrines that lead away from him."[65] In this respect, Luther's concept of Scripture, the traditional biblical canon, was far from a fundamentalist one. He did not assume that all of these books were divinely inspired and therefore unquestionably part of the canon. To the contrary, we can say that Luther focused more on Christ's incarnation than on any doctrine of inspiration.[66] As expressed by Luther: "Whatever does not teach Christ is not yet apostolic, even though Saint Peter or Saint Paul does the teaching. Again, whatever preaches Christ would be apostolic, even if Judas, Annas, Pilate and Herod were doing it."[67]

Just as Luther's thought on the divine inspiration of the biblical canon differed from a fundamentalist understanding, so does his concept of Scripture as the "Word of God." Steinmetz suggests that the "Word of God" has several meanings in Luther's thought, but for the purposes of this study, two of them are significant.[68] The first such meaning is that Jesus is the Word of God incarnate, based on the opening words in the Gospel of John. Accordingly, Luther sees Jesus as "the perfect Word that God speaks, the perfect expression of the will and intention of God, the perfect reflection of the mind and being of God." The other significant meaning is that the "Word of God" is the act of preaching.[69]

> In the words of Heinrich Bullinger in the Second Helvetic Confession (1562–1566): *Praedicatio verbi dei est verbum dei*; "The preaching of the Word of God *is* the Word of God." It does not say that the preaching of the Word of God signifies the Word of God or that the preaching of the Word of God is a witness to the Word. Preaching is more than a witness to God's word; insofar as it is an event in which the voice of God is heard again, it *is* the Word of God.[70]

For Luther, the preached word was God's *Thettel-Wort*, a word that creates something that did not exist previously, as opposed to a *Heissel-Wort*, which only names something that already exists.[71] According to Steinmetz, then, Luther's understanding of the Word of God means that to preach on Ezekiel's oracles is not an act of reporting on something that happened a long time ago, as if it were *once* a living word; "rather, at the hands of the preacher, Ezekiel's oracles become again the Word of God, powerful and lifegiving in our own time and place."[72]

Such a concept of the Word of God has far-reaching implications, all of which contradict narrow fundamentalist notions on the matter. Luther sees Scripture as "the functioning tool with which God works here and now," thus allowing it to have "a living and creative authority."[73] Furthermore, Luther could not consider the Bible to be "a closed historical record, describing what God once-upon-a-time had done" because preaching continues God's work of salvation.[74] Following the logic, then, without an interest in the Bible as a closed record, Luther was not concerned about any doctrine of infallibility to support every letter and word in Scripture.[75] Therefore, because Luther was more concerned with a dynamic and functional view of the Word of God, rather than with one that limits the Word of God to "a once-and-for-all inspired book," he did not equate the "Word of God" (*verbum*) and the "words of Scripture" (*scriptura*).[76] Given Luther's insistence that "every word in the Bible points to Jesus," it is safe to conclude that his approach to biblical interpretation was essentially theological.[77]

That same theological orientation to biblical authority and interpretation is seen in Calvin's writings. For example, Calvin's concept of biblical authority is best seen in his affirmation of the sufficiency of the Bible as the guide to Christian belief and conduct.[78] In turn, Calvin's authority of Scripture is based on its revelation of Christ:

> This is what we should . . . seek in the whole of Scripture: truly to know Jesus Christ, and the infinite riches that are comprised in him and are offered to us by him from God the Father. If one were to sift thoroughly the Law and the Prophets, he would not find a single word which would not draw and bring us to him. And for a fact, since all treasures of wisdom and understanding are hidden in him, there is not the least question of having, or turning toward, another goal. . . . [O]ur minds ought to come to a halt at the point where we learn in Scripture to know Jesus Christ and him alone, so that we may be directly led by him to the Father who contains in himself all perfection.[79]

Calvin's Christological emphasis is so strong that even biblical law is to be understood from that point of view. Calvin's distinction is clear: the law is "a dead letter if cut off from the grace of Christ," but "if it shows forth Christ, it is the word of life."[80] Calvin used that kind of distinction in his interpretation of the biblical laws against usury. Today, dictionaries define usury as the receipt of *excessive* or *illegal* rates of interest for money loaned, but in Calvin's time, usury referred to the charging of *any* interest for money loaned.[81] Because of the biblical prohibitions against usury (Exod. 22:25; Lev. 25:35–37; Deut. 23:19–20; Ps. 15:5; Prov. 28:8; Ezek. 18:8, 13, 17), it had been consistently forbidden by the Christian Church until the time of the Protestant Reformation.[82] For example, Calvin did not condemn the practice. As David Jones observes, Calvin went beyond the written words of Scripture to find the reason behind the law, and he determined that God's will is the restoration of the order of creation, and an integral part of that restoration is the expression of "authentic love in human relationships."[83] Applying that rationale to the laws on usury, Calvin concluded that they communicate a duty to display love, especially in dealings with the poor and with foreigners.[84] Given Calvin's ability to look beyond the letter of the law to investigate God's intention behind the law, he was apparently not a biblical literalist in the style of contemporary conservatives.

Calvin's theological emphasis in reading Scripture is best attested to in his writing of the *Institutes of the Christian Religion* (*Institutes*) and the subsequent revisions undertaken, all of which occurred between 1536 and 1560.[85] Calvin's objective in writing the *Institutes* was to provide a theological framework within which individual biblical texts could be understood correctly.[86]

> It has been my purpose in this labor to prepare and instruct candidates in sacred theology for the reading of the divine Word, in order that they may be able both to have easy access to it and advance in it without stumbling. For I believe I have so embraced the sum of religion in all its parts and have arranged it in such an order that if anyone rightly grasps it, it will not be difficult for him to determine what he ought especially to seek in Scripture and to what end he ought to relate its contents.[87]

In this way, the *Institutes* were to be "a guide to Scripture so that beginners could read the Bible without becoming lost in its sometimes confusing detail. The *Institutes* uncovered the architectonic structure of the Bible, the underlying plan of the whole, that placed details in their proper context."[88] Consequently, valid biblical interpretation would not consider biblical passages in isolation but would consider the larger context in which those texts would become "fully intelligible."[89]

> Just as old and bleary-eyed men and those with weak vision, if you thrust before them a most beautiful volume, even if they recognize it to be some sort of writing, yet can scarcely construe two words, but with the aid of spectacles will begin to read distinctly; so Scripture, gathering up the otherwise confused knowledge of God in our minds, having dispersed our dullness, clearly shows us the true God.[90]

In summary, Calvin's *Institutes* are the "spectacles," the necessary theological lenses, through which we can encounter the true God in Scripture.

Wesley, like Luther and Calvin, affirmed Scripture as authoritative for Christians in matters of faith and practice. He considered the Bible to be the solitary standard for measuring Christian attitudes, words, and actions (although in his practices he acknowledged the significance of the traditions of the Church of England and Christian antiquity, among other things).[91] When some early Methodists were derided for their attachment to the Bible and called "Bible-bigots," Wesley considered it to be a badge of honor.[92] Similarly, Wesley upheld the sufficiency of Scripture where Christian doctrine and practices are concerned, but he never argued that "the Bible contains all we need to know on every subject of human knowledge."[93] He was clear that the doctrine covered only "divine knowledge" concerning God and God's will for human beings, and he even acknowledged scientific contributions when they contradicted the literal sense of Scripture.[94] Also like the earlier reformers, Wesley preferred the literal or plain meaning of biblical texts, as opposed to allegories, and he felt that "most apparent contradictions between parts of the Bible could be resolved by a deeper reading of the literal sense."[95]

Wesley believed that the Scriptures were divinely inspired, although he was aware that human agents were used in the process of communication, and so their concerns and perspectives influenced how the divine message was communicated.[96] Wesley's notion of inspiration, in turn, is related to his assertions of Scripture's infallibility. As Scott Jones concluded, since Wesley supports the infallibility of Scripture, Wesley feels that "what it says must be taken seriously."[97] However, doing this would mean some of its requirements that are often ignored would have to be taken seriously, too.

> In his sermon "On Riches," he argues that the rich typically neglect Jesus' command in Luke 9:23 that all of his disciples deny themselves and take up their crosses. He [Wesley] writes: "O how hard a saying is this to those who are at ease 'in the midst of their possessions'! Yet the Scripture cannot be broken."[98]

Indeed, Wesley's emphasis on following scriptural mandates completely can be seen in his observations on what should be the differences between Christians and the Pharisees. Wesley found the Pharisees to be "blameless" because they "endeavoured to keep all the commandments."[99] However, Wesley thought that the Pharisees dispensed with some of the commandments, making their righteousness "partial." To Wesley, the righteousness of a "real Christian" is "universal"; "he does not observe one, or some parts, of the law of God, and neglect the rest; but keeps all his commandments, loves them all, values them above gold and precious stones."[100]

Furthermore, Wesley thought that Christian righteousness should not only equal but exceed that of the Pharisees by "fulfilling the spirit as well as the letter of the law, by inward as well as outward obedience."[101] Wesley distinguished between the inner and outer attributes in the following manner: "Thus to do no harm, to do good, to attend the ordinances of God (the righteousness of the Pharisee) are all external; whereas, on the contrary, poverty of spirit, mourning, meekness, hunger and thirst after righteousness, the love of our neighbor, and purity of heart (the righteousness of a Christian) are all internal."[102] Wesley, using an example from the Ten Commandments, explained how the difficulty in having the holy heart required for inner obedience should draw us closer to Christ:

> The law says, "You shall not kill," and hereby (as our Lord teaches) forbids not only outward acts but every unkind word or thought. Now the more I look into this perfect law, the more I feel how far I come short of it; and the more I feel this, the more I feel my need of his blood to atone for all my sin, and of his Spirit to purify my heart, and make me "perfect and entire, lacking nothing."[103]

As mentioned earlier, Wesley supports a third use of the law in Christian life as it helps believers progress toward fullness in Christ. For Wesley, though, the law is not just the moral law, it is Jesus Christ himself: "What is the law but divine virtue and wisdom assuming a visible form? What is it but the original ideas of truth and good, which were lodged in the uncreated mind from eternity, now drawn forth and clothed with such a vehicle as to appear even to human understanding?"[104] In this way, the law of God for Wesley is "a copy of the eternal mind," which is "the fairest offspring of the everlasting Father."[105] His notion of the law, then, is Christological.[106] As a result, Wesley finds a strong connection between the law and the gospel:

> There is therefore the closest connection that can be conceived between the law and the gospel. On the one hand the law continually makes way for and points us to the gospel; on the other the gospel continually leads us to a more exact fulfilling of the law. The law, for instance, requires us to love God, to love our neighbour, to be meek, humble, or holy. We feel that we are not sufficient for these things, yea, that with man it is impossible. But we see a promise of God to give us that love, and to make us humble, meek, and holy. We lay hold of this gospel, of these glad tidings: it is done according to our faith, and the righteousness of the law is fulfilled in us through faith in Christ Jesus.[107]

From the preceding discussion, we have identified what Jones says is "Wesley's distinctive teaching about the law," which is that "God's grace empowers us to keep the moral part of the law."[108] Jones considers this to be one of Wesley's rules for interpreting Scripture, and it is the idea that "commandments are covered promises."[109] As Jones explains it, "Any commandment which binds Christians is also a promise that God will enable the believer to do what God wants him or her to do," or stated somewhat differently, "believers must be perfect and, by God's grace, they will be perfect."[110]

Finally, Wesley affirmed the wholeness of Scripture, which for him means, among other things, that the message of God's way of salvation for human beings is consistent in the Old and the New Testaments.[111] His affirming the wholeness of Scripture also means that it has an overarching theme; and Wesley thought that "the whole Bible points to the redeeming love of God and the possibility of salvation by faith that God offers people."[112]

The Protestant Heritage and Inclusive Biblical Interpretation

The premise of this study has been that the doctrines and traditions of the Christian Church have been developed from the perspective of the *mythical norm*—the affluent, white, heterosexual male.[113] Consequently, to consider the perspectives and realities of those who are "Other" due to gender identity, sexuality, or race/ethnicity is to be outside of the historical tradition, as has been discovered by those on the margins who have attempted to make their voices heard. My goal has been to establish the basis for inclusive biblical interpretation that takes these other perspectives into account *and* is grounded in both the biblical and Protestant traditions. In the previous chapter, I outlined support for inclusive interpretation from the lives and ministries of Jesus and Paul; in this chapter, I seek to do the same thing for the major Protestant reformers: Luther, Calvin, and Wesley. With respect to Jesus and Paul, I emphasized *what* their biblical interpretations were; with respect to Luther, Calvin, and Wesley, I am emphasizing *how* they reached their biblical interpretations. Collectively, these reformers affirm the joy of faith in an eternal God who loves us as we are, the corresponding call to love others as we have been loved, the need to express that love in our treatment of those around us, and the effectiveness of the divine power that enables us to express such love. Although these reformers developed theological principles that reflected the needs of their own time and place, these same principles, with their simple but radical implications, can help us be more inclusive in our faith communities today.

Nevertheless, there is an important issue that I must address at this point. How am I able to suggest that the work of Luther, Calvin, and Wesley can be used to champion the cause of women, same-gender-loving people, and the poor? After all, their own attitudes and behaviors on these matters were less than exemplary. As discussed in chapter 1, Luther used homophobic rhetoric to vilify the Roman Catholic Church.[114] With respect to women, Luther and Calvin both understood the rape of Dinah in Genesis 34 to be an injury to her father, Jacob; they minimized the assault on her and blamed her for having gone away from the house, since that was her proper place.[115] Wesley supported the ministries of women, including their work as lay preachers, during his lifetime, but one factor in his rationale was that women could preach in biblical times in exceptional cases. That rationale was problematic because it was all too easy to say that such exceptional cases did not exist now, and after his death, the British Methodists banned women from preaching.[116]

Just as there is a mixed legacy concerning women, the Protestant reformers also left a mixed legacy concerning the poor. On the positive side, they changed dramatically the concept of poverty. In the Middle Ages, poverty was valorized, and giving alms to the poor was encouraged as a good work. As a result, a system was created in which there was "the duty of the poor to remain poor so that the salvation of the rich could be secured."[117] With his insistence that we are saved by faith and not our works, Luther's theology changed that system because voluntary poverty does not help one earn salvation, and giving alms to the poor will not do that either.[118] After Luther, involuntary poverty could be seen as a social ill to be combated and not a spiritual state to be admired.[119] For his part, Calvin advanced the notion of "the right use" of material goods that should be used to advance God's work in the world.[120] Likewise, one of the hallmarks of the early Methodist movement was its work with the poor. Wesley worked consistently to improve the lives of the poor by ministering to prisoners, starting schools and medical clinics, and establishing what we know today as microloan programs.[121] In fact, Wesley's efforts in these areas have been summed up as his "evangelical economics," and a preferential option for the poor has been identified.[122] Nevertheless, when peasants who, influenced by Luther's thought, wanted greater freedom and equality in their social and economic lives staged rebellions in 1525, Luther gave the princes and lords permission to use force against them. It is estimated that about 100,000 peasants were killed during that year.[123] Likewise, Calvin's condoning of the charging of interest has resulted in untold hardships for the poor, who have a greater need to borrow money and, since they often have difficulty in repaying it, accrue interest. Similarly, in spite of Wesley's laudable efforts on behalf of the poor, he can be faulted for his unfailing support of the state and especially the king which elevated them above any criticism, as well as his failure to support actual social and political reforms (except for the abolition of slavery) that might have improved conditions.[124]

Finally, the reformers were not very sensitive to or accepting of those who were different by reason of religion or race. Luther wrote the tract *The Jews and Their Lies* after having become frustrated by the failure of Jews to read Jesus into the Old Testament in the way that he did. Calvin was complicit in the burning at the stake of Michael Servetus in 1553; Servetus had denied the divinity of Jesus and was executed for blasphemy.[125] During his time in Georgia, Wesley "observed the extermination of the American indigenous population, but he did not focus his critique on it systematically or prophetically."[126] Obviously, I am not contending that Luther, Calvin, and Wesley are exemplary models of liberationist thought. Instead, I am only arguing that there are fundamental principles from their thought that can be reclaimed and utilized for inclusive biblical interpretation today. Such principles, though, when contextualized for our own time and place, may lead us to interpretations that go beyond those that the reformers actually had or would have had during their lifetimes. In the interest of brevity, we will explore in the following section just one constructive element that scholars have identified from these three Protestant traditions. Each of these discussions looks at how some aspect of the reformer's thought supports more inclusive biblical interpretations.

A Reformed Contribution: The Word of God

In a collection of essays on feminist and womanist thought in the Reformed (Calvinist) tradition, Dawn DeVries contributed an article on a constructive way to think about the "Word of God" today.[127] She starts off by explaining that the goal of Reformed theologians had been to align church doctrine and practices with "the true and saving knowledge of God," the source of which was to be found in "God's self-revelation in the Word." When that "Word" became identified with the canonical Scripture, the "Scripture Principle" resulted, that is, the stance that correct doctrine and practices were to be determined *sola scriptura*, by Scripture alone.[128] The problem, however, is that the actual expression *sola scriptura* does not appear in any of Calvin's writings or in those of the earliest Reformed confessions; surprisingly, the use of *sola scriptura* as a formal principle of Protestantism is actually an invention of nineteenth-century theologians.[129] DeVries's goal in writing the article, therefore, is to make a distinction between the "Word of God" and the biblicism that has held the church captive for far too long. As we know from the earlier discussions in this chapter on Luther and Calvin, they also distinguished between the ongoing Word of God and the written biblical text. In this respect, DeVries is helping us to regain a more authentic aspect of the Protestant heritage.

Using the institution of slavery in the United States, DeVries offers an example that illustrates well the difference between the "Word of God" and the biblical text. At that time, both the abolitionists and those who defended slavery argued that God was on their side, but the fact of the matter is that the defenders of slavery had the stronger biblically based argument. For their part, "abolitionists were driven to argue not from the plain sense of the words of Scripture but rather from the 'spirit' of Christ or the gospel, and such appeals were unconvincing to those who took the biblical words themselves as the Word of God."[130] As a result, DeVries presents two crucial questions:

> What would have happened had there been a different understanding of what constituted God's "Word"? The ambivalence between the extended and more restrictive usage of the descriptor "Word of God," then, may well lead us to question, Should the proper slogan for summarizing the criterion of reform have been *verbum divinum* and not *sola scriptura*?[131]

Based on her analysis, DeVries offers several propositions for redefining the "Word of God," three of which are important to mention here. One proposition affirms that "God's self-revelation in the person of Jesus is the primary form of God's Word and that other forms of revelation are to be recognized and received only in relation to it."[132] Once again, we can see readily that such a proposition is consistent with the thought of both Luther and Calvin. A second proposition is that "canonical Scripture is not so much a form of God's Word as it is the means of grace through which God's Word is ever and anew received in the Christian community."[133] Here, DeVries recognizes the ability of preaching, in the midst of the gathered community, to communicate the Word of God through Scripture.[134] The third proposition is that, "because the Bible functions primarily as a means of grace, Christian theology must treat the canon as open with regard to its normative significance for doctrine."[135] With her reference to an "open canon," DeVries is not suggesting that we add books that are not currently there. She is only pointing out that, when doctrinal decisions are made, we have seen shifts when some parts of the canon are given greater emphasis than others. As an example, she mentions that the ordination of women was traditionally precluded based on texts such as 1 Timothy 2:11–15, but in the twentieth century, many Reformed churches placed more emphasis on the language in Galatians 3:28, that "in Christ" there is "neither male nor female."[136] Consequently, the significance of the biblical canon remains constant but the significance of particular passages may change over time.

> The canon itself never changed as to its contents, but the way in which it was interpreted and the relative authority given to various passages did change. Some passages, such as Galatians 3:28, were taken to have farther-reaching significance than previously recognized, and thus to have greater right to norm church doctrine than other passages such as 1 Timothy 2:11–15. It seems to be a simple matter of historical fact, then, that what was once understood to have authorized a particular

doctrine of the ministry no longer counted in the same way: the boundaries of the canon as a critical norm, in other words, had shifted. The canon was in fact treated as an open one.[137]

DeVries's proposition here can be applied to the doctrinal issue of homosexuality's compatibility with Christianity. Historically, the usual biblical passages are used to support its condemnation. Yet, if we consider the canon to be an open one for doctrinal purposes, we could see that there are other passages that provide an alternative. For example, homosexuality is condemned because it is nonprocreative sex. Specifically, Deuteronomy 23:1–8 does exclude from the community Israelite males who are eunuchs or otherwise unable to procreate, but Isaiah 56:3–5 specifically includes them, and Acts 8:26–40 describes the inclusion of the Ethiopian eunuch. Furthermore, the Song of Songs, which is part of the canon, describes the delights of sexual pleasure for its own sake and the participants are not even married. Plus, there are biblical texts where loving relationships between people of the same sex are mentioned, such as the words of David upon hearing of Jonathan's death: "Greatly beloved were you to me; your love to me was wonderful, surpassing the love of women" (2 Sam. 1:26). My purpose in this brief discussion is not to present an exhaustive list of such texts. I just want to demonstrate that within the biblical canon itself are resources for an affirming approach to the issue of homosexuality. Adopting a more inclusive stance does not mean rejecting biblical authority or the Word of God. It simply means opening ourselves to the guidance of the Holy Spirit toward the inclusive Word of God that is already there.

A Lutheran Contribution: The Indwelling Christ

In her book *Healing a Broken World: Globalization and God*, Cynthia Moe-Lobeda seeks to counter the damaging effects of economic globalization, which include increased poverty, the elimination of cultural diversity and integrity, and mounting harm to the environment.[138] Most significantly, she identifies the loss of human agency as a problem, given that globalization forces human beings into organizational systems that benefit only a few and are inimical to the well-being of most. As a response, Moe-Lobeda proposes a "subversive moral agency," which is based on two key features of Luther's thought. One concept is the "indwelling Christ," which she identifies as the "centerpiece of Luther's ethics"; it primarily presupposes a "Christ who dwells in us, in whom we dwell, with whom we are united, and who transforms us."[139] The second concept is that Christ dwells not only within human flesh and blood but also within all creation, "the stones, fire, water, seeds, bread, and wine" of the earth, thereby associating the holy with the body and the earth, for they, too, "bear the divine."[140] In this way, Luther overturned the medieval value system that encouraged dissociation from the earth as well as from the body.[141] Taken together, Christ's presence within the community of believers means that they are transformed and the relationships that they have to each other and the environment are transformed:

> The "subversive" claim drawn from Luther's articulation of the indwelling Christ is this: The power of God's compassionate, justice-making, unquenchable love for creation may live within/among human beings and the rest of nature. Moral agency for living toward the flourishing of creation—which includes subverting economic systems that render death and destruction—may flow from embodied *communio* in which God incarnate is received and given.[142]

From a liberationist perspective, Moe-Lobeda's discussion of Luther's theology is helpful because it includes a community obligation to love one's neighbor and to resist both economic structures and ideologies "that thwart the gift of abundant life for all."[143] Consequently, she has articulated a Lutheran approach to combating ideologies, biases, and systems that privilege one group at the expense of others and cause irreversible harm to the environment in the process.

A Wesleyan Contribution: The Law of Love

Wesley's use of the law in the life of a Christian also helps to support inclusive biblical interpretations. For Wesley, our inability to live out the dictates of the moral law, the law of love, makes us more aware of our need for Christ in order to fulfill the law. Simultaneously, the law outlines what our transformed world would be and gives us the goals toward which we should strive. As John Cobb writes in his book on Wesleyan theology today:

> If we could describe the Christian life in a serious way, a way that gave it content and character, we could renew the preaching of the law. For example, if we were collectively convinced that the law of love today calls us to reduce our consumption of resources, and if we thought through, concretely, in terms of the changed lifestyle entailed, then we could hold up this demand of the gospel in a way analogous to Wesley's use of the law. If we were collectively convinced that patriarchal dominance is wrong and that children need to be brought up in a nonpatriarchal family context, and if we could see something

> of what that means concretely, we could state what is required of us by the law of love. Something like this happened in the church through Martin Luther King's leadership of the Civil Rights Movement. We did come collectively to the decision that racism is incompatible with the law of love, and we were able to preach the law, and in some measure implement it, in concrete and realistic ways.[144]

To live out the law of love, Cobb knows that we will need to remember another concept of Wesley's—entire sanctification. Entire sanctification presumes that conversion (changed behavior) is not complete in all areas of a Christian life or for all time, and that the process of repentance and conversion can take place in different ways and at different times, resulting in a "progressive Christianization of life."[145] In this way, learning to consider the realities of others, as sought here, could be understood as a process that takes shape as we learn how to live out the law of love with one another and our world.

We have seen in this chapter that the approach of Luther, Calvin, and Wesley to biblical interpretation was both theological and contextual, and that such an approach can support current efforts to include those who are traditionally marginalized because they are outside of the *mythical norm*. As God loves us, we are to love others, and in today's context, these others must be the ones whose realities and experiences have traditionally been excluded. Correspondingly, just as Christ has redeemed us, our task as Christians is to be the vehicles through which Christ's redeeming love can be shown to others. We are to bring them, as whole persons, within the household of God (Eph. 2:19). Empowered by the Holy Spirit, our theological task is to enable "the objects of someone else's history to become the subjects of their own destiny in God."[146] As further articulated by the South African theologian Steve de Gruchy:

> Our task is therefore to listen to the voices of those who are silent and silenced in the Bible. If the Bible was not written by slaves, women or gays and lesbians, then it is the contemporary task of theology to take that experience, that life, that story, as a crucial source for reflection. Indeed, it needs to be the primary source for reflection when the church addresses the concerns of slaves, women or gays and lesbians. In doing so, theology undertakes the task of enabling the objects of someone else's history to become the subjects of their own destiny in God. No longer can we talk about "them," but rather the attentive silence of the "free" heterosexual male hears the "other" into a freedom that liberates both. And if this disturbs the prevailing consensus on doctrine and dogma, then we rejoice that we are on the road to a broader vision and a wider consensus.[147]

6

Biblical Authority and the Ethics of Biblical Interpretation

As described by Audre Lorde, there is a *mythical norm* embedded in our awareness that "is usually defined as white, thin, male, young, heterosexual, Christian, and financially secure."[1] This *mythical norm* constitutes *the* normative perspective that shapes the accepted (conservative) Christian religious policies and biblical interpretations. The implicit, if not explicit, adoption of this norm has created "the Other," a term that refers collectively to all the groups that are different based on race, gender identity, sexual orientation, religion, or class. In this project, I seek to develop a way of interpreting the Bible inclusively, which means an approach that takes into account the perspectives of these groups and the consequences traditional interpretations have on them. Unfortunately, the very groups that might benefit from alternative readings of these texts and traditions identify so thoroughly with the dominant ones that there is no recognition that their own circumstances are different. Correspondingly, they are unaware that they are, in fact, being harmed by traditional stances. The African American female high school student who told me, "This is the Word of God. If it says slavery is okay, slavery is okay. If it says rape is okay, rape is okay," is an example of that complete and self-destructive identification with the operative norm.

Consequently, when introducing the concept of inclusive biblical interpretation to local church groups, I have met some resistance. One comment that I often hear is: "But we can't just pick and choose which Scripture we want to use." I find that response a bit amusing because that is exactly what we do as a people of faith. We pick and choose which Scripture we want to use or, at least, the ones we emphasize. Three examples are offered here. One example is that runaway slaves must not be returned to their owners according to Deuteronomy 23:15–16: "Slaves who have escaped to you from their owners shall not be given back to them. They shall reside with you, in your midst, in any place they choose in any one of your towns, wherever they please; you shall not oppress them." During the era of racial slavery in the United States, a runaway slave named Dred Scott fought being returned to his owner. The decision of the U.S. Supreme Court was that he had to return; the court held that as a black man, he was inferior, and "he had no rights which the white man was bound to respect."[2] For the Christians who supported slavery at that time, this was clearly a biblical law that they were choosing not to follow and, in so doing, a nonwhite male was disadvantaged.

The next two examples come from our contemporary era. According to Deuteronomy 15:1, the remission of debts is to be granted in every seventh year. However, even in our current setting in which bankruptcies and foreclosures are occurring at increasingly high rates, no one is claiming that we have rejected biblical authority by not following these laws. Those who are struggling economically in our country and who, I might add, are disproportionately people of color, would benefit greatly from interpretations that related their circumstances to those described in the Bible in this way, but that interpretation is seldom heard. Similarly, there are few if any charges that biblical authority has been abandoned when we ignore the prohibitions found in Leviticus 19:19 against the mixing of different types of animal breeds, seeds in a field, or materials in a garment: "You shall keep my statutes. You shall not let your animals breed with a different kind; you shall not sow your field with two kinds of seed; nor shall you put on a garment made of two different materials." Although such prohibitions could have a bearing on the issue of genetically modified food and its long-term safety implications for human beings and the environment, they are not brought into wider discussions, and it is important to consider why that is the case.

My point here is that, in each of these instances, the Bible takes on new and exciting meanings when the point of departure is that of "the Other" rather than the *mythical norm*. Contrary to some fears, the Bible's significance, relevance, and vitality do not cease if it is read from a stance other than the traditional one. The Bible can still yield meaning when approached from an inclusive perspective, as the previous examples show. Again, the dominant interpretations, the "authoritative" ones, are simply the ones that represent the historic interests of one particular group—that of the privileged white, Western, heterosexual male. It is from this perspective that we "pick and choose" which laws and interpretations we support. Consequently, what I am doing here is not new because of my acknowledgment that we can "pick and choose" certain laws and reject others. It is new only because I am arguing that additional realities, other than the dominant one, need to be taken into account when those determinations are made.

I am not contending that *all* males who are financially comfortable, white, Western, and heterosexual subscribe to the dominant paradigm. To the contrary, I know men within that elite category who are very committed to full inclusivity. Furthermore, I am not contending that *any* "flesh-and-blood" persons have to actively support the *mythical norm* for that norm to survive. The privileged perspective is so embedded in church systems and the national consciousness that being a part of either system means upholding past traditions, and those traditions themselves are defined by exclusion. Finally, I am not contending that *only* comfortable, white, Western, heterosexual men support the dominant stance. It can be supported by women, nonwhites, homosexuals, and those from the Two-Thirds World because exclusion is synonymous with the tradition, and maintaining the traditional stance, no matter how hurtful, allows them to remain within the familiar. I am most concerned about these latter groups, though, because in so doing they have adopted a form of Christianity and a concept of national identity that are, to a large degree, inimical to their own well-being.

That traditional and dominant perspective is most forcefully expressed around two issues: the role of women and homosexuality. Viewed from the perspective of the *mythical norm*, we can understand why these certain passages are "chosen" for application in today's context and take on crucial importance. Conservative churches gravitate toward passages that assert women should be silent in churches (1 Cor. 14:34–35) and subject to their husbands (Eph. 5:22–24), and that homosexuality is an abomination (Lev 18:22). If these passages are rejected by more liberal church groups, it becomes the basis for schisms—as seen historically with the ordination of women, slavery, and now with the full inclusion of homosexuals in the life of the church. The question has to be asked: Why do certain issues, particularly abortion and homosexuality, constitute the "line in the sand" for conservatives today? To answer that question, we need to understand the significance of these two issues to the maintenance of a patriarchal system.

As discussed earlier, the basic premise of a patriarchal system is that the male should be dominant and never subordinate, and that the female should be subordinate and never dominant. The model patriarchal social unit, then, is the nuclear family because it enshrines the male dominance structure. Because of this relationship between patriarchy and the nuclear family, Andrea

Smith uses the term "heteropatriarchy" to underscore an organizational system that presumes not just males but heterosexual males and creates a hierarchy that "rests on a gender binary system in which only two genders exist, one (male) dominating the other (female)."[3] To enforce the nuclear family, therefore, means that any attempt by women to control their own lives and their bodies (as in decisions about abortion) interferes with male control over them and contests the patriarchal norm that they should be subordinate to men. Likewise, homosexuality contests normative heterosexuality because it posits a subordinate (penetrated) male, which, in a heterosexist system, is thought to be unnatural. Simply stated, abortion has come to connote a dominant female, and homosexuality has come to connote a subordinate male. Because both phenomena contradict the basic gender hierarchy of a patriarchal system, they are seen as threats to the nuclear family.

Previously, the message seemed to be that "everyone *should* be in a nuclear family." Today, however, we have gone beyond a mere preference for the heteronormative standard, the nuclear family. Now, the message seems to be that everyone *has* to be in a nuclear family, resulting in what is referred to as "compulsory heterosexuality." It is important to understand that shift and its implications at home and abroad. Domestically, the emphasis on the nuclear family (which is coded as white, patriarchal, and suburban/middle-class) makes it possible to mask the general abandonment of urban areas. Summarizing the work of Ann Burlein, Andrea Smith writes:

> She notes that the investment in the private family makes it difficult for people to invest in more public forms of social connection. In addition, investment in the suburban private family serves to mask the public disinvestment in urban areas that makes the suburban lifestyle possible. The social decay in urban areas that results from this disinvestment is then construed as the result of deviance from the Christian family ideal rather than as the result of political and economic forces.[4]

At the same time, there are global implications to the conservative emphasis on the nuclear family. In essence, it reinforces the dominance/subordination paradigm and models to the rest of the world the dominance that the white Western heterosexual male should have over everyone else. Therefore, Smith finds that "the colonial world order depends on heteronormativity—just as the patriarchs rule the family, the elites of the nation-state rule their citizens."[5] We generally consider the nuclear family to be the positive foundation of social order, but the work of Burlein and Smith forces us to recognize that this order tends to provide benefits to the few at the expense of the many. It offers a sense of order, but it all too often fails to deliver justice.

Upholding traditional interpretations of these biblical passages on women and homosexuality, in particular, means that the perspective of the privileged white heterosexual male remains the definitive one, and there is the corresponding control over those who are "Other"—women, homosexuals, and groups of different races (or religions). From the dominant perspective, whenever any of these marginalized groups gives voice to their own experiences of God and their own readings of Scripture, they are challenging the assumption that traditional interpretations represent the opinions of *all* Christians. Consequently, conservative Christianity must exclude any contrary perspectives and avoid any considerations that might result in the "unmasking" of its putative objectivity.

As discussed more extensively in chapter 1, the ability of the *mythical norm* to speak for *all* of humanity has been successful primarily because of two things—claims that the interpretation was "divine" in church circles or "objective" in academic circles, and adopting a concept of biblical authority that is essentially based on a hierarchical "banking" model, as described by Paulo Freire. Taking these two dynamics together, the interests of the privileged elite became synonymous with the divine will in the church, and those interests were then taught as the official doctrines and interpretations to all the subordinate groups. Reflecting the interests of only that male elite, Christianity has come to define itself by the groups it excludes or subordinates. In contrast, the goal of an inclusive approach to biblical interpretation is to create Christian faith communities that are radically inclusive. Supporting the creation of inclusive communities, then, requires the unmasking of the elite's claimed neutrality, as done in chapter 1, and redefining the concepts of Scripture and biblical authority, as done in the following section.

Reconceptualizing Scripture and Biblical Authority

It is true but rarely admitted that human beings determine what constitutes Scripture. In other words, Scripture "is not a quality inherent in a given text, or type of text"; rather, it is "an interactive relation between the text and a community of persons (though such relations have been by no means constant)."[6] Succinctly put, "people—a given community—make a text into scripture, or keep it scripture, by treating it in a certain way: *scripture is a human activity*."[7] On the surface, admitting that Scripture is a human activity would seem to contradict evangelical understandings because they insist on divine inspiration and, therefore, an inherent basis for Scripture and its authority. However, upon closer examination, a similar interactive relationship between the text and the community is discernible. Brian Malley, in his study of an evangelical congregation in Michigan, found that its notion of the Bible's authority was not based primarily on the doctrine of divine inspiration:

> The doctrine of inspiration is indeed often invoked as a justification and explanation of the authority that evangelicals attribute to the Bible. Yet the relative certainty and uniformity of informants' views of biblical authority suggests that it is in fact biblical authority that is primary, and that the doctrine of divine inspiration functions psychologically as a *rationale* for *prior* belief in the Bible's authority. Psychologically, it is authority, not inspiration, that is the premise, and inspiration, not authority, that is the consequence.[8]

In this evangelical setting, Malley observed that biblical authority was "a discursive practice of framing one's speech in relation to the Bible" and that this practice was one of those "in which community members, in order to *be* community members, participate."[9] Putting together the work of Cantrell Smith and Malley allows us to say that faith communities create Scripture by engaging the Bible, specifically, by referring to it and seeking to make it relevant to their lives. Yet this is something that can and should be done by people of faith across the political and theological spectrum. Whether in liberal or conservative churches, members who engage the Bible are affirming a sense of biblical authority, that is, a sense that the Bible "carries weight."[10] Despite the apparent rhetorical differences, therefore, the concepts of "Scripture" and "biblical authority" may not be as different as we might think between conservative churches and liberal ones.

If communities determine which texts are Scripture, how do they make such determinations? According to Cantrell Smith, there must be an experience of transcendence: "The scriptural phenomena begin with people's awareness of involvement in transcendence," and that awareness has been "somehow *reduced* to speech or writing," that is, "given accessible form in words."[11] In turn, that experience of transcendence shapes the community's theology, which is essentially its notion of God and its sense of God's relationship with them and the world.

Historically, African American Christian faith communities, based on their experience of the transcendent, functioned with a theological understanding of "the universal parenthood of God which implied the universal kinship of humankind."[12] The theological premise that they were children of God empowered enslaved people to reject those portions of Scripture which contradicted such an understanding. Howard Thurman (1900–1981), once the dean of the chapel at Howard University, offers an often-quoted example of how slaves (and former slaves) resisted the slave owners' use of the Bible:

> My regular chore was to do all of the reading for my grandmother—she could neither read nor write. . . . With a feeling of great temerity I asked her one day why it was that she would not let me read any of the Pauline letters. What she told me I shall never forget. "During the days of slavery," she said, "the master's minister would occasionally hold services for the slaves. . . . Always the white minister used as his text something from Paul. At least three or four times a year he used as a text: 'Slaves be obedient to them that are your masters . . . , as unto Christ.' Then he would go on to show how, if we were good and happy slaves, God would bless us. I promised my Maker that if I ever learned to read and if freedom ever came, I would not read that part of the Bible."[13]

As Brian Blount, an African American New Testament scholar, comments on the grandmother's remarks, "This doesn't mean that the New Testament lost its sense of authority for the slaves. But it *does* mean that their perception of God in their midst was *more* authoritative."[14]

We know that faith communities shape their Scripture and its interpretation, but the problem is that the groups discussed in this study, such as women, African Americans, and homosexuals, are marginalized groups that are not allowed to fully participate in shaping that Scripture or its interpretation. They are rendered invisible, and their perspectives are ignored, although (or maybe because) they are usually different from those deemed responsible for upholding the biblical traditions. By developing their own approaches to the Bible, the formerly excluded groups are using the same process—starting with their own experience of the transcendent and the assurance that they are indeed children of God—to define what is Scripture to them. Defining Scripture is therefore primarily a theological enterprise. In this respect, "the Bible is like a sacrament, a means of grace; it mediates God's presence in the life of each of us and God's concern for the whole planet."[15]

Since faith communities determine the shape of their canons, the concept of biblical authority must be reformulated to capture a more relational dynamic between the Bible and the interpreting community. Like other Christian perspectives, a liberationist perspective holds the Bible as authoritative, but the difference is that, for liberationists, this does not imply domination. Biblical authority does not have to be authoritarian. Instead, a new model for authority is offered that rejects *authority as domination* in favor of *authority as partnership.*[16] The "authority as domination" model sees reality as a hierarchy or pyramid, with God at the top and everything else (men, then women, and then nature) assigned an order underneath. More specifically, "this paradigm reinforces ideas of authority *over* community and refuses to admit the ideas and persons that do not (wish to) fit into the established hierarchies of thought or social structures."[17]

Although this is the traditional paradigm for biblical authority, it is inadequate because it provides "a religious rationale for the domination and oppression of the weak" (those lower down the hierarchical chain), it contradicts God's welcome to all outsiders (Luke 4:16–30), and, in the midst of our contemporary diversity, "it no longer makes sense to try to fit people into such a rigid view of theological and social truth."[18] Another harmful effect of the "authority as domination" paradigm is that "it discourages cooperation in the search for meaning because it frames discussion as a competition of ideas in which all participants aim at gaining the top spot and vanquishing others."[19] The alternative is "authority as partnership"; "in this view, reality is interpreted in the form of a circle of interdependence." Similarly, authority is exercised *in* community rather than *over* it, and participation is required rather than submission:

> Ordering is explored through inclusion of diversity in a rainbow spectrum that does not require that persons submit to the "top" but, rather, that they participate in the common task of creating an interdependent community of humanity and nature. Authority is exercised *in* community and tends to reinforce ideas of cooperation, with contributions from a wide diversity of persons enriching the whole. When difference is valued and respected, those who have found themselves marginal to church or society begin to discover their own worth as human beings.[20]

Without a doubt, then, it is crucial that one specify which definition of biblical authority is being used. If authority is defined as domination, it follows that Scripture is thought to be given directly by God (thus untainted by human beings or ancient contexts), and its precepts are unchanging, unquestionable, and absolute. One submits to biblical authority. It is a hierarchical and an exclusive concept. From the liberationist perspective, however, human interests in biblical texts should be acknowledged, and the influence of ancient cultural settings should be identified and appropriately rejected as unchanging divine mandates. Correspondingly, biblical authority becomes a partnership, a process of critical engagement that requires dialogue between and within communities of faith. Instead of submitting to biblical authority, we engage biblical authority. It is a mutual and inclusive process. Obviously, these totally different approaches to biblical authority mean that people who take "biblical authority equally seriously can disagree about its meaning."[21]

Having covered the difference between biblical authority as submission and biblical authority as participation, we can now evaluate the insights on biblical authority that are offered by two prominent scholars, Stanley Hauerwas and N. T. Wright. Hauerwas, in *Unleashing the Scripture: Freeing the Bible from Captivity in America*, argues that fundamentalism (an approach of the church) and biblical criticism (an approach of academia) are "two sides of the same coin" because "each assumes that the [biblical] text should be accessible to anyone without the necessary mediation by the Church."[22] According to Hauerwas, both camps think that the text has an "objective meaning" and that the Bible "should make rational sense (to anyone), apart from the uses that the Church has for Scripture."[23] Hauerwas does not agree with the notion that "each person in the Church is given the right to interpret the Scripture." Instead, he suggests that "the 'right' reading of Scripture depends on having spiritual masters who can help the whole Church stand under the authority of God's Word."[24] Furthermore, he contends that "if we are to understand Scripture it is necessary that we place ourselves under authority, a placement that at least begins by our willingness to accept the discipline of the Church's preaching."[25]

From a liberationist perspective, a very basic question must be asked: What is the nature of God's Word that is communicated in the preaching? Does that Word include the perspectives and realities of women, the poor, and those who are different because or race/ethnicity, religious affiliation, or sexual orientation? Similarly, who are the "spiritual masters" that will preach to the church? Will they be the privileged male elite? If they are, will they be able to incorporate in their preaching the concerns and needs of those who are unlike themselves? But how could they? If they subscribe to traditional (conservative) biblical interpretations and church policies, the perspectives and concerns of these other segments of the population have been ignored. In fact, orthodox policies and practices typically have been defined by the very exclusion of these groups.

Gloria Albrecht, a white feminist theorist, describes well the concerns that are raised when the marginalized are told to submit to traditions that they had no hand in shaping:

> Feminists and womanists have learned that it is important to ask who produced this knowledge that we are taught to speak, from which social position, and for what loyalties? We must ask who has the power

> to describe and define; who has the power to produce the principles or rules being brought to bear? Who authored "our tradition"? Whose sense is "common"? And, in the production of knowledge, who has not had the power to be heard, or to speak?[26]

Equally problematic is the proposal made by N. T. Wright. He argues in his book *The Last Word: Scripture and the Authority of God* that the reading of Scripture *as taught by the church's accredited leaders* is to be strongly encouraged and enabled.[27] Although he recognizes that teaching occurs at different levels in the church, given his own Anglican tradition, he addresses his remarks to "bishops in particular" because "it is at that level that certain things need to be said."[28] Wright is concerned that bishops have become so involved with bureaucratic responsibilities that they no longer have time for the preaching, teaching, and pastoral work so needed in today's world.[29] His concern is certainly warranted.

From a liberationist perspective, however, the question is, Who will be among those "accredited church leaders"? In recent times, there has been tremendous controversy—and a schism—within the Episcopal Church, the Anglican Communion's branch in the United States.[30] The furor resulted from a combination of the denomination's selection of Katharine Jefferts Schori as its first female presiding bishop in 2005 (she is the first woman to head any national branch of the Anglican Church) and the consecration of the first openly gay bishop, Gene Robinson, in 2003. In 2007, the archbishop of Canterbury sent out the first invitations for the next year's Lambeth Conference, the gathering of the bishops of the global Anglican Communion that occurs only every ten years. Bishop Gene Robinson of New Hampshire, the only openly gay bishop in that global communion, was one of only a few duly elected bishops who did not receive an invitation. Clearly, not all of the Anglican Communion considers either Jefferts Schori or Robinson to be "accredited church leaders."

Once again, the question is who will be among the "spiritual masters," to use Hauerwas's language, or the "accredited leaders" of the church, following Wright? Those who are different from the *mythical norm* will probably not be included because the tradition has usually excluded them and their perspectives. In this way, approaches such as those of Hauerwas and Wright continue the exclusion and exploitation of marginalized groups.[31] They do not solve the problems raised here; they perpetuate them. As Albrecht suggests, a more constructive approach to Christian ethics results if the dominant learn how to use their power "for the purpose of liberating others from oppression."[32] Early in her book, Albrecht recognized that 11:00 on Sunday morning is "not only the most racially segregated hour of the week, it is all too often the most sexist, class segregated, and homophobic."[33] We should thank God that this does not always have to be so.

The Ethics of Biblical Interpretation

In my first book, *Women, Ideology, and Violence*, I argued that the laws concerning gender in the books of Exodus and Deuteronomy constructed a male dominant/female subordinate paradigm.[34] Using critical theory, I equated that paradigm with violence because of its repression of the feminine and then suggested that it is directly related to actual violence against women today. Specifically, the prevalence of rape and female battering in this country can be seen as a purposeful dynamic, supported by the dominant/subordinate paradigm, which serves to enforce the patriarchal authority of men over women.[35] In this current project, I wanted to demonstrate how biblical (and theological) interpretations in both the church and the academy have been done from the perspective of a *mythical norm*.[36] That norm, coupled with a dominant/subordinate gender paradigm, has meant that all who do not fit this norm become subordinate, that is, subject to the control of the dominant privileged elite. We must begin to see that this control is a form of violence, too.

As articulated by Gloria Albrecht, the violence that women experience is directly attributable to the dominant discourses in our social, political, economic, and, I hasten to add, religious communities.[37] For women, violence

> names the experience of being defined by dominant discourses that are embedded in the structures of our institutions, in the material practices of our social, political, and economic systems, as well as in the theories and stories that give them authenticity. . . . [W]omen have also experienced violence as coercion by the dominant within our community in shaping and forming us according to their worldview. It is a violence that takes women's lives, physically and spiritually.[38]

In chapter 1, I argued that the identifiable suppression of females easily corresponds to the suppression of any group that is "Other" than the *mythical norm*. To counter that dynamic, two things must happen. First, the particularity of the privileged elite, who have taken their perspectives and experiences as the normative ones, must be unmasked and its universality challenged. In both the church and the academy, the argument is always that it is not *their* interpretation but it is that of God, as the church says, or that they were being objective, as the academy says. Instead, an element of critical self-reflection must occur in each interpretive process so that one's own particularity is acknowledged and becomes part of that process. My point here is not that particularity itself is bad. To the contrary, we all have our own particularity. The problem is when the particularity of *one* group is allowed to be the standard against which all other human beings are measured.

Second, the impact of a decision or interpretation on any or all of the nondominant groups must be a part of the interpretive process, in addition to having critical self-awareness. For far too long, the privileged elite and the institutions that support their interests have been able to ignore the consequences of their determinations on the "Other." The harm caused to these groups and the environment has reached tragic levels, and ignoring those consequences is no longer tenable. Essentially, then, I am arguing for an ethics of biblical interpretation—an evaluative process that distinguishes between plausible interpretations that could apply in today's context versus those that are otherwise plausible but should be rejected because they result from a lack of critical self-awareness or have harmful consequences.

Fortunately, more and more biblical scholars are becoming aware of the need for ethical considerations in biblical interpretation. In her 1988 presidential address to the Society of Biblical Literature, Elisabeth Schüssler Fiorenza reported that, with multiple interpretations of texts possible, and with race, class, and gender now factors, "a double ethics" is needed.[39] Such "double ethics," she proposed, includes "an ethics of historical reading" and "an ethics of accountability." The ethics of historical reading refers to locating meaning in the ancient historical setting and includes an analysis of "the values and authority claims of the biblical text" so that they may be assessed and critically evaluated for their relevance today.[40] An "ethics of accountability" refers to the responsibility the interpreter has for the choice of interpretative models used, as well as "for the ethical consequences of the biblical text and its meanings." Therefore, interpreters must be aware of the Bible's use as a means to harmful ends.

> If scriptural texts have served not only noble causes but also to legitimate war, to nurture anti-Judaism and misogynism [*sic*], to justify the exploitation of slavery, and to promote colonial dehumanization, then biblical scholarship must take the responsibility not only to interpret biblical texts in their historical contexts but also to evaluate the construction of their historical worlds and symbolic universes in terms of a religious scale of values. . . . [That responsibility] must also include the elucidation of ethical consequences and political functions of biblical texts in their historical as well as in their contemporary sociopolitical contexts.[41]

In this way, Schüssler Fiorenza suggests that interpreters have an ethical responsibility to consider the actual consequences of their interpretations. Similarly, Daniel Patte wrote in 1995 how he had learned over time that his exegetical practices "had hurt other people instead of helping them," and that a shift in paradigm was necessary.[42] To that end, he concluded that "we, male European-American critical exegetes, must assume responsibility for the effect of our work upon various groups of people, especially when this effect is quite negative."[43]

Another helpful trend has been developments in the field of hermeneutics. A basic premise of hermeneutics, the study of interpretation, is that the reading of any text, including biblical texts, is affected by the presuppositions of readers.[44] To demonstrate differences in the presuppositions of readers, consider these following statements about the Bible, inspiration, biblical authority, and biblical interpretation:

> Statement 1
> The Bible is literally the Word of God. Scripture consists of the writings that were inspired by God, if not actually dictated by God to the biblical writers. The community of faith is to submit to biblical authority. Biblical interpretation is divine, expressing the will of God, not of human beings.

> Statement 2
> Creating Scripture is a human activity that takes place within communities of faith. Inspiration applies not only "to the origin of the text but to its transmission and interpretation among us."[45] The Bible is "inherently the live Word of God," which recognizes that it is divine communication that has been "refracted" through many different authors who spoke from their own circumstances.[46] Biblical authority is exercised *in* community rather than *over* it, and the community of faith's participation is called for rather than its submission.[47] Biblical interpretation is contextual and necessarily influenced by the human beings who do it.

These are the kinds of presuppositions that any one person or community of faith has in mind before they even open the Bible, and they will necessarily influence the meaning that is found there for Christian faith and life today. An ethical approach to biblical interpretation identifies and acknowledges such presuppositions.

Basically, "hermeneutical ethics" is now a field of inquiry, and it contributes two significant insights. First, "if social location shapes reading, then it is important to be honest and self-conscious about one's social location in approaching any act of interpretation."[48] Second, if multiple interpretations of a passage are possible, then we need to make explicit the reasons we have chosen a particular meaning. As Charles Cosgrove writes, "It is important that we identify and state not just the interpretive [methodological] reasons for the meanings we choose but also the moral and theological reasons for the interpretations we affirm."[49] Cosgrove knows that these factors are usually not articulated, but he feels that they should be "made explicit so that we can submit them to examination by ourselves and others."[50]

Current discussions in the area of hermeneutical ethics force us to realize that a given biblical interpretation is ethical only if it was reached in a particular and acknowledged context, where the community has a degree of self-awareness concerning the factors that shaped its reading (such as its own presuppositions about the Bible itself), and there is a willingness to engage in dialogues with other communities that read the biblical texts differently and are impacted differently by conventional interpretations. As a result, if one of these criteria is absent, a plausible interpretation is not an ethical one. Today, when we have to recognize that any one text can have different meanings, we must consider not just *how* meaning is derived from ancient biblical texts but *why* a particular meaning, among several plausible meanings, is chosen. Therefore, hermeneutical ethics opens up new possibilities for inclusive biblical interpretation. The factors described here unmask the privileging of traditional, so-called objective interpretations, by encouraging all interpreters to be aware of their underlying presuppositions and to addresses the impact of traditional interpretations on the "Other."

Specifying the elements of ethical biblical interpretation—assessment of the contemporary context, critical self-awareness, and an analysis of consequences on the "Other"—means that any particular interpretation can be evaluated accordingly. Dale Martin's discussion of works by Craig Keener and David Instone-Brewer on divorce provides excellent examples of interpretations that are ethically questionable.[51] Keener and Instone-Brewer identify themselves as evangelical Christians who seek a biblical basis for divorce and remarriage. Using historical-critical methods, they argue that such a basis does exist, but they fail to acknowledge that their own presuppositions influenced the way they read the biblical texts. Instead, they contend that their readings are actually *true* meanings in their ancient historical context. In stark contrast to their finding that the grounds for divorce and remarriage are found in the New Testament, Martin argues persuasively that the point of the relevant New Testament texts (Matt. 5:32 and 19:9; Luke 16:18; Mark 10:11–12; 1 Corinthians 7:10–11) is that divorce and remarriage were, in fact, forbidden:

> Divorce and remarriage were commonly seen as serving the purpose of gratifying desire. Forbidding divorce and remarriage, therefore, would have been seen as a curb on the free rein too often given to passion. I think it most likely, therefore, that the historical Jesus did forbid divorce and remarriage and that such a prohibition was interpreted along ascetic lines of self-control in expectation of the imminent kingdom of God.[52]

With Martin's alternative reading of what the text meant historically, it becomes clear that Keener and Instone-Brewer have adopted historical interpretations that serve their purposes (allowing divorce and remarriage under certain circumstances), but they fail to acknowledge that fact. To make matters worse, Keener even criticizes liberals for accepting "unscriptural divorces."[53] As Martin points out, however, Keener fails to realize that his interpretive method is the same as that used by liberals:

> Where Keener is wrong is in failing to recognize that *his* interpretations are just as creative as those of more liberal Christians, and that such creativity begins with his very *reading* of the text and not merely with the *application* of its meaning to a different situation. His reading of the texts at the base of his interpretive practice is already influenced by his more liberal beliefs about divorce and remarriage, his tendency to avoid the strictest interpretation.[54]

Similarly, Martin finds that "one of the main motivations of Instone-Brewer's tendency to deradicalize Jesus' sayings is precisely his recognition that, were the sayings to be taken strictly, the teaching would be 'impractical' for application in the lives of Christians."[55]

> [Instone-Brewer] just insists that *his* interpretation of the text must be the right one because it is more "practical" and accords better with modern Christian common sense. Even evangelical and conservative Christians *need* to be able sometimes to divorce and remarry. Instone-Brewer's mistake is that he seems actually to think that this is "what the text means" when interpreted objectively by the lights of historical criticism.[56]

Keener and Instone-Brewer are aware of their contexts, the need for a compassionate basis for divorce and remarriage, and they are aware of the harm caused by prohibitions against both. To this extent, their interpretations are ethical. However, their interpretations are ethically questionable due to a lack of critical self-awareness. Although Keener and Instone-Brewer exhibit some self-awareness because they identify their theological orientation (evangelical), it is not critical self-awareness. Specifically, they fail to see the ways in which their own presuppositions affect the way that they read the Bible and interpret what they find there. Instead, they both contend that they are unearthing the "true" and the "objective" meaning. As argued previously, such contentions merely mask the specific interests of those who make these determinations. An ethical interpretation has to be one that is transparent and where interests are acknowledged. Even though I agree that the church should deal humanely with issues of divorce and remarriage, I must conclude as Martin does that the ways in which Keener and Instone-Brewer have structured their arguments are ethically flawed.

Along the same lines, the church's condemnation of homosexuality is ethically invalid because of the lack of critical self-awareness of most interpreters who condemn it, and there is a failure to consider the harm caused. The harm caused refers to the violence of marginalization and the "closeted" existence assigned to those who deviate from the heterosexually defined norm. Most significantly, though, the lack of critical self-awareness appears as claims by such interpreters that they are simply communicating God's will or that they are being objective. Yet, as Dale Martin persuasively argues, interpreting Romans 1:18–32 to condemn homosexuality requires several logical "leaps."[57] First, Martin notes that Paul's discussion in Romans 1 assumes homosexuality is punishment for idolatry and polytheism, but few of us today would "believe that the abolition of idolatrous cults and polytheism would spell the end of homosexuality."[58]

> Modern people, even Christians, do not believe the mythological structure that provides the logic for Paul's statements about homosexuality in Romans 1. Heterosexist scholars alter Paul's reference to a myth that most modern Christians do not even know, much less believe (that is, a myth about the beginnings of idolatry), and pretend that Paul refers to a myth that many modern Christians do believe, at least on some level (the myth about the fall). Heterosexism can retain Paul's condemnation of same-sex coupling only by eliding the supporting logic of that condemnation.[59]

Second, Martin finds that modern scholars often assume Paul is addressing both homosexual activity and desire—as if both were different from heterosexuality—but, in the Greco-Roman world, "homosexual desire sprang from the same desire that motivated heterosexual sex."[60] Finally, these scholars, according to Martin, find homosexuality to be unnatural based on Romans 1, but Paul's understanding of what is natural is based on the gender hierarchy of male over female.[61] These logical "leaps" are usually not acknowledged by interpreters who still claim that they are being objective and merely adopting the original meaning of the text. Given the clear evidence that their predispositions influence the way they read the text, there is an obvious lack of critical self-awareness. I know that one's own predispositions influence how one reads the text; my point is that an ethical reading will acknowledge the relationship between the two. Consequently, I am merely challenging those who claim objectivity when they are clearly choosing a meaning that fits within their own worldviews.

In this regard, the current condemnation of homosexuality is similar to earlier interpretations that supported slavery and subordination of women. In his work *Jesus, the Bible, and Homosexuality*, Jack Rogers details the historical pattern of using the Bible to justify the oppression of black people and women.[62]

He recognizes that "for more than 200 years, most Americans, including Christians, shared three assumptions regarding slavery and segregation."[63] Furthermore, at one time these common assumptions on slavery and, as we will see, women were deemed to be "natural."

> Most people believed that (1) the Bible records God's judgment against the sin of people of African descent from their first mention in Scripture (the curse on Ham); (2) people of African descent were inferior in moral character and incapable of rising to the level of full white, "Christian civilization"; and (3) people of African descent were willfully sinful, often sexually promiscuous and threatening, and they deserved punishment for their own acts. We abhor such views now, but most Christians considered such views "natural" and "common sense" in the past.[64]

Just as whites were able to use the Bible to justify the enslavement of black people, Rogers argues that men were able to use comparable arguments against women:

> Men argued that (1) the Bible records God's judgment against the sin of women from their first mention in Scripture (the curse on Eve); (2) women were inferior in moral character and incapable of rising to the level of full white, male Christian civilization (because women were seen as emotional and not rational); and (3) women were willfully sinful, often sexually promiscuous and threatening, and deserved punishment for their own acts (women tempt men).[65]

Having drawn these parallels on issues of slavery and women, Rogers develops his argument further with the issue of homosexuality, and the results are striking—and all too familiar:

> Those who oppose homosexuality claim that (1) the Bible records God's judgment against the sin of homosexuality from its first mention in Scripture; (2) people who are homosexual are somehow inferior in moral character and incapable of rising to the level of full heterosexual "Christian civilization"; and (3) people who are homosexual are willfully sinful, often sexually promiscuous and threatening, and deserve punishment for their own acts.[66]

Rogers acknowledges that there are those who either ignore these previous misuses of the Bible or try to distinguish them from the issue of homosexuality:

> Many people who are opposed to full rights of membership for people who are homosexual ignore these historical analogies. Others immediately assert that the condition of being black or female is quite different from what they consider to be willful behavior like "homosexual practice." These people read Scripture regarding slavery and women as manifesting both a diversity of views and as evidencing hints toward the position that the church now takes. At the same time, they read Scripture as uniformly and unremittingly negative regarding any form of homosexual practice.[67]

Rogers feels, however, that "all of these arguments miss the point."[68] Based on the previous church stances on slavery and women, Rogers finds a pattern: "We accepted a pervasive societal prejudice and read it back into Scripture. We took certain Scriptures out of their context and claimed to read them literally with tragic consequences for those to whom those verses were applied."[69] Simply stated, his point is that we are making the same mistake with the issue of homosexuality. In other words, the "pervasive social prejudice" represented the perspective of the *mythical norm*, the privileged white heterosexual male, and the consequences on people of African descent, women, and homosexuals were and are ignored or minimized. For these reasons, the condemnation of homosexuality is a plausible reading of the Bible, but it is also an ethically invalid reading.

As argued throughout our discussions, biblical texts themselves and the controlling interpretations of the church encode the values and perspectives of privileged heterosexual males. Furthermore, biblical texts construct a gender paradigm of male dominance/female subordination that has been used historically to support the dominance of the white Western Christian male over those who are nonwhite, non-Christian and non-Western (from the Two-Thirds World). Under this schema, homosexuality is condemned because it connotes a subordinate male, and males should always be dominant, and females should always be subordinate and never dominant. Fundamentally, then, the struggles against sexism, homophobia, white supremacy, neocolonial dynamics, and Christian violence against non-Christians are intimately connected. As succinctly phrased by Andrea Smith, "Any liberation struggle that does not challenge heteronormativity cannot substantially challenge colonialism or white supremacy."[70]

These liberationist struggles, though, are often pitted against one another, and, as a result, momentum for transformative change is lost. Consequently, true collaboration in a push for inclusive communities can occur only if each of these groups starts to adopt strategies that incorporate the issues of another marginalized group. Instead of supporting the dominant condemnation of homosexuality, heterosexual women need to understand that the same underlying rationale for this condemnation supports the subordination of women. Therefore, fighting heterosexism and homophobia should be an integral part of a feminist agenda. Instead of supporting the dominant condemnation of homosexuality, African American church leaders need to understand that the same underlying rationale for this condemnation supports white supremacy, that is, the dominance of white people over people of color. Therefore, their continuing struggle against racism should include the struggle against heterosexism and homophobia. Instead of supporting the dominant condemnation of homosexuality, African church leaders need to understand that the same underlying rationale for this condemnation supports the dominance of the West and its exploitation of Africa's resources. Therefore, any critique of global capitalism as neocolonialism should also address heterosexism and homophobia. Similarly, instead of condemning the homophobia of African and African American communities, leaders in the lesbian/gay/bisexual/transgender (LGBT) communities need to understand that the same underlying rationale for the condemnation of homosexuality supports racism. Therefore, white LGBT leaders have every reason to struggle against racism as part of their own activities.

Historically, tremendous harm has been caused when one segment of the human population is able to cast its own perspectives as "universal," "objective," or "the will of God." If we have learned anything from the past, we should know that such a lack of critical self-awareness results in unethical and dangerous readings of the Bible and corresponding church policies. Surely, reversing the church's unethical condemnation of homosexuality would show that we have learned the appropriate lessons from the past. Such a reversal would be a significant step in creating faith communities that are defined by our radically inclusive love for all of God's creation rather than by the categories of people that we exclude. In this way, we would have faith communities that are agents of God's love here and now.

> The love of God, which can never be "vapid" or "self-indulgent," is breaking into our world here and now to bring about the eschatological restoration of his people under God's gracious reign. Such love, at one and the same time, makes a "radical and strengthening" demand for a total response, while requiring a more "relaxed" and open acceptance of all those who respond to God's call in love.[71]

7

The Need for an Inclusive Approach Continues

The United States, the Founding Fathers, and the National Identity

Unmasking the National Rhetoric of Inclusion

The need to consider the perspectives of and consequences on the "Other" that is apparent in biblical texts also exists with reference to the foundational documents of the United States. The nation's founding fathers were privileged white males who fit the *mythical norm.* Indeed, "at the time of the first Presidential election in 1789, only 6 percent of the population—white, male property owners—was eligible to vote."[1] Clearly, the authors of the Declaration of Independence did not have the poor, women, or people of color in mind when they agreed that "all men are created equal" in 1776. Barbara Jordan, the former African American congressional member from Texas, made the same observation about the Constitution succinctly and powerfully in 1974:

> Earlier today we heard the beginning of the Preamble to the Constitution of the United States, "We the People." It is a very eloquent beginning. But when that document was completed on the seventeenth of September in 1787, I was not included in that "We, the People." I felt somehow for many years that George Washington and Alexander Hamilton just left me out by mistake. But through the process of amendment, interpretation, and court decision, I have finally been included in "We the People."[2]

In her speech, Jordan implies (surely for dramatic effect) that her exclusion as a woman and an African American was accidental.[3] However, a comment made in a later speech indicates Jordan was well aware that the exclusion of women was intentional: "One may ask whether the founders were mean-spirited and just didn't like women? The answer is no. They loved women but had a very limited 18th-century notion about their role in the world."[4] As Jordan noted in her speech, African Americans (both male and female) were excluded by implication from constitutional rights and privileges, and that exclusion of people of African descent was made explicit in the *Dred Scott* decision.[5] In that decision of 1857, Justice Roger B. Taney affirmed the exclusionary intent of the founding fathers, finding that people of African descent "had no right which the white man was bound to respect."[6]

> We think that they are not included and were never intended to be included.... They had for more than a century before been regarded as being of an inferior order, and altogether unfit to associate with the white race...and so far inferior that they had not rights which the white man was bound to respect.... Accordingly, a Negro of the African race was regarded...as an article of property, and held and bought and sold as such.... No one seems to have doubted the correctness of the prevailing opinion of the time.[7]

Jordan's statement informs our current discussion in several ways because it clearly reminds us of the exclusionary intent of the founding fathers. The statement, therefore, underscores the need for an inclusive approach to our national heritage parallel to that needed in the Christian religious heritage. The statement also shows how her inclusion as an African American woman resulted from "the process of interpretation, amendment, and court decision." More specifically, the Constitution has been amended to include African Americans (the Fifteenth Amendment in 1870) and women (the Nineteenth Amendment in 1920), and greater inclusivity has resulted from court decisions such as the 1954 *Brown v. the Board of Education* decision of the Supreme Court. In other words, given the exclusionary intent of the original authors, these foundational documents could only become more inclusive through subsequent human actions, whether those actions are done through the judicial system or the congressional amendment process. Although the exclusionary influence of foundational documents remains for all later generations, such constitutional amendments and judicial decisions embody the manner through which that exclusionary influence can be nullified. Generally speaking, Jordan did not let the fact that such exclusion was intentional prevent her from seeing herself as part of "We, the People." Stated in a different way, Jordan did not consider the original and intentional exclusion of the authors to be the determinative meaning of the Constitution. Furthermore, Jordan's remarks mean that traditional customs and culturally defined limitations on the social roles for women and people of color in earlier centuries should not be determinative either.

Finally, Jordan's statement demonstrates that we challenge texts and traditions when we cherish them and want to be included within them. In the same famous speech, she said the following words: "My faith in the Constitution is whole, it is complete, it is total. I am not going to sit here and be an idle spectator to the diminution, the subversion, the destruction of the Constitution."[8] As one scholar, Barbara Holmes, writes, "Jordan's feelings about the Constitution are as personal and passionate as her biblical faith"; Holmes then mentions an anecdote shared by law professor Philip Bobbitt at Jordan's funeral.[9] Bobbitt refers to how "many . . . learned for the first time in the press accounts following Barbara Jordan's death that she carried with her a small pocket copy of the U.S. Constitution. From some apparently early point . . . this small pamphlet was always with her."[10]

Jordan was simultaneously committed to a text as written and dedicated to challenging conventional applications of the text so that those formerly excluded could be included. These dual themes of commitment and challenge have served as core values in the construction of the inclusive biblical approach sought here. Indeed, her insights about the Constitution readily apply to biblical interpretation. More precisely, human decisions concerning biblical texts are needed to include those groups formerly excluded. Unlike the Constitution, which can and has been amended, though, the Bible is a closed canon that cannot be amended literally. Therefore, the only way that exclusionary biblical texts can be made more inclusive is by interpretation, that is, through human decisions made within faith communities. Failing to allow a role for human decisions would mean that the exclusions of biblical texts remain intact. As a related point, then, we learn from Jordan's example that the original intent of the biblical authors cannot be the determinative one. In the same way, traditional customs and culturally defined practices cannot be determinative either. For example, Paul's insistence that women wear veils when prophesying (1 Cor. 11:2–16) is a culturally defined practice that need not restrict the participation of women in church life today.[11]

In 1993, Jordan was asked by the Clinton administration to chair the Commission on Immigration Reform. The person who approached her, Susan Martin, says that she told Jordan that "the immigration debate was becoming mean, and we needed someone like her to prevent an anti-immigration hysteria from developing; I told her that she could make the same difference on the Immigration Commission that she had on the Voting Rights Act by prevailing on the inclusion of Hispanics."[12] In an earlier Constitution Day naturalization ceremony, Jordan had made the following remarks: "The Constitution is alive and well in America. It is not a lifeless piece of paper resting in a dusty archive. It is a living document and what brings it to life is you, the citizens of this country, who live out its meaning."[13]

Jordan's notion of the Constitution as a "living document" is anathema to conservatives who feel that it gives judges too much latitude in rendering decisions. Such conservatives, including Supreme Court justice Antonin Scalia, prefer to look for an "original" meaning, set in the past when the document was written, and abhor notions of "evolving standards" that would take the contemporary interests into account.[14] Such an opinion is in stark contrast to those who do not consider an "original" meaning to be the definitive one.

> The philosophy that an originalist sets himself against most firmly is that of the Supreme Court Justice William Brennan, who, in 1985, argued that "the genius of the Constitution rests not in any static meaning it might have had in a world that is dead and gone, but in the adaptability of its great principles to cope with current problems." Scalia sees this approach as an expression of judicial arrogance that all too often leads to the "discovery" of bogus new rights—such as the "right to privacy" that undergirds two decisions that Scalia loathes, *Roe v. Wade* (1973) and *Lawrence v. Texas* (2003), which declared unconstitutional a law forbidding homosexual sodomy.[15]

It is no coincidence that an originalist would loathe the Supreme Court decisions that reflect the perspectives of groups that are typically ignored—women (*Roe v. Wade*) and homosexuals (*Lawrence v. Texas*). The framers of the Constitution, whether knowingly or not, functioned with the *mythical norm*—privileged, white, heterosexual males—as their parameters. Consequently, women and homosexuals, to name only two groups, are "Other," and any specified rights were not meant to apply to them. The originalist approach, then, upholds the *mythical norm,* and following this approach means that groups excluded in the past continue to be excluded in the present. Taken to an extreme, the originalist approach would mean that the framers wrote "We, the People," but since they did not have women and African Americans in mind, that phrase should not include those groups now.[16] Of course, an originalist would respond by saying that amendments *were* passed over time to include these groups. The problem is that such amendments are difficult to bring about because the "original" meaning is usually proclaimed to be the only authoritative meaning, and to contest that meaning is deemed to be going against the tradition itself. Therefore, the burden of proof, or should I say, the burden of change, is always on those who want to be included, and that is a difficult burden to discharge. Applying the originalist position to questions of biblical interpretation, the ability to add amendments that countered the exclusion encoded in the founding national documents is in stark contrast to the *inability* to add such amendments to the biblical ones. If, as the originalists claim, adding actual amendments to the wording of a text is the only way to include those formerly excluded, the biblical canon, as a historically determined document that cannot be physically amended, would be immune to change. The *only* way to include those formerly excluded in the biblical tradition, then, is through a sense of "evolving standards" that reflect the needs of all members of the faith community.

What intrigues me is that "All men are created equal" (from the Declaration of Independence) and "We, the People" (from the U.S. Constitution) are inclusive statements, but the authors intended to (and actually did) exclude women, nonwhites, and the poor. With respect to African Americans, though, a fundamental American paradox arises because "the rise of liberty and equality in this country was accompanied by the rise of slavery."[17] In fact, "the most eloquent spokesmen for freedom and equality—George Washington, James Madison, and Thomas Jefferson—were all slaveholders and remained so throughout their lives."[18] Even though slavery has long since been abolished, the pattern persists of inclusive rhetoric in the context of political, economic, and social systems that continue to exclude those outside of the *mythical norm*. Simply put, there is a contradiction between "American rhetoric" and the "American reality."[19] As a result, it is only when that inclusive rhetoric is "unmasked" and the inherent advantages for a particular segment of the society are identified—and addressed—that we will be able to achieve true equality and freedom for all.

Examples of the contraction between American rhetoric on inclusion and the American reality can be found in a close reading of presidential speeches. Vanessa Beasley, in her analysis of inaugural addresses and State of the Union addresses that mentioned the issue of race between 1885 and 2000, found that "chief executives have *sounded* inclusive without actually advocating inclusion."[20] Beasley identified three rhetorical strategies that have been used. Because her analysis is comprehensive and covers several presidencies under each rhetorical strategy, I have chosen, for the sake of brevity, to discuss only one example of each strategy. According to Beasley, an example of "exclusivist inclusion" rhetoric is found in Grover Cleveland's presidency. He argued in 1885 that the government needed to intervene to make Native Americans "capable" of citizenship. That intervention, Cleveland felt, was needed to "lead" them out of their essentially "barbaric" mind-set; he did not mention, Beasley observes, that they deserved assistance "because they had lost their homelands or been ravaged by war and disease."[21] Basically, given the shortcomings of Native Americans that are described, Beasley writes that such rhetoric raises the question: "Why would anyone want to include someone who was both dissimilar and inferior?"

> Despite its internal contradictions, the rhetoric of exclusivist inclusion persists in discussions of American diversity because it allows users to sidestep issues of responsibility and to disregard evidence of inequity. If Native Americans complain of not feeling fully included, for example, citizens can blame them rather than the government or themselves, arguing that "we gave you a chance to join us." Similarly, such a logic can be used to explain current inequities by "blaming the victim," asserting that perhaps Native Americans did not work hard enough to become American or that they clung to their tribal ways rather than embracing American individuality. Ultimately, this rhetoric promotes neither charity nor compassion but instead disinterest, making it a very uninclusive form of inclusion.[22]

Beasley uses a speech by President William McKinley as an example of the second rhetorical strategy, "exemptive inclusion." Generally speaking, she noted that Presidents Cleveland, Harrison, and McKinley hardly referred to African Americans in their State of the Union addresses: "Instead, they repeatedly reminded the existing citizenry of its ideational commitments. 'The love of the law and the sense of obedience and submission to the lawfully constituted judicial tribunals are embedded in the hearts of our people.'"[23] More specifically, in 1899, President McKinley said that "lynchings must not be tolerated in a great and civilized country like the United States. Courts, not mobs, must execute the penalties of the laws."[24] At the same time, Beasley accurately notes, lynchings of African Americans "were becoming increasingly common in the South." But McKinley did not refer to the lynching of African Americans in the speech; he referred to "the killing of eleven Italian immigrants to New Orleans eight years earlier."[25] On the whole, McKinley affirms the theoretical principles of inclusion, yet he fails to offer any specifics where such specifics would be expected, and his failure to mention African Americans renders their reality invisible. Rather than offering specifics, McKinley encourages citizens to "love the law and the sense of obedience and submission." But, as Beasley points out, if this is "the most specific thing that the citizenry might do to ensure inclusion," then McKinley's rhetoric is a call for "*in*action"—an "implicit yet important argument against more specific practices."[26] Consequently, "exemptive inclusion" basically tells the majority of U.S. citizens that they are exempt from action. From this perspective, they are taught to ignore the issue of inclusion and to say, "It's not our problem." In contrast, the exclusivist inclusion rhetoric discussed previously communicates the message that the failure of inclusion is "their problem."[27] The difference is only one of emphasis; they both function to keep exclusion in place.

The third rhetorical strategy Beasley identifies is "institutional inclusion," which communicates the message that "someone else will fix" the problem, and that "someone else" tends to be the government.[28] President Calvin Coolidge made the following statement in his third State of the Union address:

> Nearly one-tenth of our population consists of the Negro race. The progress which they have made in all the arts of civilization in the last 60 years is almost beyond belief. Our country has no more loyal citizens. But they do still need sympathy, kindness, and helpfulness. They need reassurance that the requirements of the Government and society to deal out to them even-handed justice will be met. They should be protected from all violence and supported in the peaceable enjoyment of the fruits of their labor. Those who do violence to them should be punished for their crimes.[29]

Given that Coolidge is aware that white citizens are the ones who are mistreating African Americans, Beasley does not think that he condemns their actions strongly enough. Instead, she construes Coolidge's comments to imply that the government should protect them from that violence. As she describes it, Coolidge "asserts that the government merely needed to do a better job of shielding African Americans from such elements."[30] Arguably, a different response would have been to confront more directly the whites who were committing the violent acts. In this way, Beasley concludes that the message communicated is that "governmental institutions, not the American people, are ultimately responsible for 'managing' such matters."[31] Along with the other rhetorical strategies, the end result is that the majority population is not motivated to bring about change. At the end of her chapter on rhetorical strategies and race, Beasley hopes that future national leaders will avoid the kinds of rhetorical traps seen here and convince citizens that "minority problems" are those of the "majority" as well.[32]

Beasley also examines gender as a topic of presidential speeches, and her findings differ somewhat from those on race. To be exact, she found that presidential messages about women varied widely: "(White) women can be seen as embodying the highest forms of nationalistic piety, for example, while also seeming oddly incapable of enacting citizenship in highly efficacious ways."[33] These variations in the messages about women "reinforce the notion that women are simultaneously inside and outside of the world of Americans' shared beliefs."[34] In contrast, the rhetorical strategies about race tended to exclude nonwhites almost uniformly. Beasley points out several societal trends that influenced the content of those rhetorical strategies, but only two of them are discussed here. In the late nineteenth century, (white) women were active in social, cultural, religious, and economic arenas of the United States. Yet, when Grover Cleveland gave his first State of the Union address, according to Beasley, he advanced the "true womanhood" gender paradigm, with the home (the private realm) as the primary locus of a woman's life because, among other things, the woman needs to be protected from the harshness of the public realm. Consequently, the political realm, as part of the public realm, was to be a man's domain.[35] Even though the "true womanhood" paradigm was widely accepted at that time, it contradicts the realities of those women who had extensive accomplishments outside of the home. As a result, Cleveland's expression of that gender paradigm in that historical context demonstrates the ongoing conflict between American rhetoric and American realities. In this case, though, the rhetoric excluded (white) women, while the reality was more inclusive.

In contrast, President Harry Truman spoke in the 1940s about "women as equal citizens," at a time when there were best-selling books that detailed the harm caused by women working outside of the home.[36] Therefore, the "true womanhood" paradigm was in place in some circles, as it had been in an earlier time, but Truman affirmed (white) women as equal citizens. Beasley suggests that Truman made such statements "during the Cold War years as part of a propaganda battle against the Soviets," which prompted him "to portray the United States as unified and egalitarian."[37]

The same contradiction between rhetoric and reality (or, stated alternatively, between "creed and deed") can be seen in civil rights legislation of the 1960s. George Lipsitz examined civil rights efforts in three areas: fair housing, fair hiring, and school desegregation.[38] In each instance, Lipsitz found that the legislation was basically unenforceable (or unenforced) and therefore did not substantially advance the full inclusion of African American citizens. Lipsitz argues that the Fair Housing Act of 1968 contained procedural provisions that made it virtually unenforceable. He quotes Patricia Roberts Harris, former secretary of the Department of Housing and Urban Development, as having said, "Our society does not often respond to crime by limiting authorities to asking the discovered lawbreaker whether he wants to discuss the matter."[39] Lipsitz cites statistics that present the depth of the problem:

> A 1980 study showed that only 35 percent of cases brought to HUD reached agreement and that half of those were settled in favor of the party accused of discrimination. A total of only four hundred fair housing cases have been decided since 1986; by 1980 only five victims of discrimination had received damages in excess of thirty-five hundred dollars. Most experts believe that more than two million cases of housing discrimination occur each year, but the law is so weak that no action can be taken.[40]

Based on his analysis, Lipsitz concluded that discriminatory housing patterns and lax enforcement policies provide whites with economic advantages that black Americans who often pay higher interest rates on their mortgages, among other things, do not have.[41]

Similarly, Lipsitz found that the Fair Hiring Act of 1968 "contained provisions that undermined its stated goals; in addition to weak enforcement it also provided explicit special protection for the beneficiaries of past discrimination."[42] In the same way, Lipsitz argues that *Brown v. Board of Education* struck down de jure segregation, but the plaintiffs did not get what they sought—which was for black students to receive the same educational resources and opportunities routinely provided to white students. The decision failed to accomplish this "because it outlawed only one technique of inequality—de jure segregation—without addressing the ways in which discrimination in housing, employment, and access to public services enabled whites to resegregate the schools by moving to suburban districts."[43] Due to "white flight" from the cities to the suburbs, de jure segregation (legal) in America's schools was simply replaced with de facto segregation (by tradition).[44] Michael Seidman has said, therefore, that the *Brown* decision "brought about a transformation without real change":

> Separate facilities were now simply proclaimed to be inherently unequal. But the flip side of the aphorism was that once white society was willing to make facilities legally non-separate, the demand for equality had been satisfied and blacks no longer had just cause for complaint. The mere existence of *Brown* thus served to legitimate current arrangements. True, many blacks remained poor and disempowered. But their status was no longer a result of the denial of equality. Instead, it marked a personal failure to take advantage of one's definitionally equal status.[45]

Given the preceding discussion, we have seen that there is indeed a fundamental paradox in the American consciousness that has been with us since the nation's founding. This paradox refers to the existence of the "official" inclusive rhetoric that exists (creeds) while social and economic systems are in place that keep nonwhites, women, and the poor relatively marginalized (deeds). On this basic contradiction between "creed" and "deed," Beasley remembers the words of the sociologist Gunnar Myrdal, who thought that the American creed would ultimately prevail.[46] Because this has not happened, though, Beasley thinks that "the American people have learned how to live comfortably with their contradictions." Indeed, Beasley surmises that this ability to live comfortably with contradictions is because "they have come to understand American beliefs—and, by implication, American identity—in a way that has helped to ease the cognitive dissonance that has presumably accompanied the glaring discrepancies between their creed and their conduct."[47]

I agree with Beasley's analysis. I think that our American identity has been and continues to be equated with the *mythical norm*, as Audre Lorde refers to it—"a norm that is defined as white, thin, male, young, heterosexual, Christian, and financially secure."[48] There are two consequences that result from this implicit norm. First, those who do not fit that norm tend to be excluded from the mainstream and have to struggle to participate in the "American dream." In fact, those who are viewed as threatening that norm may have difficulty entering the United States at all. For example, immigration is a "hot topic" right now. Although the United States has benefited economically from immigration more than it has been hurt by it, many Americans still deeply resent immigrants.[49] Opposition to immigrants has revolved primarily around perceived economic issues, but such fear is often accompanied by cultural concerns, that is, that "immigrants are a threat to American culture in general and to the predominance of the English language in particular."[50] Consequently, those Americans are most troubled by increasing numbers of Spanish-speaking immigrants. We have also feared immigrants who are non-Protestant (Catholics in the nineteenth century) or non-Christian (Jews in the nineteenth and early twentieth century, and Muslims since September 11, 2001).[51] What all these groups have in common is that they differ in some way from the *mythical norm* that has come to define American identity.

Groups outside of the *mythical norm* do not fare any better when they are citizens rather than immigrants. As we saw in Beasley's work *You, the People*, the presidential rhetoric concerning American Indians and African Americans appeared to be inclusive, but it actually excluded those groups. Because the presidential rhetoric both shapes and reflects popular sentiment, similar exclusionary attitudes are seen in the general population. Correspondingly, in the post–civil rights era, the white population seeks to retain its own privileges and has little interest in broadening opportunities for nonwhites. Referring to the work of Gary Orfield, Lipsitz summarizes the attitudes of suburban whites in the following way:

> In Orfield's words, "Whites tell pollsters that they believe that blacks are offered equal opportunities, but fiercely resist any efforts to make them send their children to the schools they insist are good enough for blacks." At the same time, "the people who oppose busing minority students to the suburbs also tend to oppose sending suburban dollars to city schools."[52]

Finally, there are privileges that accrue to those who fit that norm (especially those who are white and financially secure), and those privileges have come to be expected and are not challenged—not even by the ones who do *not* benefit from those same privileges. For example, with all the controversy concerning affirmative action admissions policies of colleges and universities that favor nonwhites, it is noteworthy that no issue has been made about special admissions plans that favor whites, that is, the legacy admission practices. The legacy programs give preferences to the children of alumni and large donors to a school, and quite a few students benefit from the practice in any one year. According to one study, the Harvard class of 1992 had 200 legacy admits, who "outnumbered their class's combined total of Puerto Rican, Mexican American, Native American and African American students."[53] The silence surrounding this issue speaks volumes. Clearly, one reason we accept the contradiction between "rhetoric and reality" is that we just assume those in a certain category will have advantages that other groups will not have.

Working toward Real Inclusion: Participatory Democracy and the Prophetic Tradition

To succeed in today's environment, those who are outside of the *mythical norm* must downplay any attitudes or behaviors that would mark them as different. Kenji Yoshino refers to this phenomenon as "covering," where "to cover is to tone down a disfavored identity to fit into the mainstream." He thinks, as did Audre Lorde in an earlier time, that "all of us are outside of the mainstream in some way; but being deemed mainstream is a necessity of social life."[54] He then offers examples of famous persons who "covered," that is, made accommodations to fit the mainstream:

> Famous examples of covering abound. Ramón Estévez covered his ethnicity when he changed his name to Martin Sheen, as did Krishna

> Bhanji when he changed his name to Ben Kingsley. Margaret Thatcher covered her status as a woman when she trained with a voice coach to lower the timbre of her voice. Long after they came out as lesbians, Rosie O'Donnell and Mary Cheney still covered, keeping their same-sex partners out of the public eye. Issur Danielovitch Demsky covered his Judaism when he became Kirk Douglas, as did Joseph Levitch when he became Jerry Lewis. Franklin Delano Roosevelt covered his disability by ensuring his wheelchair was always hidden behind a desk before his Cabinet entered.[55]

Yoshino doubts that any of these individuals covered themselves willingly; he "suspects they were all bowing to an unjust reality that required them to tone down their stigmatized identities to get along in life."[56] In this way, Yoshino argues, covering forces groups to deny who they are to some extent and constitutes "a hidden assault on our civil rights," where "the aspiration of civil rights has always been to permit people to pursue their human flourishing without limitations based on bias."[57] As part of his analysis, Yoshino has identified the underlying dynamics that necessitate covering:

> The reason racial minorities are pressured to "act white" is because of white supremacy. The reason women are told to downplay their child-care responsibilities in the workplace is because of patriarchy. And the reason gays are asked not to "flaunt" is because of homophobia. So long as such covering demands persist, American civil rights will not have completed its work.[58]

Accordingly, Yoshino proposes a new civil rights movement that cuts across "old-fashioned group-based identity politics" and addresses the issue of covering "because it applies to us all." The "common cause" that we share, he contends, is "the desire for authenticity, our common human wish to express ourselves without being impeded by unreasoning demands for conformity."[59] From my perspective, those demands have the *mythical norm* as their point of reference; those who differ from it by race, religion, gender, or sexuality are forced to comply. Yoshino, therefore, is advocating an inclusive notion of the American national identity that takes into account the perspectives and realities of its "Other" citizens. Simply stated, then, "covering is a form of assimilation."[60]

In the civil rights struggle of the 1960s, assimilation was referred to as "integration," and the objective was "integrating the Negro into the mainstream institutions of the society from which he has been traditionally excluded."[61] The criticism of integration, even then, was that it allowed "a small group of Negroes with middle-class aspirations" to be "siphoned off" into the surrounding middle-class white communities and so "sapped the black community of leadership and know-how."[62] Similarly, an additional charge was that the struggle for integration "allowed the nation to focus on a handful of Southern black children who get into white schools at a great price and to ignore the ninety-four percent who are left in unimproved all-black schools."[63] Furthermore, it was felt that "the goal is not to take black children out of the black community and expose them to white middle-class values; the goal is to build and strengthen the black community."[64] In many respects, as James Cone contends, integration was a strategy—a practical approach that permitted some black advancement and that "many whites accepted as reasonable and just."[65] As we have seen in the fifty years since the *Brown* decision, however, integration did not address the systemic problems that contributed to the marginalization of black people. Evidently, another approach is needed to address those problems.

In feminist theory, two types of women's interests can be identified, and the difference between them is pertinent here. Maxine Molyneux differentiates between practical and strategic gender interests.[66] Strategic gender interests "are derived deductively, that is, from the analysis of women's subordination and from the formulation of an alternative, more satisfactory set of arrangements to those which exist."[67] The objective of strategic gender interests is to overcome women's subordination, including "the removal of institutionalized forms of discrimination" and "the adoption of adequate measures against male violence and control over women," among other things.[68] In contrast, practical gender interests "are given inductively and arise from the concrete conditions of women's positioning within the gender division of labor" and are "usually a response to an immediate perceived need." Moreover, they do not "generally entail a strategic goal such as women's emancipation or gender equality." In fact, "practical interests do not in themselves challenge the prevailing forms of gender subordination."[69] Shelters for battered women offer a good example of the difference between practical and strategic interests. If services are provided to women in crisis, then they meet a practical interest because they are a response to a perceived need. But when the shelters become sites where the causes of violence against women are disscussed, including, the male dominance/female subordination paradigm that contributes to such violence, work has begun "toward changing an entire system of power and control."[70] In this latter case, the strategic interests of women are at work.

Applying Molyneux's distinction to the issue of integration, we can see that racial integration serves practical interests—it meets perceived needs such as providing better education for some African Americans. In this sense, Cone's description of integration as *practical* is indeed fortuitous![71] However, meeting practical needs will not encourage questions or prompt the kind of analysis that will work against the underlying economic and political systems that harm this same community. To do that kind of analytical work, a strategic approach is needed. It stands to reason, then, that integration should not be the ultimate goal, if full inclusion of African Americans (or any other marginalized group) is sought. Instead, critical and crucial questions must be raised about the *mythical norm*, its association with dominant concepts of the national identity, and the exclusionary impact of that association on those who are "Other."

As a national agenda, those who do not fit the *mythical norm* and are on the margins of society must be empowered to participate in our democratic processes. From a liberationist perspective, then, "we want more than a representative democracy; we want a participatory democracy."[72] As it is now, poor people tend not to vote. In the 1994 elections, only 7.7 percent of the voters came from families with incomes under $15,000 per year, down from 13.8 percent in 1990, and that small number votes because the political parties are not reflecting the interests of Americans in the lower income brackets.[73] In their book, *The Miner's Canary*, Lani Guinier and Gerald Torres outline some of the issues that poor communities and brown and black communities face—such as high incarceration rates, greater policing, and fewer educational opportunities.[74] Developing strategies to improve the situation in these communities, based on the perspectives and priorities of the poor rather than the privileged, though, is seldom a priority in political campaigns. Nevertheless, Guinier and Torres feel that race is like the miner's canary, and what is happening to these communities of color is a sign of future danger to the general society:

> Miners often carried a canary into the mine alongside them. The canary's more fragile respiratory system would cause it to collapse from noxious gases long before humans were affected, thus alerting the miners to danger. The canary's distress signaled that it was time to get out of the mine because the air was becoming too poisonous to breathe.
>
> Those who are racially marginalized are like the miner's canary: their distress is the first sign of a danger that threatens us all. It is easy enough to think that when we sacrifice this canary, the only harm is to communities of color. Yet others ignore problems that converge around racial minorities at their own peril, for these problems are symptoms warning us that we are all at risk.[75]

As for the church's role in addressing these social ills today, Cornel West reminds us of the prophetic tradition in American Christianity, naming leaders such as Walter Rauschenbusch of the Social Gospel movement in the early twentieth century, Dorothy Day, Philip and Daniel Berrigan, William Sloane Coffin, as well as Martin Luther King Jr. and others within the black prophetic tradition of which he was a part.[76] For West, it is significant that prophetic leaders such as these "preserve[d] their Christianity and its democratic commitments, without coercing others and conflating church and state spheres."[77] West argues further that "the most influential social movements for justice in America have been led by prophetic Christians," such as the abolitionists, women's suffrage, trade union movements in the nineteenth century, and the civil rights movement in the twentieth century.[78] To West, "prophetic Christianity is an ecumenical force for good," and it must be recaptured and reasserted in public life if the democratic tendencies of this country are to be revitalized.[79] Basically, he argues that religious discourse should be heard in the public square.[80] Contrary to some theorists, West asserts that Christians must acknowledge and affirm "the gains of modernity procured by prophetic religious and progressive secular citizens" and not withdraw from the world: "To be a prophetic Christian is not to be against the world in the name of church purity; it is to be in the world but not of the world's nihilism, in the name of a loving Christ who proclaims the this-worldly justice of a kingdom to come."[81]

West is aware that the efforts of prophetic Christians are "underfunded and unpopular" in today's context, but he knows that such Christians "must become more visible and vocal."[82] To do so is a challenge that must be met nevertheless:

> To be a Christian is to live dangerously, honestly, and freely—to step in the name of love as if you may land on nothing, yet to keep on stepping because that something that sustains you no empire can give you and no empire can take it away. This is the kind of vision and courage required to enable the renewal of prophetic, democratic Christian identity in the age of the American empire.[83]

For me, the metaphor that best describes the end product of a prophetic Christian identity is the creation of the beloved community. The theological motivation for the civil rights movement, which was separate and distinct from its political motivation, was to establish the kingdom of God. In turn, the kingdom of God "grounds, frames, and surrounds the pursuit of the beloved community" and "gives it a memory that sharpens its focus, inspires action, and sustains hope."[84] As Charles Marsh describes it, the beloved community "is a way of talking about the redemptive and reconciling spaces whose real history is the church but which cannot be contained by the church or brought fully under its management."[85] If the church is to be the beloved community, though, it must "welcome all those who come to the work of mercy and justice out of different faiths and convictions."[86] It is significant that Marsh uses a concept of the beloved community that is not synonymous with the church. Therefore, if the church fails to carry out the tasks of redemption and reconciliation, that failure does not limit God's actions. In his analysis, the beloved community can exist separately from the church, if necessary, because "God may nurture and fortify the beloved community through the activity of the Holy Spirit."[87] Marsh's expansive vision of the beloved community means that marginalization is a theological point of departure. As a result, "our faith begins and ends in places of exclusion and struggle. Our sojourn into a violent and hurting world is shaped by the memory of Christ who was born in a stable because there was no room for him at the inn."[88] A democratic national identity that is also prophetic and Christian in our pluralistic environment, therefore, would have in mind "those places of exclusion and struggle" as we live, work, and dream in our communities, our institutions, and our world.

Notes

CHAPTER 1

1. Thomas Bartlett, "I Suffer Not a Woman to Teach," *Chronicle of Higher Education*, April 13, 2007.

2. Jason Burke, "Pope's Move on Latin Mass 'A Blow to Jews,'" *Guardian* (UK), July 8, 2007.

3. Subsequently, the language of the mass was revised to some degree, but it still called for Jews to recognize Jesus Christ as their savior and so retained a call for their conversion to Catholicism. See Philip Pullella, "Vatican Seeks to Reassure Jews on Good Friday Prayer," April 4, 2008, http://www.reuters.com/article/worldNews/idUSL0483119020080404?feedType=RSS&feedName=worldNews (accessed April 24, 2008).

4. Information on the Matthew Shepard Act is taken from the Web site of the Human Rights Campaign, http://www.hrc.org.

5. Greg Garrison, "Conservative Anglicans Heading to Birmingham," *Birmingham News*, January 8, 2006; quoted in Elizabeth Adams, *Going to Heaven: The Life and Election of Bishop Gene Robinson* (Brooklyn, NY: Soft Skull Press, 2006), 247.

6. Elisabeth Schüssler Fiorenza, "An Invitation to 'Dance' in the Open House of Wisdom: Feminist Study of the Bible," in *Engaging the Bible: Critical Readings from Contemporary Women*, ed. Cho Hee An and Katheryn Pfisterer Darr (Minneapolis, MN: Fortress Press, 2006), 83.

7. Charles H. Cosgrove, *Appealing to Scripture in Moral Debate: Five Hermeneutical Rules* (Grand Rapids, MI: Eerdmans, 2002), 91.

8. Elisabeth Schüssler Fiorenza, "The Will to Choose or to Reject: Continuing Our Critical Work," in *Feminist Interpretation of the Bible*, ed. Letty M. Russell (Philadelphia: Westminster Press, 1985), 130.

9. Judith Fetterley, *The Resisting Reader: A Feminist Approach to American Fiction* (Bloomington: Indiana University Press, 1978).

10. W. Randolph Tate, *Interpreting the Bible: A Handbook of Terms and Methods* (Peabody, MA: Hendrickson, 2006), 174.

11. Schüssler Fiorenza, "Invitation to 'Dance,'" 84 (italics in the original).

12. Paulo Freire, *Pedagogy of the Oppressed,* thirtieth anniversary edition, trans. Myra Bergman Ramos (New York: Continuum, 2003).

13. Ibid., 72.

14. Ibid., 73.

15. Letty M. Russell, *Household of Freedom: Authority in Feminist Theology* (Philadelphia: Westminster, 1987); Phyllis A. Bird, "The Authority of the Bible," in *The New Interpreter's Bible,* vol. 1 (Nashville, TN: Abingdon Press, 1994), 33–64.

16. Letty M. Russell, "Authority and the Challenge of Feminist Interpretation," in *Feminist Interpretation of the Bible,* ed. Letty M. Russell (Philadelphia: Westminster Press, 1985), 137–146.

17. Bird, "Authority of the Bible," 63.

18. Eric H. F. Law, *Inclusion: Making Room for Grace* (St. Louis, MO: Chalice Press, 2000), 42.

19. Bruce C. Birch, *Let Justice Roll Down: The Old Testament, Ethics, and Christian Life* (Louisville, KY: Westminster John Knox Press, 1991), 43.

20. Ibid.

21. Ibid.

22. Cosgrove, *Appealing to Scripture,* 109.

23. Ibid.

24. Bird, "Authority of the Bible," 63. See also Phyllis A. Bird, *The Bible as the Church's Book* (Philadelphia: Westminster Press, 1982).

25. Alice Ogden Bellis, *Helpmates, Harlots, and Heroes: Women's Stories in the Hebrew Bible,* 2nd ed. (Louisville, KY: Westminster John Knox Press, 2007).

26. Gale A. Yee, *Poor Banished Children of Eve: Woman as Evil in the Hebrew Bible* (Minneapolis, MN: Fortress Press, 2003).

27. Frances Taylor Gench, *Back to the Well: Women's Encounters with Jesus in the Gospels* (Louisville, KY: Westminster John Knox Press, 2004).

28. Wilda C. Gafney, *Daughters of Miriam: Women Prophets in Ancient Israel* (Minneapolis, MN: Fortress Press, 2008).

29. See, for example, Renita J. Weems, *Just a Sister Away,* revised and updated (New York: Warner Books, 2005).

30. Muriel Orevillo-Montenegro, *The Jesus of Asian Women: Women from the Margins* (Maryknoll, NY: Orbis Books, 2006).

31. Barbara E. Reid, O.P., *Taking Up the Cross: New Testament Interpretations through Latina and Feminist Eyes* (Minneapolis, MN: Fortress Press, 2007).

32. Brian K. Blount, ed., *True to Our Native Land: An African American New Testament Commentary* (Minneapolis, MN: Fortress Press, 2007).

33. Mary F. Foskett and Jeffrey Kah-Jin Kuan, eds., *Ways of Being, Ways of Reading: Asian American Biblical Interpretation* (St. Louis, MO: Chalice Press, 2006).

34. See, for example, Ernesto Cardenal, *The Gospel in Solentiname*, 4 vols., trans. Donald D. Walsh (Maryknoll: Orbis Books, 1976–1982); Jorge V. Pixley, *The Bible, the Church, and the Poor* (Maryknoll, NY: Orbis Books, 1989).

35. See, for example, Gerald O. West, ed., *Reading Other-Wise: Socially Engaged Biblical Scholars Reading with Their Local Communities* (Atlanta: Society of Biblical Literature, 2007).

36. See, for example, R. S. Sugirtharajah, *Postcolonial Criticism and Biblical Interpretation* (Oxford: Oxford University Press, 2002).

37. See, for example, Stephen D. Moore and Fernando F. Segovia, eds., *Postcolonial Biblical Criticism: Interdisciplinary Intersections* (London: T&T Clark, 2005).

38. Musa W. Dube, *Postcolonial Feminist Interpretation of the Bible* (St. Louis, MO: Chalice Press, 2000); Laura E. Donaldson and Kwok Pui-lan, eds., *Postcolonialism, Feminism and Religious Discourse* (New York: Routledge, 2002).

39. Tod Linafelt, ed., *Strange Fire: Reading the Bible after the Holocaust* (Sheffield: Sheffield Academic Press, 2000); Linafelt, ed., *A Shadow of Glory: Reading the New Testament after the Holocaust* (New York: Routledge, 2002).

40. See, for example, Ken Stone, ed., *Queer Commentary and the Hebrew Bible* (Cleveland: Pilgrim Press, 2001); Robert E. Goss and Mona West, eds., *Take Back the Word: A Queer Reading of the Bible* (Cleveland: Pilgrim Press, 2000); Deryn Guest, Robert E. Goss, Mona West, and Thomas Bohache, eds., *The Queer Bible Commentary* (London: SCM Press, 2006).

41. Barry Harvey, "Anti-Postmodernism," in *Handbook of Postmodern Biblical Interpretation*, ed. A. K. M. Adam (St. Louis, MO: Chalice Press, 2000), 1–7.

42. Allan G. Johnson, *The Gender Knot: Unraveling Our Patriarchal Legacy*, revised and updated (Philadelphia: Temple University Press, 2005), 5 (italics in the original).

43. Ibid.

44. Ibid., 7.

45. Ibid., 10.

46. Ibid., 14. For a contemporary legal analysis of such control, see Debran Rowland, *The Boundaries of Her Body: The Troubling History of Women's Rights in America* (Naperville, IL: Sphinx, 2004).

47. Johnson, *Gender Knot*, 15.

48. Ibid.

49. Schüssler Fiorenza, "Invitation to 'Dance,'" 82.

50. Audre Lorde, "Age, Race, Class, and Sex: Women Redefining Difference," in *Sister Outsider* (Freedom, CA: Crossing Press, 1984), 114–123, 115. For a more extensive discussion of classism today, see Michael Zweig, *The Working Class Majority: America's Best Kept Secret* (Ithaca, NY: ILR Press, 2000); Zweig, *What's Class Got to Do with It: American Society in the Twenty-first Century* (Ithaca, NY: ILR Press, 2004).

51. Patricia Beattie Jung and Ralph F. Smith, *Heterosexism: An Ethical Challenge* (Albany: State University of New York Press, 1993), 13.

52. Ibid., 14 (italics in the original).

53. Ibid.

54. Ibid.

55. Suzanne Pharr, *Homophobia: A Weapon of Sexism* (Inverness, CA: Chardon Press, 1988), 26.

56. Joane Nagel, *Race, Ethnicity, and Sexuality: Intimate Intersections, Forbidden Frontiers* (New York: Oxford University Press, 2003), 1.

57. Ibid., 9–10. See Judith Halberstam, *Female Masculinity* (Durham, NC: Duke University Press, 1998).

58. Nagel, *Race, Ethnicity, and Sexuality*, 10.

59. Beverly Wildung Harrison, *Making the Connections: Essays in Feminist Social Ethics*, ed. Carol S. Robb (Boston: Beacon Press, 1985), 140.

60. Daniel Boyarin, *Unheroic Conduct: The Rise of Heterosexuality and the Invention of the Jewish Man* (Berkeley: University of California Press, 1997), xiii.

61. Richard L. Rubenstein and John K. Roth, *Approaches to Auschwitz: The Holocaust and Its Legacy*, rev. ed. (Louisville, KY: Westminster John Knox Press, 2003), 2–3.

62. See, for example, James Carroll, *Constantine's Sword: The Church and the Jews* (Boston: Houghton Mifflin, 2001).

63. Diana L. Eck, *A New Religious America: How a "Christian Country" Has Now Become the Most Religiously Diverse Nation* (San Francisco: HarperSanFrancisco, 2001).

64. Quoted in Dube, *Postcolonial Feminist Interpretation of the Bible*, 3.

65. Funso Afolayan, *Culture and Customs of South Africa* (Westport, CT: Greenwood Press, 2004), 73.

66. Nagel, *Race, Ethnicity, and Sexuality*, 1.

67. Laurel C. Schneider, "Changing the Missionary Position: Facing Up to Racism, Sexism, and Nationalism in G(LBT) Liberation," Tenth Anniversary Gilberto Castaneda Lecture, Chicago Theological Seminary, May 3, 2007, 5–6 (italics in the original), http://www.ctschicago.edu/pdf/Casta%F1edaLecture2007.pdf (accessed December 2007). GLBT is an acronym for gay, lesbian, bisexual, and transgender persons.

68. Ibid., 7.

69. Ibid. (italics in the original).

70. Mayra Rivera Rivera, "En-gendered Territory: U.S. Missionaries' Discourse in Puerto Rico (1898–1920)," in *New Horizons in Hispanic/Latino(a) Theology*, ed. Benjamin Valentin (Cleveland: Pilgrim Press, 2003), 79–97.

71. *Year Book*, 1906, 25; quoted in ibid., 88.

72. Rivera, "En-gendered Territory," 88.

73. Ibid., 95.

74. Rosemary Radford Ruether, *New Woman, New Earth: Sexist Ideologies and Human Liberation* (New York: Seabury Press, 1975), 204.

75. Ibid.

76. Executive Summary, Toxic Wastes and Race at Twenty 1987–2007, United Church of Christ (February 2007). Available: http://www.ejrc.cau.edu/2007%20UCC%20Executive%20Summary.pdf (accessed December 2007), 4.

77. Andrea Smith, *Conquest: Sexual Violence and American Indian Genocide* (Cambridge, MA: South End Press, 2005), 55.

78. Schüssler Fiorenza, "Invitation to 'Dance,'" 83 and 140 n. 5.

79. See Karen Brodkin, *How Jews Became White Folks and What That Says about Race in America* (New Brunswick, NJ: Rutgers University Press, 1998).

80. Naomi Zack, *Thinking about Race,* 2nd ed. (Belmont, CA: Thomson Wadsworth, 2006), 26.

81. Andrea Smith, "Heteropatriarchy and the Three Pillars of White Supremacy: Rethinking Women of Color Organizing," in Incite! Women of Color Against Violence, *Color of Violence: The Incite! Anthology* (Cambridge, MA: South End Press, 2006), 66.

82. Rev. Kelvin Calloway, quoted in Kelly Brown Douglas, "Heterosexism and the Black American Church Community: A Complicated Reality," in *Heterosexism in Contemporary World Religion: Problem and Prospect,* ed. Marvin M. Ellison and Judith Plaskow (Cleveland: Pilgrim Press, 2007), 199.

83. Pharr, *Homophobia,* 64.

84. Jung and Smith, *Heterosexism,* 167–186.

85. Warren J. Blumenfeld, ed., *Homophobia: How We All Pay the Price* (Boston: Beacon Press, 1992), 37–38.

86. For a reconsideration of "justice" in the current sociopolitical context, see Joerg Rieger, "That's Not Fair: Upside-Down Justice in the Midst of Empire," in *Interpreting the Postmodern: Responses to "Radical Orthodoxy,"* ed. Rosemary Radford Ruether and Marion Grau (New York: T&T Clark, 2006).

87. Lorde, "Age, Race, Class, and Sex," 116.

88. Cosgrove, *Appealing to Scripture,* 91.

89. Donald K. McKim, *What Christians Believe about the Bible* (Nashville, TN: Thomas Nelson, 1985), 56.

90. Ibid., 55.

91. Ibid. (italics in the original).

92. Craig D. Allert, *A High View of Scripture? The Authority of the Bible and the Formation of the New Testament Canon* (Grand Rapids, MI: Baker Academic, 2007), 151. See also Clark H. Pinnock with Barry L. Callen, *The Scripture Principle: Reclaiming the Full Authority of the Bible,* 2nd ed. (Grand Rapids, MI: Baker Academic, 2006).

93. Allert, *High View of Scripture?* 151.

94. Daniel J. Harrington, S.J., "Introduction to the Canon," in *The New Interpreter's Bible,* vol. 1 (Nashville, TN: Abingdon Press, 1994), 7–21.

95. Ibid., 14–15.

96. "The Gospel of Mary," in Bart D. Ehrman, *Lost Scriptures: Books That Did Not Make It into the New Testament* (New York: Oxford University Press, 2003), 35–37. See also Ehrman, *Lost Christianities: The Battles for Scripture and the Faiths We Never Knew* (New York: Oxford University Press, 2003).

97. See Theodore W. Jennings Jr., *The Man Jesus Loved: Homoerotic Narratives from the New Testament* (Cleveland: Pilgrim Press, 2003).

98. Allert, *High View of Scripture?* 147–148.

99. Ibid., 148.

100. John Rogerson, "Can a Translation of the Bible Be Authoritative?" in *Bible Translation on the Threshold of the Twenty-first Century: Authority, Reception, Culture and*

Religion, ed. Athalya Brenner and Jan Willem van Henten (London: Sheffield Academic Press, 2002), 22.

101. Randall C. Bailey, "The Danger of Ignoring One's Own Cultural Bias in Interpreting the Text," in *The Postcolonial Bible*, ed. R. S. Sugirtharajah (Sheffield: Sheffield Academic Press, 1998), 76.

102. Ibid.

103. Ibid.

104. Ibid., 76–77.

105. David W. King, *The Bible in History: How the Texts Have Shaped the Times* (New York: Oxford University Press, 2004), 120.

106. Jack B. Rogers and Donald K. McKim, *The Authority and Interpretation of the Bible: An Historical Approach* (San Francisco: Harper and Row, 1979), 76.

107. King, *Bible in History*, 120.

108. Steven Ozment, *The Age of Reform 1250–1550: An Intellectual and Religious History of Late Medieval and Reformation Europe* (New Haven, CT: Yale University Press, 1980, 71 (italics in the original).

109. Eric W. Gritsch, "The Jews in Reformation Theology," in *Jewish-Christian Encounters over the Centuries: Symbiosis, Prejudice, Holocaust, and Dialogue*, ed. Marvin Perry and Frederick M. Schweitzer (New York: Peter Lang, 1994), 199.

110. *Luther's Works* (*LW*), vol. 47: 267–268.

111. William L. Shirer, *The Rise and Fall of the Third Reich: A History of Nazi Germany* (New York: Simon and Schuster, 1960), 236.

112. Michael Carden, "It's Lonely at the Top: Patriarchal Models, Homophobic Vilification and the Heterosexual Household in Luther's Commentaries," in *Redirected Travel: Alternative Journeys and Places in Biblical Studies*, ed. Roland Boer and Edgar W. Conrad (London: T&T Clark, 2003), 193.

113. Caroline Walker Bynum, ". . .And Woman His Humanity," in *Gender and Religion: On the Complexity of Symbols*, ed. Caroline Walker Bynum et al. (Boston: Beacon Press, 1986), 268–269; quoted in Margaret Bendroth, *Fundamentalism and Gender, 1875 to the Present* (New Haven, CT: Yale University Press, 1993), 6.

114. Carden, "It's Lonely at the Top," 193.

115. Ibid., 195. Luther, however, does think that Lot's offering his daughters to the mob is somewhat problematic, but he remains committed to the authority of the male head of household. Ibid., 196–198.

116. Ibid., 195–196.

117. Max L. Stackhouse, "Covenantal Marriage: Protestant Views and Contemporary Life," in *Covenant Marriage in Comparative Perspective*, ed. John Witte Jr. and Eliza Ellison (Grand Rapids, MI: Eerdmans, 2005), 159.

118. Bendroth, *Fundamentalism and Gender*, 6.

119. Ibid.

120. Ibid., 7.

121. Ibid., 36–37.

122. Ibid., 8. For more on evangelical feminism, see Donald W. Dayton, *Discovering an Evangelical Heritage* (New York: Harper and Row, 1976).

123. Bendroth, *Fundamentalism and Gender*, 131 n. 23.

124. Ibid., 8, 36.

125. Ibid., 8.

126. Laurence Moore, *Religious Outsiders and the Makings of Americans* (New York: Oxford University Press, 1986), 163–172; quoted in Bendroth, *Fundamentalism and Gender*, 5.

127. Dale B. Martin, *Sex and the Single Savior: Gender and Sexuality in Biblical Interpretation* (Louisville, KY: Westminster John Knox Press, 2006).

128. Ibid., 1.

129. Ibid.

130. Ibid. (italics in the original).

131. Ibid., 2.

132. Ibid., 5–6.

133. Ibid., 9–10 (italics in the original).

134. Ibid., 2 (italics in the original).

135. Martin Luther King Jr., sermon, "Where Do We Go from Here?," in *A Testament of Hope: The Essential Writings of Martin Luther King, Jr.*, ed. James M. Washington (San Francisco: Harper and Row, 1986), 252.

136. Sandra M. Schneiders, *The Revelatory Text: Interpreting the New Testament as Sacred Scripture* (San Francisco: HarperSanFrancisco, 1991), 32.

137. Elisabeth Schüssler Fiorenza, *In Memory of Her: A Feminist Theological Reconstruction of Christian Origins*, 10th anniversary edition (New York: Crossroad, 1994), 33.

138. Rosemary Radford Ruether, "Feminist Interpretation: A Method of Correlation," in *Feminist Interpretation of the Bible*, ed. Letty M. Russell (Philadelphia: Westminster Press, 1985), 115.

139. Ibid.

CHAPTER 2

1. Lorde, "Age, Race, Class, and Sex," 116.

2. Cheryl B. Anderson, *Women, Ideology, and Violence: Critical Theory and the Construction of Gender in the Book of the Covenant and the Deuteronomic Law* (London: T&T Clark, 2004).

3. Ibid., 126.

4. Issues about the dating of these law collections are often addressed in scholarly studies but are not relevant here. Similarly, the version of the Ten Commandments found in Exodus 20 is not the only one. A comparable one is found in Deuteronomy 5:6–21, and, arguably, others exist but are not of concern here either. See Dale Patrick, *Old Testament Law* (Atlanta: John Knox Press, 1985), 36–39; Walter J. Harrelson, *The Ten Commandments and Human Rights* (Philadelphia: Fortress Press, 1980), 33–40.

5. Carolyn Pressler, *The View of Women Found in Deuteronomic Family Laws* (Berlin: W. de Gruyter, 1993), 38.

6. Anderson, *Women, Ideology, and Violence*, 88.

7. Walter Brueggemann, "Exodus," in *The New Interpreter's Bible Commentary*, vol. 1 (Nashville, TN: Abingdon Press, 1994), 867.

8. Ibid.

9. The husband's control over his wife's body continues even after his death. In Deut. 25:5–10, the law of levirate marriage is described in which the widow of a deceased man who has no sons is to marry her husband's brother, and their firstborn becomes the deceased brother's heir so that his name will not be "blotted out of Israel." See Anderson, *Women, Ideology, and Violence*, 46–47.

10. Ibid., 89.

11. Ibid.

12. Judith Hauptman, "Rabbinic Interpretation of Scripture," in *A Feminist Companion to Reading the Bible: Approaches, Strategies and Methods*, ed. Athalya Brenner and Carole Fontaine (Sheffield: Sheffield Academic Press, 1997), 474; quoted in Anderson, *Women, Ideology, and Violence*, 99.

13. John Rogerson and Philip Davies, *The Old Testament World* (Englewood Cliffs, NJ: Prentice Hall, 1989); cited in Frank S. Frick, *A Journey through the Hebrew Scriptures* (Fort Worth, TX: Harcourt Brace, 1995), 242.

14. Pressler, *Family Laws*, 42–43.

15. Ibid., 31; Anderson, *Women, Ideology, and Violence*, 42–43.

16. Danna Nolan Fewell and David Miller Gunn, *Gender, Power, and Promise: The Subject of the Bible's First Story* (Nashville, TN: Abingdon Press, 1993), 106.

17. Ibid.

18. Ibid., 107.

19. See Frederick J. Gaiser, "A New Word on Homosexuality? Isaiah 56:1–8 as Case Study," *Word and World* 14 (Summer 1994): 280–293.

20. Fewell and Gunn, *Gender, Power, and Promise*, 108.

21. Ibid.

22. Dale B. Martin, "Arsenokoitês and Malakos: Meanings and Consequences," in *Biblical Ethics and Homosexuality: Listening to Scripture*, ed. Robert L. Brawley (Louisville, KY: Westminster John Knox Press, 1996), 124.

23. Ibid., 127.

24. Ibid., 124.

25. Ibid., 129.

26. Ibid.

27. Bernadette J. Brooten, *Love between Women: Early Christian Responses to Female Homoeroticism* (Chicago: University of Chicago Press, 1996), 250.

28. Ibid., 252.

29. Ibid., 256.

30. Anderson, *Women, Ideology, and Violence*, 46–47, 54–56.

31. Harold V. Bennett, *Injustice Made Legal: Deuteronomic Law and the Plight of Widows, Strangers, and Orphans in Ancient Israel* (Grand Rapids, MI: Eerdmans, 2002).

32. Ibid., 124; Anderson, *Women, Ideology, and Violence*, 56.

33. Bennett, *Injustice Made Legal*, 124; Anderson, *Women, Ideology, and Violence*, 56.

34. William Robert Domeris, *Touching the Heart of God: The Social Construction of Poverty among Biblical Peasants* (London: T&T Clark, 2007), 168.

35. Cyril S. Rodd, *Glimpses of a Strange Land: Studies in Old Testament Ethics* (Edinburgh: T&T Clark, 2001), 184.

36. Ibid.

37. Ibid.

38. Leslie J. Hoppe, O.F.M, *There Shall Be No Poor among You: Poverty in the Bible* (Nashville, TN: Abingdon Press, 2004), 173–174.

39. Michael Prior, C.M., *The Bible and Colonialism: A Moral Critique* (Sheffield: Sheffield Academic Press, 1999), 34.

40. Ibid.

41. Norman K. Gottwald, *Tribes of Yahweh: A Sociology of Religion of Liberated Israel, 1250–1050 B.C E.* (Maryknoll, NY: Orbis Books, 1979); Brueggemann, "Exodus," 878.

42. Brueggemann, "Exodus," 878.

43. B. S. J. Isserlin, *The Israelites* (Minneapolis, MN: Fortress Press, 2001), 93; quoted in Johanna van Wijk-Bos, *Making Wise the Simple: The Torah in Christian Faith and Practice* (Grand Rapids, MI: Eerdmans, 2005), 46.

44. Susan Niditch, *War in the Hebrew Bible: A Study in the Ethics of Violence* (New York: Oxford University Press, 1993); Rodd, *Glimpses of a Strange Land*, 191–193.

45. Van Wijk-Bos, *Making Wise the Simple*, 26–27.

46. Ibid., 31 (italics in the original).

47. Patrick D. Miller, *The Way of the Lord: Essays in Old Testament Theology* (Grand Rapids, MI: Eerdmans, 2004), 3.

48. J. David Pleins, *The Social Visions of the Hebrew Bible: A Theological Introduction* (Louisville, KY: Westminster John Knox Press, 2001), 56.

49. Ibid.

50. Nancy J. Duff, "Should the Ten Commandments Be Posted in the Public Realm? Why the Bible and the Constitution Say, 'No,'" in *The Ten Commandments: The Reciprocity of Faithfulness*, ed. William P. Brown (Louisville, KY: Westminster John Knox Press, 2004), 166.

51. Ibid.

52. Wilma Ann Bailey, *"You Shall Not Kill" or "You Shall Not Murder"? Assault on a Biblical Text* (Collegeville, MN: Liturgical Press, 2005).

53. Athalya Brenner, "An Afterword: The Decalogue—Am I an Addressee?" in *A Feminist Companion to Exodus to Deuteronomy*, ed. Athalya Brenner (Sheffield: Sheffield Academic Press, 1994), 255–258.

54. Ibid., 257.

55. Ibid., 258.

56. David J. A. Clines, "The Ten Commandments, Reading from Left to Right," in *Interested Parties: The Ideology of Writers and Readers of the Hebrew Bible* (Sheffield: Sheffield Academic Press, 1995), 26–45, 33–34.

57. Janzen's basic definition of "paradigm" is "something used as a model or example for other cases where a basic principle remains unchanged, though details differ." Waldemar Janzen, *Old Testament Ethics: A Paradigmatic Approach* (Louisville, KY: Westminster John Knox Press, 1994), 26. That definition is taken from Christopher J.

H. Wright's book *An Eye for an Eye: The Place of the Old Testament Ethics Today* (Downers Grove, IL: InterVarsity Press, 1983), 43.

58. Janzen, *Old Testament Ethics*, 2.

59. Ibid., 3.

60. Ibid., 10.

61. Ibid., 33.

62. Ibid., 37.

63. Ibid.

64. Fewell and Gunn, *Gender, Power, and Promise*, 41.

65. Amy-Jill Levine, "Ruth," in *Women's Bible Commentary*, expanded edition, ed. Carol A. Newsom and Sharon H. Ringe (Louisville, KY: Westminster John Knox Press, 1998), 84–90, 90.

66. Janzen, *Old Testament Ethics*, 35.

67. Musa W. Dube, "The Unpublished Letters of Orpah to Ruth," in *Ruth and Esther, A Feminist Companion to the Bible*, second series, ed. Athalya Brenner (Sheffield: Sheffield Academic Press, 1999), 145–150.

68. Ibid., 150.

69. Janzen, *Old Testament Ethics*, 37.

70. The biblical laws would in fact make that distinction. Homosexual acts are punishable by death, but the rape of the daughter of one's host, if she were not married or betrothed, meant only that the perpetrator had to marry the daughter (Deut. 22:28–29).

71. Janzen, *Old Testament Ethics*, 51 n. 29.

72. Ibid., 52 n. 31.

73. John Rogerson, "The Family and Structures of Grace in the Old Testament," in *Theory and Practice in Old Testament Ethics*, ed. M. Daniel Carroll R. (London: T&T Clark, 2004), 132.

74. Ibid., 132.

75. Ibid., 133.

76. Ibid.

77. Stephen C. Barton, "Marriage and Family Life as Christian Concerns," in *New Occasions Teach New Duties: Christian Ethics for Today*, ed. Cyril S. Rodd (Edinburgh: T&T Clark, 1995), 168–170.

78. Christopher J. H. Wright, *Old Testament Ethics for the People of God* (Downers Grove, IL: InterVarsity Press, 2004), 11–12.

79. Ibid., 14–15 (italics in the original).

80. Ibid., 473–474.

81. Ibid., 475–476. See also C. S. Cowles et al., *Show Them No Mercy: Four Views on God and Canaanite Genocide* (Grand Rapids, MI: Zondervan, 2003).

82. Robert Allen Warrior, "A Native American Perspective: Canaanites, Cowboys, and Indians," in *Voices from the Margin: Interpreting the Bible in the Third World*, ed. R. S. Sugirtharajah (Maryknoll, NY: Orbis, 1997), 279.

83. Wright, *Old Testament Ethics*, 479.

84. Warrior, "Native American Perspective," 284. It is striking that Wright assumes the annihilation actually took place yet sees the action as unproblematic, whereas Warrior thinks that the story itself, regardless of its historicity, is problematic.

85. Today postcolonial criticism examines the ways in which the Bible has been used to facilitate European imperialism. See, for example, Dube, *Postcolonial Feminist Interpretation of the Bible.*

86. Warrior, "Native American Perspective," 283.

87. Walter Brueggemann, *An Introduction to the Old Testament: The Canon and Christian Imagination* (Louisville, KY: Westminster John Knox Press, 2003), 10.

88. Wright, *Old Testament Ethics*, 475.

89. Robert A. Oden Jr., *The Bible without Theology: The Theological Tradition and Alternatives to It* (San Francisco: Harper and Row, 1987), 153.

90. Randall C. Bailey, "They're Nothing but Incestuous Bastards: The Polemical Use of Sex and Sexuality in Hebrew Canon Narratives," in *Reading from This Place: Social Location and Biblical Interpretation in the United States*, vol. 1, ed. Fernando F. Segovia and Mary Ann Tolbert (Minneapolis, MN: Fortress, 1995), 137.

91. Ibid., 124. See also Bailey, "He Didn't Even Tell Us the Worst of It!" *Union Seminary Quarterly Review* 59 (2005): 15–24.

92. Warrior, "Native American Perspective," 283.

93. Ibid., 284.

94. John Barton, *Understanding Old Testament Ethics: Approaches and Explorations* (Louisville, KY: Westminster John Knox Press, 2003), 47.

95. Pressler, *Family Laws*, 42–43.

96. Birch, *Let Justice Roll Down*, 43.

97. Barton, *Understanding Old Testament Ethics*, 48.

98. Ibid., 50.

99. Ibid., 34–37.

100. Ibid., 52.

101. Ibid., 40.

102. Rodd, *Glimpses of a Strange Land*, 184.

103. Barton, *Understanding Old Testament Ethics*, 51.

104. Ibid.

105. Ibid., 53.

106. Rodd, *Glimpses of a Strange Land*, 68.

107. Ibid., 68, 69.

108. Ibid., 76.

109. Miguel A. De La Torre, *Doing Christian Ethics from the Margins* (Maryknoll, NY: Orbis Books, 2004), 12.

110. Ibid., 13.

111. Ibid., 14.

112. Cheryl B. Anderson, "The Eighth Commandment: A Way to King's Beloved Community?" in *The Ten Commandments*, ed. William P. Brown (Louisville, KY: Westminster John Knox Press, 2004).

113. Walter J. Harrelson, *The Ten Commandments for Today* (Louisville, KY: Westminster John Knox Press, 2006), 67–68.

114. Ibid., 68.

115. Terence E. Fretheim, *God and World in the Old Testament: A Relational Theology of Creation* (Nashville, TN: Abingdon Press, 2005), 134–135.

116. Ibid., 153 (italics in the original).

117. Ibid.

118. Ibid., 154.

119. Ibid., 154–155.

120. Ibid., 156.

CHAPTER 3

1. Harrington, "Canon," 7.

2. Bruce C. Birch, Walter Brueggemann, Terence E. Fretheim, and David L. Petersen, *A Theological Introduction to the Old Testament*, 2nd ed. (Nashville, TN: Abingdon Press, 2005), 449.

3. Ibid., 429.

4. Madipoane Masenya (ngwana' Mphahlele), "Ruth," in *Global Bible Commentary*, ed. Daniel Patte (Nashville, TN: Abingdon Press, 2004), 86.

5. Ibid., 89.

6. Julie L. C. Chu, "Returning Home: The Inspiration of the Role Dedifferentiation in the Book of Ruth for Taiwanese Women," *Semeia* 78 (1997): 50–51.

7. Ibid., 51–52. In contrast, Amy-Jill Levine finds ambivalence in the relationship between Ruth and Naomi and a lack of appreciation on Naomi's part for her daughter-in-law's efforts. See Levine, "Ruth," 84–90. See also Ellen Van Wolde, "Texts in Dialogue with Texts: Intertextuality in the Ruth and Tamar Narratives," *Biblical Interpretation* 5 (1997): 1–28.

8. Sarojini Nadar, "A South African Indian Womanist Reading of the Character of Ruth," in *Other Ways of Reading: African Women and the Bible*, ed. Musa W. Dube (Atlanta: Society of Biblical Literature, 2001), 171.

9. Ibid.

10. Kwok Pui-lan, "Finding a Home for Ruth: Gender, Sexuality, and the Politics of Otherness," in *New Paradigms for Bible Study: The Bible in the Third Millennium*, ed. Robert M. Fowler, Edith Blumhofer, and Fernando F. Segovia (New York: T&T Clark, 2004), 141.

11. Kwok, "Finding a Home," 141. See also Danna Nolan Fewell and David Miller Gunn, *Compromising Redemption: Relating Characters in the Book of Ruth* (Louisville, KY: Westminster John Knox Press, 1990).

12. Madipoane Masenya, "Struggling with Poverty/Emptiness: Rereading the Naomi-Ruth Story in African-South Africa," *Journal of Theology for Southern Africa* 120 (November 2004): 58.

13. Ibid.

14. Anna May Say Pa, "Reading Ruth 3:1–15 from an Asian Woman's Perspective," in *Engaging the Bible in a Gendered World: An Introduction to Feminist Biblical Interpretation in Honor of Katharine Doob Sakenfeld*, ed. Linda Day and Carolyn Pressler (Louisville, KY: Westminster John Knox Press, 2006), 47–59.

15. Kwok, "Finding a Home," 141.

16. Masenya, "Struggling with Poverty/Emptiness."

17. Laura E. Donaldson, "The Sign of Orpah: Reading Ruth through Native Eyes," in *Ruth and Esther: A Feminist Companion to the Bible*, ed. Athalya Brenner, 2nd ser. (Sheffield: Sheffield Academic Press, 1999), 132.

18. Levine, "Ruth," 86.

19. Rebecca Alpert, "Finding Our Past: A Lesbian Reading of the Book of Ruth," in *Reading Ruth: Contemporary Women Reclaim a Sacred Story*, ed. Judith A. Kates and Gail Twersky Reimer (New York: Ballantine Books, 1994), 91–96.

20. Ibid.

21. For a bisexual reading that challenges reading Ruth as a story about *either* a heterosexual relationship (Ruth and Boaz) *or* a homosexual one (Ruth and Naomi), see Celena M. Duncan, "The Book of Ruth: On Boundaries, Love, and Truth," in *Take Back The Word: A Queer Reading of the Bible*, ed. Robert E. Goss and Mona West (Cleveland: Pilgrim Press, 2000), 92–102.

22. Weems, *Just a Sister Away*, 27.

23. Ibid., 36.

24. Bailey, "They're Nothing but Incestuous Bastards."

25. Smith, *Conquest*, 7–33.

26. Yee, *Poor Banished Children of Eve*, 159.

27. Levine, "Ruth," 85.

28. Donaldson, "Sign of Orpah," 137–138.

29. Ibid., 142.

30. Ibid., 143. See also Judith E. McKinlay, *Reframing Her: Biblical Women in Postcolonial Focus* (Sheffield: Sheffield Phoenix Press, 2004), 37–56.

31. Dube, "Unpublished Letters."

32. Ibid., 150.

33. Musa W. Dube, "Divining Ruth for International Relations," in *Other Ways of Reading: African Women and the Bible*, ed. Musa W. Dube (Atlanta: Society of Biblical Literature, 2001), 179–195.

34. Ibid., 192.

35. Ibid., 194.

36. Carolyn Pressler, *Joshua, Judges, and Ruth* (Louisville, KY: Westminster John Knox Press, 2002), 264 (italics in the original).

37. Sidnie Ann White Crawford, "Esther," in *Women's Bible Commentary*, ed. Carol A. Newsom and Sharon H. Ringe, expanded edition (Louisville, KY: Westminster John Knox Press, 1998), 133.

38. Carey A. Moore, *Esther*, Anchor Bible 7B (Garden City, NY: Doubleday, 1971), lii; White Crawford, "Esther," 133.

39. Lewis Bayles Paton, *A Critical and Exegetical Commentary on the Book of Esther* (Edinburgh: T&T Clark, 1908), 96; White Crawford, "Esther," 133.

40. See, for example, Katheryn Pfisterer Darr, *Far More Precious Than Jewels: Perspectives on Biblical Women* (Louisville, KY: Westminster John Knox Press, 1991), 164–193; Jon L. Berquist, *Reclaiming Her Story: The Witness of Women in the Old Testament* (St. Louis, MO: Chalice Press, 1992), 154–166.

41. Susan Niditch, "Esther: Folklore, Wisdom, Feminism, and Authority," in *A Feminist Companion to Esther, Judith, and Susanna*, ed. Athalya Brenner (Sheffield: Sheffield Academic Press, 1995), 33.

42. Ibid.

43. Itumeleng J. Mosala, "The Implications of the Text of Esther for African Women's Struggle for Liberation in South Africa," *Semeia* 59 (1992): 136.

44. Ibid.

45. Nicole Duran, "Who Wants to Marry a Persian King? Gender Games and Wars and the Book of Esther," in *Pregnant Passion: Gender, Sex, and Violence in the Bible*, ed. Cheryl A. Kirk-Duggan, Semeia Studies 44 (Atlanta: Society of Biblical Literature, 2003), 81.

46. Linda M. Day, *Esther*, Abingdon Old Testament Commentaries (Nashville, TN: Abingdon Press, 2005), 42.

47. Mieke Bal, "Lots of Writing," in *Ruth and Esther: A Feminist Companion to the Bible*, ed. Athalya Brenner, 2nd ser. (Sheffield: Sheffield Academic Press, 1999), 227 n. 27.

48. Weems, *Just a Sister Away*, 118.

49. White Crawford, "Esther," *New Interpreter's Bible*, vol. 3 (Nashville, TN: Abingdon Press, 1999), 889.

50. Duran, "Who Wants to Marry a Persian King," 73.

51. Sarojini Nadar, "'Texts of Terror': The Conspiracy of Rape in the Bible, Church, and Society: The Case of Esther 2:1–18," in *African Women, Religion, and Health*, ed. Isabel Apawo Phiri and Sarojini Nadar (Maryknoll, NY: Orbis Books, 2006), 88.

52. Ibid., 88–89.

53. Ibid., 89–90. See also Anderson, *Women, Ideology, and Violence*, 101–117.

54. Duran, "Who Wants to Marry a Persian King?" 84 (italics in the original).

55. There is no assumption here that racism no longer exists. For a discussion of contemporary forms of racism, see Patricia Hill Collins, *Black Sexual Politics: African Americans, Gender, and the New Racism* (New York: Routledge, 2005).

56. For a full discussion of "passing" and African American gays and lesbians, see Horace L. Griffin, *Their Own Receive Them Not: African American Lesbians and Gays in Black Churches* (Cleveland: Pilgrim Press, 2006).

57. Gary David Comstock, *Gay Theology without Apology* (Cleveland: Pilgrim Press, 1993), 56.

58. Ibid.

59. Day, *Esther*, 43.

60. Ibid.

61. White Crawford, "Esther," 133. To the contrary, Randall Bailey finds in his reading of the text a condemnation of the king and Haman, as well as of those Jews, Esther and Mordecai, who collaborate with the imperial regime. See "That's Why They Didn't Call the Book Hadassah! Intersec(ct)/(x)ionality of Race/Ethnicity, Gender, and Sexuality in the Book of Esther,". *They Were All Together in One Place? Toward Minority Biblical Criticism*, Semeia Studies 57, ed. Randall C. Bailey, Tat-siong Benny Liew, and Fernando F. Segovia (Atlanta: Society of Biblical Literature, 2009), 227–250. I would

like to thank Professor Bailey for making a copy of his paper available to me in advance of publication.

62. See, for example, R. S. Sugirtharajah, *The Postcolonial Bible* (Sheffield: Sheffield Academic Press, 1998); Dube, *Postcolonial Feminist Interpretation of the Bible*. For a survey of recent postcolonial feminist writings, see Susanne Scholz, *Introducing the Women's Hebrew Bible* (New York: T&T Clark, 2007). I am grateful to Professor Scholz for giving me an advance copy of her manuscript.

63. Madipoane Masenya, "Esther and Northern Sotho Stories: An African-South African Woman's Commentary," in *Other Ways of Reading: African Women and the Bible*, ed. Musa W. Dube (Atlanta: Society of Biblical Literature, 2001), 47.

64. Ibid.

65. Day, *Esther*, 21.

66. Ibid.

67. Timothy K. Beal, *The Book of Hiding: Gender, Ethnicity, Annihilation, and Esther* (London: Routledge, 1997), 12.

68. Wong Wai Ching Angela, "Esther," in *Global Bible Commentary*, ed. Daniel Patte (Nashville, TN: Abingdon Press, 2004), 137.

69. Ibid., 139.

70. Ibid., 137.

71. Ibid., 140.

72. Johanna van Wijk-Bos, *Ruth and Esther: Women in Alien Lands* (New York: General Board of Global Ministries of the United Methodist Church, 1988), 2, 4.

73. Ibid., 4.

74. Leviticus 25–27, Numbers 18, as well as the law of levirate marriage found in Deuteronomy 25:5–10 and alluded to in Ruth.

75. Katharine Doob Sakenfeld, "Ruth 4, an Image of Eschatological Hope: Journeying with a Text," in *Liberating Eschatology: Essays in Honor of Letty M. Russell*, ed. Margaret A. Farley and Serene Jones (Louisville, KY: Westminster John Knox Press, 1999), 63.

76. Ibid.

77. Ibid.

78. Ibid., 56.

79. Johanna van Wijk-Bos, *Ruth, Esther, Jonah* (Atlanta: John Knox Press, 1986), 3.

80. Ibid., 41.

81. Fewell and Gunn, *Compromising Redemption*, 105.

82. Jacqueline Lapsley, *Whispering the Word: Hearing Women's Stories in the Old Testament* (Louisville, KY: Westminster John Knox Press, 2005), 105.

83. Lapsley, *Whispering the Word*, 105.

84. Dube, *Postcolonial Feminist Interpretation of the Bible*, 185.

85. Ibid., 186.

86. Scott M. Langston, *Exodus through the Centuries*, Blackwell Bible Commentaries (Malden, MA: Blackwell, 2006), 4–8.

87. Mary Ann Tolbert, "Afterwords: Christianity, Imperialism, and the Decentering of Privilege," in *Reading from This Place*, vol. 2, *Social Location and Biblical Interpre-*

tation in Global Perspective, ed. Fernando F. Segovia and Mary Ann Tolbert (Minneapolis MN: Fortress Press, 1995), 347–348.

88. Ibid., 348–349.

89. Ibid., 350.

90. Ibid.

91. Ibid., 351.

92. Sharon H. Ringe, "Asian Readings of the Bible: A North American Feminist Response," *Biblical Interpretation* 2 (1994): 376.

93. Phyllis A. Bird, "A North American Feminist Response," in *Other Ways of Reading: African Women and the Bible,* ed. Musa W. Dube (Atlanta: Society of Biblical Literature, 2001), 200.

94. Ibid. 200.

95. Antoinette Clark Wire, "A North American Perspective," *Semeia* 78 (2001): 148–149.

96. Ringe, "North American Feminist Response," 375.

97. Ibid.

98. Tolbert, "Afterwords," 355.

99. Ibid., 356 (italics in the original).

100. Ibid., 359.

101. Ibid., 360.

CHAPTER 4

1. Geza Vermes, *The Religion of Jesus the Jew* (Minneapolis, MN: Fortress Press, 1993), 18.

2. As E. P. Sanders notes, "The stories of healing on the Sabbath (the Man with the Withered Hand, Matt. 12:9–14/Mark 3:1–6/Luke 6:6–11; the Woman with a Spirit of Infirmity, Luke 13:10–17; the Healing of a Man with Dropsy, Luke 14:1–6) also reveal no instance in which Jesus transgressed the Sabbath law." Sanders explains that "the matter is quite simple: no work was performed," and "the laying on of hands (Luke 13:13) is not work, and no physical action of any kind is reported in the other stories." Sanders, *Jesus and Judaism* (Philadelphia: Fortress Press, 1985), 266.

3. Vermes, *Religion of Jesus the Jew,* 23.

4. Ibid., 24–26.

5. Ibid., 25. For the dating of the book of Acts, see Bart D. Ehrman, *The New Testament: A Historical Introduction to the Early Christian Writings,* 3rd ed. (New York: Oxford University Press, 2004), 148.

6. Bruce J. Malina and Richard L. Rohrbaugh, *Social-Science Commentary on the Synoptic Gospels,* 2nd ed. (Minneapolis, MN: Fortress Press, 2003), 427.

7. Ibid.

8. Ibid.

9. Ibid.

10. See, for example, Amy-Jill Levine, *The Misunderstood Jew: The Church and the Scandal of the Jewish Jesus* (New York: HarperSanFrancisco, 2006); Bruce Chilton, *Rabbi*

Jesus: An Intimate Biography: The Jewish Life and Teachings That Inspired Christianity (New York: Doubleday, 2000); Chilton, *Rabbi Paul: An Intellectual Biography* (New York: Doubleday, 2004).

11. George W. E. Nickelsburg, *Ancient Judaism and Christian Origins: Diversity, Continuity, and Transformation* (Minneapolis, MN: Fortress Press, 2003), 162; Jacob Neusner, *From Politics to Piety: The Emergence of Pharisaic Judaism*, 2nd ed. (New York: Ktav, 1979).

12. Nickelsburg, *Ancient Judaism and Christian Origins*, 162–163.

13. Ibid., 162.

14. Ehrman, *New Testament*, 235–236.

15. Ibid., 236.

16. Ibid.

17. Ibid.

18. Ibid.

19. Malina and Rohrbaugh, *Social-Science Commentary*, 175.

20. Ibid.

21. Ibid.

22. William R. Herzog II, *Jesus, Justice, and the Reign of God: A Ministry of Liberation* (Louisville, KY: Westminster John Knox Press, 2000), 149–155; Herzog, *Prophet and Teacher: An Introduction to the Historical Jesus* (Louisville, KY: Westminster John Knox Press, 2005), 175–177.

23. Malina and Rohrbaugh, *Social-Science Commentary*, 175.

24. Nickelsburg, *Ancient Judaism and Christian Origins*, 165.

25. See, for example, Levine, *Misunderstood Jew*; Jacob Neusner, *A Rabbi Talks with Jesus: An Intermillennial, Interfaith Exchange* (New York: Doubleday, 1993); Robert M. Grant with David Tracy, *A Short History of the Interpretation of the Bible*, 2nd ed., rev. and enl. (Philadelphia: Fortress Press, 1984), 8–16.

26. Ehrman, *New Testament*, 72.

27. Ibid.

28. Ibid.

29. Ibid.

30. Pheme Perkins, "The Gospel of Mark," *New Interpreter's Bible Commentary*, vol. 8 (Nashville, TN: Abingdon Press, 1995), 606.

31. Ibid., 607.

32. Herzog, *Prophet and Teacher*, 43–69.

33. Ibid., 134.

34. Ibid.

35. Ibid., 69.

36. William R. Herzog II, *Parables as Subversive Speech: Jesus as Pedagogue of the Oppressed* (Louisville, KY: Westminster John Knox Press, 1994), 264.

37. Ibid.

38. Perkins, "Mark," 606.

39. Herzog, *Prophet and Teacher*, 78.

40. Ibid.

41. M. Eugene Boring, "The Gospel of Matthew," *The New Interpreter's Bible*, vol. 8 (Nashville, TN: Abingdon Press, 1995), 426.

42. Ibid.

43. Ibid., 425.

44. Malina and Rohrbaugh, *Social-Science Commentary*, 84.

45. Herzog, *Prophet and Teacher*, 68.

46. Ibid., 160.

47. Malina and Rohrbaugh, *Social-Science Commentary*, 84.

48. Herzog, *Prophet and Teacher*, 160.

49. Herzog, *Jesus, Justice, and the Reign of God*, 165–166.

50. Herzog, *Prophet and Teacher*, 22, 196.

51. Ibid., 196.

52. Boring, "Matthew," 426.

53. Ehrman, *New Testament*, 170–173.

54. Jack Nelson-Pallmeyer, *Jesus against Christianity: Reclaiming the Missing Jesus* (Harrisburg, PA: Trinity Press International, 2001), 314.

55. Ibid.

56. Ibid., 315–316.

57. In my reference to "liberating Paul" I have in mind Neil Elliott's book *Liberating Paul: The Justice of God and the Politics of the Apostle* (Sheffield: Sheffield Academic Press, 1995).

58. Ehrman, *New Testament*, 288.

59. Ibid., 287.

60. Ibid.

61. Ibid. For more information on the concept of later redactions and other topics covered in the academic study of the Bible, see V. George Skillington, *Reading the Sacred Text: An Introduction to Biblical Studies* (London: T&T Clark, 2002).

62. Clarice J. Martin, "The *Haustafeln* (Household Codes) in African American Biblical Interpretation: 'Free Slaves' and 'Subordinate Women,'" in *Stony the Road We Trod: African American Biblical Interpretation*, ed. Cain Hope Felder (Minneapolis, MN: Fortress Press, 1991), 209.

63. Ibid.; Schüssler Fiorenza, *In Memory of Her*, 255, 263.

64. Martin, "The *Haustafeln* (Household Codes)," 211, 213.

65. Joanna Dewey, "1 Timothy," in *Women's Bible Commentary*, exp. ed., ed. Carol A. Newsom and Sharon Ringe (Louisville, KY: Westminster John Knox Press, 1998), 447.

66. Ibid.

67. Jonathan P. Burridge, *Imitating Jesus: An Inclusive Approach to New Testament Ethics* (Grand Rapids, MI: Eerdmans, 2007), 122.

68. J. Paul Sampley, "First Corinthians," *New Interpreter's Bible Commentary*, vol. 10 (Nashville, TN: Abingdon Press, 2002), 969 (italics in the original).

69. Ibid., 970. For a critique of arguments by Antoinette Clark Wire and Elisabeth Schüssler Fiorenza in favor of the authenticity of this pericope, see Elliott, *Liberating Paul*, 52–54.

70. Burridge, *Imitating Jesus*, 123.

71. Brian K. Blount, *Then the Whisper Put on Flesh: New Testament Ethics in an African American Context* (Nashville, TN: Abingdon Press, 2001), 140.

72. Ibid.

73. Martin, The *Haustafeln* (Household Codes), 213; Charles Hodge, "The Fugitive Slave Law," in *Cotton Is King and Pro-slavery Arguments Compromising the Writings of Hammond, Harper, Christy, Hodge, Bledsoe, and Cartwright on This Important Subject*, ed. E.N. Elliott (Augusta, GA: Pritchard, Abbott and Loomis, 1860), 809–840.

74. Martin, "The *Haustafeln* (Household Codes)," 216.

75. Ibid.

76. Elliott, *Liberating Paul*, 32. See also Brad Braxton, *The Tyranny of Resolution: 1 Corinthians 7:17–24* (Atlanta: Society of Biblical Literature, 2000), 220–234.

77. Elliott, *Liberating Paul*, 36.

78. Burridge, *Imitating Jesus*, 135.

79. Ibid.

80. Lloyd A. Lewis, "An African American Appraisal of the Philemon-Paul-Onesimus Triangle," in *Stony the Road We Trod: African American Biblical Interpretation*, ed. Cain Hope Felder (Minneapolis, MN: Fortress Press, 1991), 232–246.

81. Ibid.

82. Jouette M. Bassler, "First Corinthians," in *Women's Bible Commentary*, ed. Carol A. Newsom and Sharon H. Ringe, expanded edition (Louisville, KY: Westminster John Knox Press, 1998), 413–414.

83. Ibid., 413.

84. Martin, *Sex and the Single Savior*, 65 (italics in the original).

85. Ibid., 56.

86. Ibid., 56–57 (italics in the original).

87. Ibid., 58; Martii Nissinen, *Homoeroticism in the Biblical World: A Historical Perspective* (Minneapolis, MN: Fortress Press, 1998), 103–113.

88. See, for example, the resources listed in Burridge, *Imitating Jesus*, 129 n. 204

89. Ibid., 129.

90. Ibid., 84.

91. Ibid., 85.

92. David G. Horrell, *Solidarity and Difference: A Contemporary Reading of Paul's Ethics* (London: T&T Clark International, 2005), 102, 106.

93. Ibid., 139.

94. Ibid.

95. James D. G. Dunn, *The Theology of Paul the Apostle* (Grand Rapids, MI: Eerdmans, 1998), 144.

96. Richard B. Hays, "Galatians," in *The New Interpreter's Bible*, Vol. 11 (Nashville, TN: Abingdon Press, 2000), 184–185.

97. Jouette M. Bassler, *Navigating Paul: An Introduction to Key Theological Concepts* (Louisville, KY: Westminster John Knox, 2007), 18 (italics in the original).

98. Ibid., 18–19.

99. Ibid., 21 (italics in the original).

100. Ehrman, *New Testament*, 324. Although Ehrman has a question mark about class differences, Dunn thinks that social tensions were involved. Dunn, *Theology of Paul the Apostle*, 701–702.

101. Ehrman, *New Testament*, 324–325.

102. Sampley, "First Corinthians," 901–902.

103. Horrell, *Solidarity and Difference*, 174.

104. Ibid., 184–185. It is worth mentioning that, even though the observance of Jewish law was at stake, Horrell thinks that both the "strong" and the "weak" groups would have contained Jews and Gentiles.

105. Ibid., 186, 188.

106. Ibid., 188.

107. Sampley, "First Corinthians," 814, 934.

108. Elliott, *Liberating Paul*, 206–211.

109. Richard A. Horsley, "First Corinthians: A Case Study of Paul's Assembly as an Alternative Society," in *Paul and Empire: Religion and Power in Roman Imperial Society*, ed. Richard Horsley (Harrisburg, PA: Trinity Press International, 1997), 252. See also Richard A. Horsley, "Submerged Biblical Histories and Imperial Biblical Studies," in *The Postcolonial Bible*, ed. R.S. Sugirtharajah (Sheffield: Sheffield Academic Press, 1998), 152–173; Richard A. Horsley, ed., *Paul and the Roman Imperial Order* (Harrisburg, PA: Trinity Press International, 2004).

110. Burridge, *Imitating Jesus*, 107.

111. Ibid., 107–108.

112. Ibid., 108.

113. Ibid., 109.

114. Bassler, *Navigating Paul*, 19 (italics in the original).

115. Dunn, *Theology of Paul the Apostle*, 631–658; quoted in Burridge, *Imitating Jesus*, 115.

116. Burridge, *Imitating Jesus*, 115.

117. Ibid., 40.

118. Ibid., 89.

119. Ibid., 50, 105.

120. Cosgrove, *Appealing to Scripture*, 158.

121. Ibid., 161. The references here are to Augustine, *De Doctrina Christiana*, book 1 (1.84–85) [XXXV–XXXVI] and to the Second Helvetic Confession of 1566 (5.010).

122. Cosgrove, *Appealing to Scripture*, 174 n. 77; Richard B. Hays, *The Moral Vision of the New Testament: A Contemporary Introduction to New Testament Ethics* (San Francisco: HarperSanFrancisco, 1996).

123. Martin, *Sex and the Single Savior*, 165; Stanley Hauerwas, *Vision and Virtue: Essays in Christian Ethical Reflection* (Notre Dame, IN: Fides, 1974).

124. Martin, *Sex and the Single Savior*, 167.

125. Ibid., 168 (italics in the original).

126. Burridge, *Imitating Jesus*, 50–51. Burridge also mentions here Matt. 5:38–48 and Luke 6:27–36.

127. Law, *Inclusion*, 42.

128. See, for example, Yvette A. Flunder, *Where the Edge Gathers: Building A Community of Radical Inclusion* (Cleveland: Pilgrim Press, 2005).

CHAPTER 5

1. For general information about these reformers, see Heiko A. Oberman, *Luther: Man between God and the Devil*, trans. Eileen Walliser-Schwarzbart (New Haven, CT: Yale University Press, 1989); T. H. L. Parker, *Calvin: A Biography* (Louisville, KY: Westminster John Knox Press, 2007); Kenneth J. Collins, *A Real Christian: The Life of John Wesley* (Nashville, TN: Abingdon Press, 1999).

2. Martin Luther, *Lectures on Galatians: 1535: Chapters 1–4*, vol. 26 of *Luther's Works* (St. Louis, MO: Concordia, 1963), 308.

3. Ibid.

4. Ibid., 308–309.

5. Ibid., 309–310.

6. Ibid., 309.

7. John Calvin, *Commentaries on the Epistles of Paul to the Galatians and the Ephesians*, trans. William Pringle (Edinburgh: Calvin Translation Society, 1854), 108.

8. John Calvin, *Institutes of the Christian Religion in Two Volumes*, ed. John T. McNeill and Ford Lewis Battles, Library of Christian Classics, vol. 20 (Philadelphia: Westminster Press, 1960), 354, 357.

9. Ibid., 1:358.

10. Ibid., 1:360.

11. Ibid., 1:360–361.

12. Edward A. Dowey, "Law in Luther and Calvin," *Theology Today* 41 (1984): 153; quoted in Patrick D. Miller, "Old Testament Exegesis in the Reformed Perspective: The Case of the Commandments," in *Reformed Theology: Identity and Ecumenicity II: Biblical Interpretation in the Reformed Tradition*, ed. Wallace M. Alston Jr. and Michael Welker (Grand Rapids, MI: Eerdmans, 2007), 221.

13. John B. Cobb Jr., *Grace and Responsibility: A Wesleyan Theology for Today* (Nashville, TN: Abingdon Press, 1995), 118.

14. John Wesley, "On the Original, Nature, Property, and Use of the Law," in *Sermons II: 34–70*, vol. 2 of *The Works of John Wesley*, ed. Albert C. Outler (Oxford: Clarendon Press, 1975), 17.

15. Ibid., 16. Interestingly, Wesley does not refer to a political use of the law as Luther and Calvin did. See Cobb, *Grace and Responsibility*, 186 n. 3; Ronald H. Stone, *John Wesley's Life and Ethics* (Nashville, TN: Abingdon Press, 2001), 213.

16. John Wesley, "Of Preaching Christ," in *John Wesley*, ed. Albert C. Outler (New York: Oxford University Press, 1964), 233; quoted in Cobb, *Grace and Responsibility*, 118–119.

17. Calvin, *Institutes*, 1:421.

18. Philip Turner, "The Ten Commandments in the Church in a Postmodern World," in *I Am the Lord Your God: Christian Reflections on the Ten Commandments*, ed. Carl E. Braaten and Christopher R. Seitz (Grand Rapids, MI: Wm. B. Eerdmans,

2005), 8. See also Paul Althaus, *The Ethics of Martin Luther* (Philadelphia: Fortress Press, 1972).

19. Turner, "Ten Commandments," 10.

20. Ibid.

21. Ibid.; Calvin, *Institutes*, 2:8, 404–405.

22. Elsie Ann McKee, "The Character and Significance of John Calvin's Teaching on Social and Economic Issues," in *John Calvin Rediscovered: The Impact of His Social and Economic Thought*, ed. Edward Dommen and James D. Bratt (Louisville, KY: Westminster John Knox Press, 2007), 3–22, see 5–6.

23. Cobb, *Grace and Responsibility*, 119; Wesley, "On The Original, Nature, Property, and Use of the Law," 10.

24. Cobb, *Grace and Responsibility*, 119.

25. Carter Lindberg, *The European Reformations* (Oxford: Blackwell, 1996), 63.

26. Ibid.

27. Ibid., 67.

28. Ibid.

29. Ibid., 74–75.

30. Ibid., 75.

31. Ibid.

32. Ibid., 75–76.

33. Ibid., 76.

34. Ibid., 67.

35. Ibid., 70.

36. Ibid., 249.

37. Ozment, *Age of Reform*, 375.

38. Ibid., 376; Martin Luther, "Sermon on the Sum of Christian Life: 1 Tim 1:5–7," in *Sermons I*, ed. and trans. John W. Doberstein, vol. 51 of *Luther's Works* (Philadelphia: Muhlenberg Press, 1959), 284.

39. Calvin, *Institutes*, 1:785; quoted in Ozment, *Age of Reform*, 378.

40. Ozment, *Age of Reform*, 378–379.

41. Ibid., 379.

42. Lindberg, *Reformations*, 266.

43. Ibid., 266–267.

44. Ibid., 267. Calvin's concept of predestination appears in book 3, chapter 21, of the *Institutes*, but later Calvinists emphasized it as a primary theological principle.

45. J. Wesley Bready, *England: Before and after Wesley: The Evangelical Revival and Social Reform* (London: Hodder and Stoughton, 1938), 127.

46. John Wesley, "Thoughts on the Present Scarcity of Provisions," in *The Works of the Rev. John Wesley A.M.*, ed. Thomas Jackson, vol. 11 (London: J. Mason, 1830), 53–59; quoted in Pamela D. Couture, *Blessed Are the Poor: Women's Poverty, Family Policy, and Practical Theology* (Nashville, TN: Abingdon Press, 1991), 126.

47. Cobb, *Grace and Responsibility*, 90.

48. Stone, *John Wesley's Life and Ethics*, 155–156.

49. Cobb, *Grace and Responsibility*, 90–91.

50. John Wesley, *The Journal of the Rev. John Wesley, A.M.*, ed. Nehemiah Curnock, 8 vols. (London: Epworth Press, 1909–1916), 1:476 (May 24, 1738); quoted in Cobb, *Grace and Responsibility*, 91.

51. Manfred Marquardt, *John Wesley's Social Ethics: Praxis and Principles*, trans. John E. Steely and W. Stephen Gunther (Nashville, TN: Abingdon Press, 1992), 120–121.

52. Ernst Troeltsch, *The Social Teaching of the Christian Churches*, trans. Olive Wyon, 2 vols. (New York: Macmillan, 1931), 2:724; quoted in Marquardt, *Wesley's Social Ethics*, 121.

53. Martin Luther, *Word and Sacrament 1*, ed. E. Theodore Bachmann, vol. 35 of *Luther's Works* (Philadelphia: Muhlenberg Press, 1960), 236; quoted in David C. Steinmetz, "Luther, the Reformers, and the Bible," in *Living Traditions of the Bible: Scripture in Jewish, Christian, and Muslim Practice*, ed. James E. Bowley (St. Louis: Chalice Press, 1999), 163–176, 174. See also Steinmetz, *Luther in Context*, 2nd ed. (Grand Rapids, MI: Baker Academic, 2002).

54. Heinrich Bornkamm, *Luther and the Old Testament*, trans. Eric W. and Ruth C. Gritsch (Mifflintown, PA: Sigler Press, 1997), 250.

55. Ibid., 257.

56. Found in Robert M. Grant, *A Short History of the Interpretation of the Bible* (New York, Macmillan, 1963), 95; quoted in Ozment, *Age of Reform*, 66.

57. Ozment, *Age of Reform*, 66.

58. Ibid.

59. William S. Campbell, "Martin Luther and Paul's Epistle to the Romans," in *The Bible as Book: The Reformation*, ed. Orlaith O'Sullivan (New Castle, DE: Oak Knoll Press, 2000), 108.

60. Steinmetz, "Luther, the Reformers, and the Bible," 172; Campbell, "Martin Luther and Paul's Epistle to the Romans," 106.

61. Bornkamm, *Luther and the Old Testament*, 88.

62. Ibid., 98–100.

63. Steinmetz, "Luther, the Reformers, and the Bible," 175.

64. Ibid., 175–176.

65. Willem Jan Kooiman, *Luther and the Bible*, trans. John Schmidt (Philadelphia: Muhlenberg Press, 1961), 225–226.

66. Ibid., 237.

67. Luther, *Word and Sacrament 1*, 396.

68. Steinmetz, "Luther, the Reformers, and the Bible," 168.

69. Ibid., 168–169.

70. Ibid. (italics in the original).

71. Ibid.

72. Ibid., 169.

73. Kooiman, *Luther and the Bible*, 236–237.

74. Ibid., 237.

75. Ibid.

76. Ibid.; B. A. Gerrish, *The Old Protestantism and the New: Essays on the Reformation Heritage* (Chicago: University of Chicago Press, 1982), 66.

77. Campbell, "Martin Luther and Paul's Epistle to the Romans," 106.

78. Gerrish, *Old Protestantism and the New,* 61.

79. John Calvin, "Preface to Olivétan's New Testament," in *Calvin's Commentaries,* ed. Joseph Haroutunian, Library of Christian Classics, vol. 23 (Philadelphia: Westminster Press, 1958), 70; quoted in Gerrish, *Old Protestantism and the New,* 61.

80. Gerrish, *Old Protestantism and the New,* 61.

81. David W. Jones, *Reforming the Morality of Usury: A Study of the Differences That Separated the Protestant Reformers* (Lanham, MD: University Press of America, 2004), 3 (italics in the original).

82. Ibid., ix.

83. Ibid., 84–85.

84. John Calvin, *Commentaries on the Four Last Books of Moses: Arranged in the Form of a Harmony,* vols. 2–3 of *Calvin's Commentaries,* trans. Charles William Bingham (Grand Rapids, MI: Baker Books, 2003), 3:127–128, 132; *Commentary on the Book of Psalms,* vols. 4–6 of *Calvin's Commentaries,* trans. Henry Beveridge (Grand Rapids, MI: Baker Books, 2003), 1:213–214; Jones, *Reforming the Morality of Usury,* 85–86.

85. David C. Steinmetz, "John Calvin as an Interpreter of the Bible," in *Calvin and the Bible,* ed. Donald K. McKim (Cambridge: Cambridge University Press, 2006), 291. See also Steinmetz, *Calvin in Context* (Oxford: Oxford University Press, 1995).

86. Steinmetz, "John Calvin as an Interpreter of the Bible," 291.

87. Calvin, *Institutes,* 1:4.

88. Steinmetz, "John Calvin as an Interpreter of the Bible," 291.

89. Ibid.

90. Calvin, *Institutes,* 1:70.

91. Wesley, "On God's Vineyard," *Sermons III: 71–114,* vol. 3 of *The Works of John Wesley,* ed. Albert C. Outler (Nashville, TN: Abingdon Press, 1986), 502–517, par. 1.1; Scott J. Jones, *John Wesley's Conception and Use of Scripture* (Nashville, TN: Kingswood Books, 1995), 31.

92. Jones, *John Wesley's Conception and Use of Scripture,* 31.

93. Ibid., 38–39.

94. Ibid., 39.

95. Jones, "The Rule of Scripture," in *Wesley and the Quadrilateral: Renewing the Conversation,* ed. W. Stephen Gunter et al. (Nashville, TN: Abingdon Press, 1997), 56.

96. Ibid., 50.

97. Ibid., 51.

98. Ibid.; John Wesley, "On Riches," in *Sermons III: 71–114,* vol. 3 of *The Works of John Wesley* (Nashville, TN: Abingdon Press, 1986), 527.

99. John Wesley, "Upon Our Lord's Sermon on the Mount, V," *Sermons 1:1–33,* vol. 1 of *The Works of John Wesley,* ed. Albert C. Outler (Nashville, TN: Abingdon Press, 1984), 567–568.

100. Ibid., 567–571.

101. Ibid., 568.

102. Ibid.

103. Wesley, "On The Original, Nature, Property, and Use of the Law," 17–18.

104. Ibid., 9–10.

105. Ibid, 10.

106. D. Stephen Long, *Living the Discipline: United Methodist Theological Reflection on War, Civilization, and Holiness* (Grand Rapids, MI: Eerdmans, 1992), 93.

107. Wesley, "Sermon on the Mount, V," 554.

108. Jones, "Rule of Scripture," 57.

109. Ibid. (italics in the original).

110. Ibid.

111. Ibid., 53–54.

112. Ibid., 55.

113. Lorde, "Age, Race, Class, and Sex," 116.

114. Carden, "It's Lonely at the Top," 185–200.

115. Joy A. Schroeder, *Dinah's Lament: The Biblical Legacy of Sexual Violence in Christian Interpretation* (Minneapolis, MN: Fortress Press, 2007), 11–55. See also Michael Parsons, *Luther and Calvin on Old Testament Narratives: Reformation Thought and Narrative Text* (Lewiston, ME: Edwin Mellen Press, 2004); John L. Thompson, *Writing the Wrongs: Women of the Old Testament among Biblical Commentators from Philo through the Reformation* (New York: Oxford University Press, 2001); Thompson, *Reading the Bible with the Dead: What You Can Learn from the History of Exegesis That You Can't Learn from Exegesis Alone* (Grand Rapids, MI: Eerdmans, 2007).

116. Paul W. Chilcote, *She Offered Them Christ: The Legacy of Women Preachers in Early Methodism* (Nashville, TN: Abingdon Press, 1993), 110–122.

117. Bonnie Pattison, *Poverty in the Theology of John Calvin* (Eugene, OR: Pickwick Publications, 2006), 81–82.

118. Ibid., 82–83.

119. Carter Lindberg, "Luther's Struggle with Social-Ethical Issues," in *The Cambridge Companion to Martin Luther*, ed. Donald K. McKim (Cambridge: Cambridge University Press, 2003), 171.

120. Pattison, *Poverty in the Theology of John Calvin*, 134–137.

121. Richard Heitzenrater, ed., *The Poor and the People Called Methodist* (Nashville, TN: Kingswood Press, 2002).

122. Theodore W. Jennings Jr., *Good News to the Poor: John Wesley's Evangelical Economics* (Nashville TN: Abingdon Press, 1990).

123. Ozment, *Age of Reform*, 272–289.

124. Marquardt, *Wesley's Social Ethics*, 133–134.

125. Ozment, *Age of Reform*, 369–371.

126. Stone, *John Wesley's Life and Ethics*, 187.

127. Dawn DeVries, "'Ever to Be Reformed According to the Word of God': Can the Scripture Principle Be Redeemed for Feminist Theology?" in *Feminist and Womanist Essays in Reformed Dogmatics*, ed. Amy Plantinga Pauw and Serene Jones (Louisville, KY: Westminster John Knox Press, 2006), 40–57.

128. Ibid.

129. Ibid., 44.

130. Ibid., 47.

131. Ibid.

132. Ibid., 53.

133. Ibid., 52.

134. Ibid., 52–53.

135. Ibid., 54.

136. Ibid., 54–55.

137. Ibid., 55.

138. Cynthia D. Moe-Lobeda, *Healing a Broken World: Globalization and God* (Minneapolis, MN: Fortress Press, 2002).

139. Ibid., 74–75.

140. Ibid., 83.

141. Ibid.

142. Ibid., 109.

143. Ibid.

144. Cobb, *Grace and Responsibility*, 126.

145. Ibid., 128.

146. Steve de Gruchy, "Human Being in Christ: Resources for an Inclusive Anthropology," in *Aliens in the Household of God: Homosexuality and Christian Faith in South Africa*, ed. Paul Germond and Steve de Gruchy (Cape Town: David Philip, 1997), 235.

147. De Gruchy, "Human Being in Christ," 235.

CHAPTER 6

1. Lorde, "Age, Race, Class, and Sex," 116.

2. *Dred Scott v. Sandford*, 60 U.S. 393 (1857).

3. Smith, "Heteropatriarchy," 72.

4. Ibid.; Ann Burlein, *Lift High the Cross: Where White Supremacy and the Christian Right Converge* (Durham, NC: Duke University Press, 2002).

5. Smith, "Heteropatriarchy," 72.

6. Wilfred Cantwell Smith, *What Is Scripture?* (Minneapolis, MN: Fortress Press, 1993), ix.

7. Ibid., 18.

8. Brian Malley, *How the Bible Works: An Anthropological Study of Evangelical Biblicism* (Walnut Creek, CA: AltaMira Press, 2004), 136 (italics in the original).

9. Ibid., 140.

10. Cosgrove, *Appealing to Scripture*, 2.

11. Wilfred Cantrell Smith, *What Is Scripture?* 231.

12. Peter Paris, "The Bible and the Black Churches," in *The Bible and Social Reform*, ed. Ernest Sandeen (Philadelphia: Fortress Press, 1982), 135.

13. Howard Thurman, *Jesus and the Disinherited* (Nashville, TN: Abingdon Press, 1949), 30–31; quoted in Brian K. Blount, "The Last Word on Biblical Authority," in *Struggling with Scripture*, ed. Walter Brueggemann, William C. Placher, and Brian K. Blount (Louisville, KY: Westminster John Knox Press, 2002), 58.

14. Ibid., 59 (italics in the original).

15. William Sloane Coffin, "Introduction," in *Struggling with Scripture*, ed. Walter Brueggemann, William C. Placher, and Brian Blount (Louisville, KY: Westminster John Knox Press, 2002), 3.

16. Russell, "Authority," 143 (italics in the original).

17. Ibid. (italics in the original).

18. Ibid.

19. Ibid., 144.

20. Ibid.

21. William C. Placher, "Struggling with Scripture," in *Struggling with Scripture*, ed. Walter Brueggemann, William C. Placher, and Brian Blount (Louisville, KY: Westminster John Knox Press, 2002), 42.

22. Stanley Hauerwas, *Unleashing the Scripture: Freeing the Bible from Captivity in America* (Nashville, TN: Abingdon Press, 1993), 17.

23. Ibid., 18.

24. Ibid., 16.

25. Ibid., 38.

26. Gloria Albrecht, *The Character of Our Communities: Toward an Ethic of Liberation for the Church* (Nashville, TN: Abingdon Press, 1995), 97; Sharon Welch, *A Feminist Ethic of Risk* (Minneapolis, MN: Fortress Press, 1990), 150.

27. N. T. Wright, *The Last Word: Scripture and the Authority of God—Getting beyond the Bible Wars* (New York: HarperCollins, 2005), 137 (italics in the original).

28. Ibid.

29. Ibid., 140.

30. See, for example, Matt Curry, "Episcopalians Contemplate Divided Future—Conservative Bishops Reject Authority of Incoming Leader, in Part for Gay Stance," *Washington Post*, August 26, 2006, B7. In the international setting, Anglicans who objected to the inclusive developments of the Episcopal Church gathered in June 2008 at the Global Anglican Future Conference (GAFCON).

31. Albrecht, *Character of Our Communities*, 137.

32. Ibid., 169.

33. Ibid., 28.

34. Anderson, *Women, Ideology, and Violence*, 66–76.

35. Ibid., 105–110.

36. Lorde, "Age, Race, Class, and Sex," 116.

37. Albrecht, *Character of Our Communities*, 96–97.

38. Ibid.

39. Elisabeth Schüssler Fiorenza, "The Ethics of Biblical Interpretation: Decentering Biblical Scholarship," *Journal of Biblical Literature* 107 (1988): 3–17. A more detailed construction of her ethical project is in her book *Rhetoric and Ethic: The Politics of Biblical Studies* (Minneapolis, MN: Fortress Press, 1999).

40. Schüssler Fiorenza, "Ethics of Biblical Interpretation," 14.

41. Ibid., 15.

42. Daniel Patte, *Ethics of Biblical Interpretation: A Reevaluation* (Louisville, KY: Westminster John Knox Press, 1995), ix.

43. Ibid., 1–2.

44. David Jasper, *A Short Introduction to Hermeneutics* (Louisville, KY: Westminster John Knox Press, 2004), 20–24.

45. Walter Brueggemann, "Biblical Authority," in *Struggling with Scripture*, eds. Walter Brueggemann, William C. Placher, and Brian Blount (Louisville, KY: Westminster John Knox Press, 2002), 24. Reprinted in Brueggemann, *The Book That Breathes New Life: Scriptural Authority and Biblical Theology* (Minneapolis, MN: Fortress Press, 2005), 20–36.

46. Brueggemann, "Biblical Authority," 11–12.

47. Russell, "Authority," 144 (italics in the original).

48. Charles H. Cosgrove, "Introduction," in *The Meanings We Choose: Hermeneutical Ethics, Indeterminacy and the Conflict of Interpretations*, ed. Charles H. Cosgrove (London: T&T Clark, 2004), 3.

49. Ibid., 7.

50. Ibid., 7–8.

51. Martin, *Sex and the Single Savior*, 143–146; Craig S. Keener, *And Marries Another: Divorce and Remarriage in the Teaching of the New Testament* (Peabody, MA: Hendrickson, 1991); David Instone-Brewer, *Divorce and Remarriage in the Bible: The Social and Literary Context* (Grand Rapids, MI: Eerdmans, 2002).

52. Martin, *Sex and the Single Savior*, 132.

53. Keener, *And Marries Another*, xi–xii; Martin, *Sex and the Single Savior*, 144.

54. Martin, *Sex and the Single Savior*, 144 (italics in the original).

55. Ibid., 146.

56. Ibid.

57. Ibid., 51–64.

58. Ibid., 55.

59. Ibid.

60. Ibid., 55–56.

61. Ibid., 59–60.

62. Jack Rogers, *Jesus, the Bible, and Homosexuality: Explode the Myths, Heal the Church* (Louisville, KY: Westminster John Knox Press, 2006), 17–34.

63. Ibid., 18.

64. Ibid.

65. Ibid., 25.

66. Ibid., 34.

67. Ibid., 17.

68. Ibid., 18.

69. Ibid.

70. Smith, "Heteropatriarchy," 72.

71. Burridge, *Imitating Jesus*, 55.

CHAPTER 7

1. The Charters of Freedom exhibit at the National Archives, http://www.archives.gov/national-archives-experience/charters (accessed January 2008).

2. Barbara Jordan, "Opening Statement to the House Judiciary Committee Proceedings on Impeachment of Richard Nixon," 93rd Cong., 2nd sess., 111, Washington, DC, July 25, 1974; quoted in Barbara Holmes, *A Private Woman in Public Spaces: Barbara Jordan's Speeches on Ethics, Public, Religion, and Law* (Harrisburg, PA: Trinity Press International, 2000), 48. See also Max Sherman, *Barbara Jordan: Speaking the Truth with Eloquent Thunder* (Austin: University of Texas Press, 2007), 27.

3. Jordan was also a closeted lesbian who, when she died, had been with her "longtime companion" for more than twenty years. The issue of including those who are different from the *mythical norm* because of gender identity or sexual orientation remains before us. J. Jennings Moss, "Barbara Jordan: The Other Life," *Advocate*, March 5, 1996, 38–45; quoted in Griffin, *Their Own Receive Them Not*, 131–134.

4. Barbara Jordan, "Women and the Constitution: The Challenge," remarks, February 11, 1988, Atlanta, Georgia; quoted in Barbara Holmes, *Private Woman*, 48.

5. *Dred Scott v. Sandford*, 60 U.S. 393 (1857).

6. Holmes, *Private Woman*, 48.

7. *Dred Scott v. Sandford*, 60 U.S. 393, 405, 407–408; quoted in Holmes, *Private Woman*, 48.

8. Barbara Jordan, "Testimony House Judiciary Committee," July 25, 1974, Washington, DC; quoted in Holmes, *A Private Woman*, 95. See also Sherman, *Barbara Jordan*, 27.

9. Holmes, *Private Woman*, 94.

10. Philip C. Bobbitt, "Barbara Jordan: Constitutional Conscience," *Texas Journal of Women and the Law* 5 (1996): 171–73; quoted in Holmes, *Private Woman*, 94.

11. See, for example, Dale B. Martin, *The Corinthian Body* (New Haven, CT: Yale University Press, 1995), 229–249.

12. Susan Martin, as reported in Mary Beth Rogers, *Barbara Jordan: American Hero* (New York: Bantam Books, 1998), 343–344.

13. Barbara Jordan, "It's More Than a Lifeless Archive," remarks on Constitutional Day naturalization ceremony, September 17, 1987, RJT Archives, Houston, Texas; quoted in Holmes, *Private Woman*, 94.

14. Margaret Talbot, "Supreme Confidence: The Jurisprudence of Antonin Scalia," *New Yorker*, March 28, 2005, 40–55. See also Vincent Crapanzano, *Serving the Word: Literalism in America from the Pulpit to the Bench* (New York: New Press, 2000), 279–303; Jaroslav Pelikan, *Interpreting the Bible and the Constitution* (New Haven, CT: Yale University Press, 2004), 76–114.

15. Talbot, "Supreme Confidence," 42.

16. Obviously, a literal reading of the phrase would mean that African American males, as men, might have been included, and women as well, if the term "men" is synonymous with "human beings." It is probably more accurate to say that the framers had a "public meaning" in mind that automatically excluded women and people of African descent, even though their literal language seems inclusive. See Charles H. Cosgrove, "The Declaration of Independence in Constitutional Interpretation: A Selective History and Analysis," *University of Richmond Law Review* 32, no. 1 (1998): 127–128.

17. Edmund S. Morgan, "Slavery and Freedom: The American Paradox," in *Colonial Southern Slavery*, ed. Paul Finkelman (New York: Garland, 1989), 261.

18. Morgan, "Slavery and Freedom," 262.

19. Vanessa B. Beasley, *You, the People: American National Identity in Presidential Rhetoric* (College Station: Texas A&M University Press, 2004), 95. See also Cornel West, *Race Matters*, with a new preface (Boston: Beacon Press, 2001).

20. Beasley, *You, the People*, 96.

21. Ibid., 98, 100.

22. Ibid., 105.

23. Ibid., 106.

24. William McKinley, in *The State of the Union Messages of the Presidents, 1790–1966*, ed. Fred L. Israel, (New York: Chelsea House, 1966), 2:1969; quoted in Beasley, *You, the People*, 106.

25. Beasley, *You, the People*, 106.

26. Ibid., 107 (italics in the original).

27. Ibid., 97, 105.

28. Ibid., 111.

29. Calvin Coolidge, in Israel, ed., State of the Union Messages, 3:2689; quoted in Beasley, *You, the People*, 112.

30. Beasley, *You, the People*, 112.

31. Ibid.

32. Ibid., 120.

33. Ibid., 124.

34. Ibid.

35. Ibid., 126.

36. Ibid., 142.

37. Ibid.

38. George Lipsitz, "Civil Rights Rhetoric and White Identity Politics," in *Cultural Pluralism, Identity Politics, and the Law*, ed. Austin Sarat and Thomas R. Kearns (Ann Arbor: University of Michigan Press, 1999), 111–138.

39. Patricia Roberts Harris quoted in Douglas S. Massey and Nancy A. Denton, *American Apartheid: Segregation and the Making of the Underclass* (Cambridge, MA: Harvard University Press, 1993), 196; quoted in Lipsitz, "Civil Rights Rhetoric," 116.

40. Lipsitz, "Civil Rights Rhetoric," 116.

41. Ibid., 120.

42. Ibid., 127.

43. Ibid., 120–121.

44. Gloria J. Browne-Marshall, *Race, Law, and American Society: 1607 to Present* (New York: Routledge, 2007), 36–38.

45. Michael Seidman, "Brown and Miranda," *California Law Review* 80 (1992): 717; quoted in Derrick A. Bell Jr., "*Brown* Reconceived: An Alternative Scenario," in *Brown at 50: The Unfinished Legacy*, ed. Deborah L. Rhode and Charles J. Ogletree Jr. (Chicago: American Bar Association, 2004), 59–69.

46. David Southern, *Gunnar Myrdal and Black-White Relations: The Use and Abuse of an American Dilemma, 1944–1969* (Baton Rouge: Louisiana State University Press, 1987), 33–34; quoted in Beasley, *You, the People*, 26.

47. Beasley, *You, the People*, 26.

48. Lorde, "Age, Race, Class, and Sex," 116.

49. Vanessa B. Beasley, "Introduction," in *Who Belongs in America? Presidents, Rhetoric, and Immigration*, ed. Vanessa B. Beasley (College Station: Texas A&M University Press, 2006), 10. See Roger Daniels, "Two Cheers for Immigration," in *Debating American Immigration, 1882–Present*, ed. Roger Daniels and Otis L. Graham (Lanham: Rowman and Littlefield, 2001); James P. Smith and Barry Edmonston, eds., *The New Americans: Economic, Demographic, and Fiscal Effects of Immigration* (Washington, DC: National Academy Press, 1997).

50. Daniels, "Two Cheers for Immigration," 65, 66; quoted in Beasley, *Who Belongs in America?* 11.

51. Beasley, *Who Belongs in America?* 12–13.

52. Gary Oldfield, "School Desegregation after Two Generations: Race, Schools, and Opportunity in Urban Society," in *Race in America: The Struggle for Equality*, ed. Herbert Hill and James E. Jones Jr. (Madison: University of Wisconsin Press, 2003), 240, 245; quoted in Lipsitz, "Civil Rights Rhetoric," 123.

53. John Larew, "Why Are Droves of Unqualified, Unprepared Kids Getting into Our Top Colleges?" *Washington Monthly*, June 1991; quoted in Lipsitz, "Civil Rights Rhetoric," 124–125.

54. Kenji Yoshino, *Covering: The Hidden Assault on Our Civil Rights* (New York: Random House, 2006), ix.

55. Ibid., ix–x.

56. Ibid., x.

57. Ibid., xi.

58. Ibid.

59. Ibid., xii.

60. Ibid., x.

61. Stokely Carmichael and Charles V. Hamilton, "Black Power: Its Need and Substance," in *What Country Have I? Political Writings by Black Americans*, ed. Herbert J. Storing (New York: St. Martin's Press, 1970), 165–181, 179. See also Carmichael and Hamilton, *Black Power* (New York: Random House, 1967).

62. Carmichael and Hamilton, "Black Power," 179.

63. Ibid., 180.

64. Ibid.

65. James H. Cone, *Martin and Malcolm and America: A Dream or a Nightmare* (New York: Orbis Books, 1991), 16.

66. Maxine Molyneux, "Mobilization with Emancipation? Women's Interests, the State, and Revolution in Nicaragua," *Feminist Studies* 11, no. 2 (Summer 1985): 227–254. See also Shireen Hassim, *Women's Organizations and Democracy in South Africa: Contesting Authority* (Madison: University of Wisconsin Press, 2006), 4–8.

67. Molyneux, "Mobilization with Emancipation?," 232.

68. Ibid., 232–233.

69. Ibid., 233.

70. Pharr, *Homophobia*, 24–25.

71. Cone, *Martin and Malcolm and America*, 16.

72. Lani Guinier, *Lift Every Voice: Turning a Civil Rights Setback into a New Vision of Social Justice* (New York: Simon and Schuster, 1998), 252.

73. Curtis Gans, director of the Committee for the Study of the American Electorate in Washington, DC; quoted in Guinier, *Lift Every Voice*, 253.

74. Lani Guinier and Gerald Torres, *The Miner's Canary: Enlisting Race, Resisting Power, and Transforming Democracy* (Cambridge, MA: Harvard University Press, 2002), 258–283.

75. Ibid., 11.

76. Cornel West, *Democracy Matters: Winning the Fight against Imperialism* (New York: Penguin Press, 2004), 153–157.

77. West, *Democracy Matters*, 163. See also Jeffrey Stout, *Democracy and Tradition* (Princeton, NJ: Princeton University Press, 2003).

78. West, *Democracy Matters*, 152.

79. Ibid.

80. Ibid., 162–163.

81. Ibid., 162.

82. Ibid., 164.

83. Ibid., 172.

84. Charles Marsh, *The Beloved Community: How Faith Shapes Social Justice from the Civil Rights Movement to Today* (New York: Basic Books, 2005), 211.

85. Ibid., 208.

86. Ibid., 210.

87. Ibid., 208.

88. Ibid., 210.

Selected Bibliography

Adams, Elizabeth. *Going to Heaven: The Life and Election of Bishop Gene Robinson*. Brooklyn, NY: Soft Skull Press, 2006.

Afolayan, Funso. *Culture and Customs of South Africa*. Westport, CT: Greenwood Press, 2004.

Albrecht, Gloria. *The Character of Our Communities: Toward an Ethic of Liberation for the Church*. Nashville, TN: Abingdon Press, 1995.

Allert, Craig D. *A High View of Scripture? The Authority of the Bible and the Formation of the New Testament Canon*. Grand Rapids, MI: Baker Academic, 2007.

Alpert, Rebecca. "Finding Our Past: A Lesbian Reading of the Book of Ruth." In *Reading Ruth: Contemporary Women Reclaim a Sacred Story*, ed. Judith A. Kates and Gail Twersky Reimer, 91–96. New York: Ballantine Books, 1994.

Althaus, Paul. *The Ethics of Martin Luther*. Philadelphia: Fortress Press, 1972.

Anderson, Cheryl B. "The Eighth Commandment: A Way to King's Beloved Community?" In *The Ten Commandments: The Reciprocity of Faithfulness*, ed. William P. Brown, 276–289. Louisville, KY: Westminster John Knox Press, 2004.

———. *Women, Ideology, and Violence: Critical Theory and the Construction of Gender in the Book of the Covenant and the Deuteronomic Law*. London: T&T Clark, 2004.

———. "Biblical Laws: Challenging the Principles of Old Testament Ethics." In *Character Ethics and the Old Testament: Moral Dimensions of Scripture*, ed. M. Daniel Carroll R and Jacqueline E. Lapsley, 37–49. Louisville, KY: Westminster John Knox Press, 2007.

Bailey, Randall C. "They're Nothing but Incestuous Bastards: The Polemical Use of Sex and Sexuality in Hebrew Canon Narratives." In *Reading from*

This Place: Social Location and Biblical Interpretation in the United States, vol. 1, ed. Fernando F. Segovia and Mary Ann Tolbert, 121–138. Minneapolis, MN: Fortress Press, 1995.

Bailey, Randall C. "The Danger of Ignoring One's Own Cultural Bias in Interpreting the Text." In *The Postcolonial Bible*, ed. R.S. Sugirtharajah, 66–90. Sheffield: Sheffield Academic Press, 1998.

———. "He Didn't Even Tell Us the Worst of It!" *Union Seminary Quarterly Review* 59 (2005): 15–24.

———. "That's Why They Didn't Call the Book Hadassah! Intersec(ct)/(x)ionality of Race/Ethnicity, Gender, and Sexuality in the Book of Esther." In *They Were All Together in One Place? Toward Minority Biblical Criticism*. Semeia Studies 57, ed. Randall Bailey, Tat-siong Benny Liew, and Fernando F. Segovia, 227–250. Atlanta: Society of Biblical Literature, 2009.

Bailey, Wilma Ann. *"You Shall Not Kill" or "You Shall Not Murder"?: Assault on a Biblical Text*. Collegeville, MN: Liturgical Press, 2005.

Bal, Mieke. "Lots of Writing." In *Ruth and Esther: A Feminist Companion to the Bible*, 2nd ser., ed. Athalya Brenner, 212–238. Sheffield: Sheffield Academic Press, 1999.

Barton, John. *Holy Writings, Sacred Text: The Canon in Early Christianity*. Louisville, KY: Westminster John Knox Press, 1997.

———. *Ethics and the Old Testament*. Harrisburg, PA: Trinity Press International, 1998.

———. *Understanding Old Testament Ethics: Approaches and Explorations*. Louisville, KY: Westminster John Knox Press, 2003.

Barton, Stephen C. "Marriage and Family Life as Christian Concerns." In *New Occasions Teach New Duties: Christian Ethics for Today*, ed. Cyril S. Rodd, 168–170. Edinburgh: T&T Clark, 1995.

Bassler, Jouette M. "First Corinthians." In *Women's Bible Commentary*, expanded edition, ed. Carol A. Newsom and Sharon H. Ringe, 411–419. Louisville, KY: Westminster John Knox Press, 1998.

———. *Navigating Paul: An Introduction to Key Theological Concepts*. Louisville, KY: Westminster John Knox Press, 2007.

Beal, Timothy K. *The Book of Hiding: Gender, Ethnicity, Annihilation, and Esther*. London: Routledge, 1997.

Beasley, Vanessa B. *You, the People: American National Identity in Presidential Rhetoric*. College Station: Texas A&M University Press, 2004.

———. "Introduction." In *Who Belongs in America? Presidents, Rhetoric, and Immigration*, ed. Vanessa B. Beasley, 3–18. College Station: Texas A&M University Press, 2006.

Bell, Derrick A., Jr. "*Brown* Reconceived: An Alternative Scenario." In *Brown at 50: The Unfinished Legacy*, ed. Deborah L. Rhode and Charles J. Ogletree Jr., 59–69. Chicago: American Bar Association, 2004.

Bellis, Alice Ogden. *Helpmates, Harlots, and Heroes: Women's Stories in the Hebrew Bible*. 2nd ed. Louisville, KY: Westminster John Knox Press, 2007.

Bendroth, Margaret. *Fundamentalism and Gender, 1875 to the Present*. New Haven, CT: Yale University Press, 1993.

Bennett, Harold V. *Injustice Made Legal: Deuteronomic Law and the Plight of Widows, Strangers, and Orphans in Ancient Israel.* Grand Rapids, MI: Eerdmans, 2002.

Berquist, Jon L. *Reclaiming Her Story: The Witness of Women in the Old Testament.* St. Louis, MO: Chalice Press, 1992.

Birch, Bruce C. *What Does the Lord Require? The Old Testament Call to Social Witness.* Philadelphia: Westminster Press, 1985.

———. *Let Justice Roll Down: The Old Testament, Ethics, and Christian Life.* Louisville, KY: Westminster John Knox Press, 1991.

Birch, Bruce C., Walter Brueggemann, Terence E. Fretheim, and David L. Petersen. *A Theological Introduction to the Old Testament,* 2nd ed. Nashville, TN: Abingdon Press, 2005.

Birch, Bruce C., and Larry L. Rasmussen. *Bible and Ethics in the Christian Life.* Revised and expanded edition. Minneapolis, MN: Augsburg Fortress, 1989.

Bird, Phyllis A. *The Bible as the Church's Book.* Philadelphia: Westminster Press, 1982.

———. "The Authority of the Bible." In *The New Interpreter's Bible,* vol. 1, 33–64. Nashville: Abingdon Press, 1994.

———. "A North American Feminist Response." In *Other Ways of Reading: African Women and the Bible,* ed. Musa W. Dube, 199–206. Atlanta: Society of Biblical Literature, 2001.

Blount, Brian K. *Then the Whisper Put on Flesh: New Testament Ethics in an African American Context.* Nashville, TN: Abingdon Press, 2001.

———. "The Last Word on Biblical Authority." In *Struggling with Scripture,* ed. Walter Brueggemann, William C. Placher, and Brian K. Blount, 51–69. Louisville, KY: Westminster John Knox Press, 2002.

Blumenfeld, Warren J., ed. *Homophobia: How We All Pay the Price.* Boston: Beacon Press, 1992.

Boring, M. Eugene. "The Gospel of Matthew" In *The New Interpreter's Bible.* Vol. 8. Nashville, TN: Abingdon Press, 1995.

Bornkamm, Heinrich. *Luther and the Old Testament* Trans. Eric W. and Ruth C. Gritsch. Mifflintown, PA: Sigler Press, 1997.

Boyarin, Daniel. *Unheroic Conduct: The Rise of Heterosexuality and the Invention of the Jewish Man.* Berkeley: University of California Press, 1997.

Braxton, Brad. *The Tyranny of Resolution: 1 Corinthians 7:17–24.* Atlanta: Society of Biblical Literature, 2000.

Bready, J. Wesley. *England: Before and after Wesley: The Evangelical Revival and Social Reform.* London: Hodder and Stoughton, 1938.

Brenner, Athalya. "An Afterword: The Decalogue—Am I an Addressee?" In *A Feminist Companion to Exodus to Deuteronomy,* ed. Athalya Brenner, 255–258. Sheffield: Sheffield Academic Press, 1994.

Brenner, Athalya, and Jan Willem van Henten, eds. 2002. *Bible Translation on the Threshold of the Twenty-first Century.* London: Sheffield Academic Press.

Brodkin, Karen. *How Jews Became White Folks and What That Says about Race in America.* New Brunswick, NJ: Rutgers University Press, 1998.

Brooten, Bernadette J. *Love between Women: Early Christian Responses to Female Homoeroticism.* Chicago: University of Chicago Press, 1996.

Browne-Marshall, Gloria J. *Race, Law, and American Society: 1607 to Present.* New York: Routledge, 2007.

Brueggemann, Walter. "Exodus." In *The New Interpreter's Bible Commentary.* Vol. 1. Nashville, TN: Abingdon Press, 1994.

———. *An Introduction to the Old Testament: The Canon and Christian Imagination.* Louisville, KY: Westminster John Knox Press, 2003.

———. *The Book That Breathes New Life: Scriptural Authority and Biblical Theology.* Minneapolis, MN: Fortress Press, 2005.

Burke, Jason. "Pope's Move on Latin Mass 'A Blow to Jews.'" *Guardian* (UK), July 8, 2007.

Burlein, Ann. *Lift High the Cross: Where White Supremacy and the Christian Right Converge.* Durham, NC: Duke University Press, 2002.

Burnside, Jonathan P. 2003. *The Signs of Sin: Seriousness of Offence in Biblical Law.* London: Sheffield Academic Press.

Burridge, Richard A. *Imitating Jesus: An Inclusive Approach to New Testament Ethics.* Grand Rapids, MI: Eerdmans, 2007.

Bynum, Caroline Walker, et al., eds. *Gender and Religion: On the Complexity of Symbols.* Boston: Beacon Press, 1986.

Calvin, John. *Commentaries on the Epistles of Paul to the Galatians and the Ephesians.* Trans. William Pringle. Edinburgh: Calvin Translation Society, 1854.

———. "Preface to Olivétan's New Testament." In *Calvin's Commentaries,* ed. Joseph Haroutunian. Library of Christian Classics, vol. 23. Philadelphia: Westminster Press, 1958.

———. *Institutes of the Christian Religion in Two Volumes.* Ed. John T. McNeill and Ford Lewis Battles. Library of Christian Classics, vols. 20–21. Philadelphia: Westminster Press, 1960.

———. *Commentary on the Book of Psalms.* Trans. Henry Beveridge. Vols. 4–6 of *Calvin's Commentaries.* Grand Rapids, MI: Baker Books, 2003.

———. *Commentaries on the Four Last Books of Moses: Arranged in the Form of a Harmony.* Trans. Charles William Bingham. Vols. 2–3 of *Calvin's Commentaries.* Grand Rapids, MI: Baker Books, 2003.

Campbell, William S. "Martin Luther and Paul's Epistle to the Romans." In *The Bible as Book: The Reformation,* ed. Orlaith O'Sullivan, 103–114. New Castle, DE: Oak Knoll Press, 2000.

Carden, Michael. "It's Lonely at the Top: Patriarchal Models, Homophobic Vilification and the Heterosexual Household in Luther's Commentaries." In *Redirected Travel: Alternative Journeys and Places in Biblical Studies,* ed. Roland Boer and Edgar W. Conrad, 185–200. London: T&T Clark, 2003.

Cardenal, Ernesto. *The Gospel in Solentiname.* 4 vols., Trans. Donald D. Walsh. Maryknoll, NY: Orbis Books, 1976–1982.

Carmichael, Stokely, and Charles V. Hamilton. *Black Power.* New York: Random House, 1967.

———. "Black Power: Its Need and Substance." In *What Country Have I? Political Writings by Black Americans*, ed. Herbert J. Storing, 165–181. New York: St. Martin's Press, 1970.

Carroll, James. *Constantine's Sword: The Church and the Jews*. Boston: Houghton Mifflin, 2001.

Chilcote, Paul W. *She Offered Them Christ: The Legacy of Women in Early Methodism*. Nashville, TN: Abingdon Press, 1993.

Chilton, Bruce. *Rabbi Jesus: An Intimate Biography: The Jewish Life and Teachings That Inspired Christianity*. New York: Doubleday, 2000.

———. *Rabbi Paul: An Intellectual Biography*. New York: Doubleday, 2004.

Chu, Julie L. C. "Returning Home: The Inspiration of the Role Dedifferentiation in the Book of Ruth for Taiwanese Women." *Semeia* 78 (1997): 50–51.

Clines, David J. A. "The Ten Commandments, Reading from Left to Right." In *Interested Parties: The Ideology of Writers and Readers of the Hebrew Bible*, 26–45. Sheffield: Sheffield Academic Press, 1995.

Cobb, John B., Jr. *Grace and Responsibility: A Wesleyan Theology for Today*. Nashville, TN: Abingdon Press, 1995.

Coffin, William Sloane. "Introduction." In *Struggling with Scripture*, ed. Walter Brueggemann, William C. Placher, and Brian Blount, 1–3. Louisville, KY: Westminster John Knox Press, 2002.

Collins, Kenneth J. *A Real Christian: The Life of John Wesley*. Nashville, TN: Abingdon Press, 1999.

Collins, Patricia Hill. *Black Sexual Politics: African Americans, Gender, and the New Racism*. New York: Routledge, 2005.

Comstock, Gary David. *Gay Theology without Apology*. Cleveland: Pilgrim Press, 1993.

Cone, James H. *Martin and Malcolm and America: A Dream or a Nightmare*. New York: Orbis Books, 1991.

Cosgrove, Charles H. "The Declaration of Independence in Constitutional Interpretation: A Selective History and Analysis." *University of Richmond Law Review* 32, no. 1 (1998): 107–164.

———. *Appealing to Scripture in Moral Debate: Five Hermeneutical Rules*. Grand Rapids, MI: Eerdmans, 2002.

———. "Introduction." In *The Meanings We Choose: Hermeneutical Ethics, Indeterminacy and the Conflict of Interpretations*, ed. Charles H. Cosgrove, 1–22. London: T&T Clark, 2004.

Couture, Pamela D. *Blessed Are the Poor: Women's Poverty, Family Policy, and Practical Theology*. Nashville, TN: Abingdon Press, 1991.

Cowles, C. S., et al. *Show Them No Mercy: Four Views on God and Canaanite Genocide*. Grand Rapids, MI: Zondervan, 2003.

Crapanzano, Vincent. *Serving the Word: Literalism in America from the Pulpit to the Bench*. New York: New Press, 2000.

Curry, Matt. "Episcopalians Contemplate Divided Future—Conservative Bishops Reject Authority of Incoming Leader, in Part for Gay Stance." *Washington Post*, August 26, 2006, B7.

Daniels, Roger. "Two Cheers for Immigration." In *Debating American Immigration, 1882–Present,* ed. Roger Daniels and Otis L. Graham, 5–69. Lanham, MD: Rowman and Littlefield, 2001.

Darr, Katheryn Pfisterer. *Far More Precious Than Jewels: Perspectives on Biblical Women.* Louisville, KY: Westminster John Knox Press, 1991.

Day, Linda M. *Esther.* Abingdon Old Testament Commentaries. Nashville, TN: Abingdon Press, 2005.

Dayton, Donald W. *Discovering an Evangelical Heritage.* New York: Harper and Row, 1976.

De Gruchy, Steve. "Human Being in Christ: Resources for an Inclusive Anthropology." In *Aliens in the Household of God: Homosexuality and Christian Faith in South Africa,* ed. Paul Germond and Steve de Gruchy, 233–269. Cape Town: David Philip, 1997.

De La Torre, Miguel A. *Doing Christian Ethics from the Margins.* Maryknoll, NY: Orbis Books, 2004.

DeVries, Dawn. "'Ever to Be Reformed According to the Word of God': Can the Scripture Principle Be Redeemed for Feminist Theology?" In *Feminist and Womanist Essays in Reformed Dogmatics,* ed. Amy Plantinga Pauw and Serene Jones, 40–57. Louisville, KY: Westminster John Knox Press, 2006.

Dewey, Joanna. "1 Timothy." In *Women's Bible Commentary,* expanded edition, ed. Carol A. Newsom and Sharon Ringe, 444–449. Louisville, KY: Westminster John Knox Press, 1998.

Domeris, William Robert. *Touching the Heart of God: The Social Construction of Poverty among Biblical Peasants.* London: T&T Clark, 2007.

Donaldson, Laura E. "The Sign of Orpah: Reading Ruth through Native Eyes." In *Ruth and Esther, A Feminist Companion to the Bible,* 2nd ser., ed. Athalya Brenner, 130–144. Sheffield: Sheffield Academic Press, 1999.

Donaldson, Laura E., and Kwok Pui-lan, eds. *Postcolonialism, Feminism and Religious Discourse.* New York: Routledge, 2002.

Douglas, Kelly Brown. "Heterosexism and the Black American Church Community: A Complicated Reality." In *Heterosexism in Contemporary World Religion: Problem and Prospect,* ed. Marvin M. Ellison and Judith Plaskow, 177–200. Cleveland: Pilgrim Press, 2007.

Dowey, Edward A. "Law in Luther and Calvin." *Theology Today* 41 (1984): 146–153.

Dube, Musa W. "The Unpublished Letters of Orpah to Ruth." In *Ruth and Esther, A Feminist Companion to the Bible,* 2nd ser., ed. Athalya Brenner, 145–150. Sheffield: Sheffield Academic Press, 1999.

———. *Postcolonial Feminist Interpretation of the Bible.* St. Louis, MO: Chalice Press, 2000.

———. "Divining Ruth for International Relations." In *Other Ways of Reading: African Women and the Bible,* ed. Musa W. Dube, 179–195. Atlanta: Society of Biblical Literature, 2001.

Duff, Nancy J. "Should the Ten Commandments Be Posted in the Public Realm? Why the Bible and the Constitution Say, 'No.'" In *The Ten Commandments: The*

Reciprocity of Faithfulness, ed. William P. Brown, 159–170. Louisville, KY: Westminster John Knox Press, 2004.

Duncan, Celena M. "The Book of Ruth: On Boundaries, Love, and Truth." In *Take Back the Word: A Queer Reading of the Bible*, ed. Robert E. Goss and Mona West, 92–102. Cleveland: Pilgrim Press, 2000.

Dunn, James D. G. *The Theology of Paul the Apostle*. Grand Rapids, MI: Eerdmans, 1998.

Duran, Nicole. "Who Wants to Marry a Persian King?: Gender Games and Wars and the Book of Esther." In *Pregnant Passion: Gender, Sex, and Violence in the Bible*, ed. Cheryl A. Kirk-Duggan, 71–84. *Semeia Studies* 44. Atlanta: Society of Biblical Literature, 2003.

Eck, Diana L. *A New Religious America: How a "Christian Country" Has Now Become the Most Religiously Diverse Nation*. San Francisco: HarperSanFrancisco, 2001.

Ehrman, Bart D. *Lost Christianities: The Battles for Scripture and the Faiths We Never Knew*. New York: Oxford University Press, 2003.

———. *Lost Scriptures: Books That Did Not Make It into the New Testament*. New York: Oxford University Press, 2003.

———. *The New Testament: A Historical Introduction to the Early Christian Writings*. 3rd ed. New York: Oxford University Press, 2004.

Elliott, Neil. *Liberating Paul: The Justice of God and the Politics of the Apostle*. Sheffield: Sheffield Academic Press, 1995.

Fetterley, Judith. *The Resisting Reader: A Feminist Approach to American Fiction*. Bloomington: Indiana University Press, 1978.

Fewell, Danna Nolan, and David Miller Gunn. *Compromising Redemption: Relating Characters in the Book of Ruth*. Louisville, KY: Westminster John Knox Press, 1990.

———. *Gender, Power, and Promise: The Subject of the Bible's First Story*. Nashville, TN: Abingdon Press, 1993.

Flunder, Yvette A. *Where the Edge Gathers: Building a Community of Radical Inclusion*. Cleveland: Pilgrim Press, 2005.

Foskett, Mary F., and Jeffrey Kah-Jin Kuan, eds. *Ways of Being, Ways of Reading: Asian American Biblical Interpretation*. St. Louis, MO: Chalice Press, 2006.

Freire, Paulo. *Pedagogy of the Oppressed*. Thirtieth anniversary edition. Trans. Myra Bergman Ramos. New York: Continuum, 2003.

Fretheim, Terence E. *God and World in the Old Testament: A Relational Theology of Creation*. Nashville, TN: Abingdon Press, 2005.

Frick, Frank S. *A Journey through the Hebrew Scriptures*. Fort Worth, TX: Harcourt Brace, 1995.

Gafney, Wilda C. *Daughters of Miriam: Women Prophets in Ancient Israel*. Minneapolis, MN: Fortress Press, 2008.

Gaiser, Frederick J. "A New Word on Homosexuality? Isaiah 56:1–8 as Case Study." *Word and World* 14 (Summer 1994): 280–293.

Gench, Frances Taylor. *Back to the Well: Women's Encounters with Jesus in the Gospels*. Louisville, KY: Westminster John Knox Press, 2004.

Gerrish, B. A. *The Old Protestantism and the New: Essays on the Reformation Heritage*. Chicago: University of Chicago Press, 1982.

Goss, Robert E., and Mona West, eds. *Take Back the Word: A Queer Reading of the Bible.* Cleveland: Pilgrim Press, 2000.

Gottwald, Norman K. *Tribes of Yahweh: A Sociology of Religion of Liberated Israel, 1250–1050 B.C.E.* Maryknoll, NY: Orbis Books, 1979.

Grant, Robert M. *A Short History of the Interpretation of the Bible.* New York, Macmillan, 1963.

Grant, Robert M., with David Tracy. *A Short History of the Interpretation of the Bible.* 2nd ed., revised. and enlarged. Philadelphia: Fortress Press, 1984.

Griffin, Horace L. *Their Own Receive Them Not: African American Lesbians and Gays in Black Churches.* Cleveland: Pilgrim Press, 2006.

Gritsch, Eric W. "The Jews in Reformation Theology." In *Jewish-Christian Encounters over the Centuries: Symbiosis, Prejudice, Holocaust, and Dialogue,* ed. Marvin Perry and Frederick M. Schweitzer, 197–213. New York: Peter Lang, 1994.

Guest, Deryn, Robert E. Goss, Mona West, and Thomas Bohache, eds. *The Queer Bible Commentary.* London: SCM Press, 2006.

Guinier, Lani. *Lift Every Voice: Turning a Civil Rights Setback into a New Vision of Social Justice.* New York: Simon and Schuster, 1998.

Guinier, Lani, and Gerald Torres. *The Miner's Canary: Enlisting Race, Resisting Power, and Transforming Democracy.* Cambridge, MA: Harvard University Press, 2002.

Halberstam, Judith. *Female Masculinity.* Durham, NC: Duke University Press, 1998.

Harrelson, Walter J. *The Ten Commandments and Human Rights.* Philadelphia: Fortress Press, 1980.

———. *The Ten Commandments for Today.* Louisville, KY: Westminster John Knox Press, 2006.

Harrington, Daniel J., S.J. "Introduction to the Canon." In *The New Interpreter's Bible.* Vol. 1. Nashville, TN: Abingdon Press, 1994.

Harrison, Beverly Wildung. *Making the Connections: Essays in Feminist Social Ethics.* Ed. Carol S. Robb. Boston: Beacon Press, 1985.

Harvey, Barry. "Anti-postmodernism." In *Handbook of Postmodern Biblical Interpretation,* ed. A. K. M. Adam, 1–7. St. Louis, MO: Chalice Press, 2000.

Hassim, Shireen. *Women's Organizations and Democracy in South Africa: Contesting Authority.* Madison: University of Wisconsin Press, 2006.

Hauerwas, Stanley. *Vision and Virtue: Essays in Christian Ethical Reflection.* Notre Dame, IN: Fides, 1974.

———. *Unleashing the Scripture: Freeing the Bible from Captivity in America.* Nashville, TN: Abingdon Press, 1993.

Hauerwas, Stanley, and William H. Willimon. *Where Resident Aliens Live.* Nashville, TN: Abingdon Press, 1996.

Hauptman, Judith. "Rabbinic Interpretation of Scripture." In *A Feminist Companion to Reading the Bible: Approaches, Strategies and Methods,* ed. Athalya Brenner and Carole Fontaine, 472–486. Sheffield: Sheffield Academic Press, 1997.

Havea, Jione. *Elusions of Control: Biblical Law on the Words of Women.* Leiden: Brill, 2003.

Hays, Richard B. *The Moral Vision of the New Testament: A Contemporary Introduction to New Testament Ethics.* San Francisco: HarperSanFrancisco, 1996.

———. "Galatians." In *The New Interpreter's Bible*. Vol. 11. Nashville, TN: Abingdon Press, 2000.

Heitzenrater, Richard, ed. *The Poor and the People Called Methodist*. Nashville, TN: Kingswood Press, 2002.

Herzog, William R., II. *Parables as Subversive Speech: Jesus as Pedagogue of the Oppressed*. Louisville, KY: Westminster John Knox Press, 1994.

———. *Jesus, Justice, and the Reign of God: A Ministry of Liberation*. Louisville, KY: Westminster John Knox Press, 2000.

———. *Prophet and Teacher: An Introduction to the Historical Jesus*. Louisville, KY: Westminster John Knox Press, 2005.

Hodge, Charles. "The Fugitive Slave Law." In *Cotton Is King and Pro-slavery Arguments Compromising the Writings of Hammond, Harper, Christy, Hodge, Bledsoe, and Cartwright on This Important Subject*, ed. E. N. Elliott, 809–840. Augusta, GA: Pritchard, Abbott and Loomis, 1860.

Holmes, Barbara. *A Private Woman in Public Spaces: Barbara Jordan's Speeches on Ethics, Public, Religion, and Law*. Harrisburg, PA: Trinity Press International, 2000.

Hoppe, Leslie J., O.F.M, *There Shall Be No Poor among You: Poverty in the Bible*. Nashville, TN: Abingdon Press, 2004.

Horrell, David G. *Solidarity and Difference: A Contemporary Reading of Paul's Ethics*. London: T&T Clark International, 2005.

Horsley, Richard A. *Jesus and the Spiral of Violence: Popular Jewish Resistance in Roman Palestine*. San Francisco: Harper and Row, 1987.

———. "First Corinthians: A Case Study of Paul's Assembly as an Alternative Society." In *Paul and Empire: Religion and Power in Roman Imperial Society*, ed. Richard Horsley, 242–252. Harrisburg, PA: Trinity Press International, 1997.

———. "Submerged Biblical Histories and Imperial Biblical Studies." In *The Postcolonial Bible*, ed. R. S. Sugirtharajah, 152–173. Sheffield: Sheffield Academic Press, 1998.

———, ed. *Paul and the Roman Imperial Order*. Harrisburg, PA: Trinity Press International, 2004.

Instone-Brewer, David. *Divorce and Remarriage in the Bible: The Social and Literary Context*. Grand Rapids, MI: Eerdmans, 2002.

Isserlin, B. S. J. *The Israelites*. Minneapolis, MN: Fortress Press, 2001.

Janzen, Waldemar. *Old Testament Ethics: A Paradigmatic Approach*. Louisville, KY: Westminster John Knox Press, 1994.

Jasper, David. *A Short Introduction to Hermeneutics*. Louisville, KY: Westminster John Knox Press, 2004.

Jennings, Theodore W., Jr. *Good News to the Poor: John Wesley's Evangelical Economics*. Nashville, TN: Abingdon Press, 1990.

———. *The Man Jesus Loved: Homoerotic Narratives from the New Testament*. Cleveland: Pilgrim Press, 2003.

———. *Jacob's Wound: Homoerotic Narrative in the Literature of Ancient Israel*. New York: Continuum, 2005.

Johnson, Allan G. *The Gender Knot: Unraveling Our Patriarchal Legacy.* Revised and updated. Philadelphia: Temple University Press, 2005.

Jones, David W. *Reforming the Morality of Usury: A Study of the Differences That Separated the Protestant Reformers.* Lanham, MD: University Press of America, 2004.

Jones, Scott J. *John Wesley's Conception and Use of Scripture.* Nashville, TN: Kingswood Books, 1995.

———. "The Rule of Scripture." In *Wesley and the Quadrilateral: Renewing the Conversation,* ed. W. Stephen Gunter et al., 39–61. Nashville, TN: Abingdon Press, 1997.

Jordan, Barbara. "Opening Statement to the House Judiciary Committee Proceedings on Impeachment of Richard Nixon." 93rd Cong., 2nd sess., 111, July 25, 1974.

Jung, Patricia Beattie, and Ralph F. Smith. *Heterosexism: An Ethical Challenge.* Albany: State University of New York Press, 1993.

Keener, Craig S. *And Marries Another: Divorce and Remarriage in the Teaching of the New Testament.* Peabody, MA: Hendrickson, 1991.

King, David W. *The Bible in History: How the Texts Have Shaped the Times.* New York: Oxford University Press, 2004.

King, Martin Luther Jr. Sermon: "Where Do We Go from Here?" In *A Testament of Hope: The Essential Writings of Martin Luther King, Jr.,* ed. James M. Washington, 245–252. San Francisco: Harper and Row, 1986.

Kooiman, Willem Jan. *Luther and the Bible.* Trans. John Schmidt. Philadelphia: Muhlenberg Press, 1961.

Kwok, Pui-lan. "Finding a Home for Ruth: Gender, Sexuality, and the Politics of Otherness." In *New Paradigms for Bible Study: The Bible in the Third Millennium,* ed. Robert M. Fowler, Edith Blumhofer, and Fernando F. Segovia, 135–154. New York: T&T Clark, 2004.

Langston, Scott M. *Exodus through the Centuries.* Blackwell Bible Commentaries. Malden, MA: Blackwell, 2006.

Lapsley, Jacqueline. *Whispering the Word: Hearing Women's Stories in the Old Testament.* Louisville, KY: Westminster John Knox Press, 2005.

Law, Eric H. F. *Inclusion: Making Room for Grace.* St. Louis, MO: Chalice Press, 2000.

Levine, Amy-Jill. "Ruth." In *Women's Bible Commentary,* expanded edition, ed. Carol A. Newsom and Sharon H. Ringe, 84–90. Louisville, KY: Westminster John Knox Press, 1998.

———. *The Misunderstood Jew: The Church and the Scandal of the Jewish Jesus.* New York: HarperSanFrancisco, 2006.

Lewis, Lloyd A. "An African American Appraisal of the Philemon-Paul-Onesimus Triangle." In *Stony the Road We Trod: African American Biblical Interpretation,* ed. Cain Hope Felder, 232–246. Minneapolis, MN: Fortress Press, 1991.

Linafelt, Tod, ed. *Strange Fire: Reading the Bible after the Holocaust.* Sheffield: Sheffield Academic Press, 2000.

———. *A Shadow of Glory: Reading the New Testament after the Holocaust.* New York: Routledge, 2002.

Lindberg, Carter. *The European Reformations.* Oxford: Blackwell, 1996.

———. "Luther's Struggle with Social-Ethical Issues." In *The Cambridge Companion to Martin Luther*, ed. Donald K. McKim, 165–178. Cambridge: Cambridge University Press, 2003.

Lipsitz, George. "Civil Rights Rhetoric and White Identity Politics." In *Cultural Pluralism, Identity Politics, and the Law*, ed. Austin Sarat and Thomas R. Kearns, 111–138. Ann Arbor: University of Michigan Press, 1999.

Long, D. Stephen. *Living the Discipline: United Methodist Theological Reflection on War, Civilization, and Holiness*. Grand Rapids, MI: Eerdmans, 1992.

Lorde, Audre. "Age, Race, Class, and Sex: Women Redefining Difference." In *Sister Outsider*, 114–123. Freedom, CA: Crossing Press, 1984.

Luther, Martin. "Sermon on the Sum of Christian Life: 1 Tim 1:5–7." In *Sermons I*, ed. and trans. John W. Doberstein. Vol. 51 of *Luther's Works*, 257–288. Philadelphia: Muhlenberg Press, 1959.

———. *Word and Sacrament 1*. Ed. E. Theodore Bachmann. Vol. 35 of *Luther's Works*. Philadelphia: Muhlenberg Press, 1960.

———. *Lectures on Galatians: 1535: Chapters 1–4*. Ed. Jaroslav Pelikan. Vol. 26 of *Luther's Works*. St. Louis, MO: Concordia, 1963.

Malina, Bruce J., and Richard L. Rohrbaugh. *Social-Science Commentary on the Synoptic Gospels*. 2nd ed. Minneapolis, MN: Fortress Press, 2003.

Malley, Brian. *How the Bible Works: An Anthropological Study of Evangelical Biblicism*. Walnut Creek, CA: AltaMira Press, 2004.

Marquardt, Manfred. *John Wesley's Social Ethics: Praxis and Principles*. Trans. John E. Steely and W. Stephen Gunther. Nashville, TN: Abingdon Press, 1992.

Marsh, Charles. *The Beloved Community: How Faith Shapes Social Justice from the Civil Rights Movement to Today*. New York: Basic Books, 2005.

Martin, Clarice J. "The *Haustafeln* (Household Codes) in African American Biblical Interpretation: 'Free Slaves' and 'Subordinate Women.'" In *Stony the Road We Trod: African American Biblical Interpretation*, ed. Cain Hope Felder, 206–231. Minneapolis, MN: Fortress Press, 1991.

Martin, Dale B. *The Corinthian Body*. New Haven, CT: Yale University Press, 1995.

———. "Arsenokoitês and Malakos: Meanings and Consequences." In *Biblical Ethics and Homosexuality: Listening to Scripture*, ed. Robert L. Brawley, 117–136. Louisville, KY: Westminster John Knox Press, 1996.

———. *Sex and the Single Savior: Gender and Sexuality in Biblical Interpretation*. Louisville: Westminster John Knox Press, 2006.

Masenya, Madipoane (ngwana' Mphahlele). "Esther and Northern Sotho Stories: An African-South African Woman's Commentary." In *Other Ways of Reading: African Women and the Bible*, ed. Musa W. Dube, 27–49. Atlanta: Society of Biblical Literature, 2001.

———. "Ruth." In *Global Bible Commentary*, ed. Daniel Patte, 86–91. Nashville, TN: Abingdon Press, 2004.

———. "Struggling with Poverty/Emptiness: Rereading the Naomi-Ruth Story in African-South Africa." *Journal of Theology for Southern Africa* 120 (November 2004): 46–59.

Massey, Douglas S., and Nancy A. Denton. *American Apartheid: Segregation and the Making of the Underclass.* Cambridge, MA: Harvard University Press, 1993.

Matthews, Victor H., Bernard M. Levinson, and Tikva Frymer-Kensky, eds. *Gender and Law in the Hebrew Bible and the Ancient Near East.* London: Sheffield Academic Press, 1998.

McKee, Elsie Ann. "The Character and Significance of John Calvin's Teaching on Social and Economic Issues." In *John Calvin Rediscovered: The Impact of His Social and Economic Thought,* ed. Edward Dommen and James D. Bratt, 3–24. Louisville, KY: Westminster John Knox Press, 2007.

McKim, Donald K. *What Christians Believe about the Bible.* Nashville, TN: Thomas Nelson, 1985.

McKinlay, Judith E. *Reframing Her: Biblical Women in Postcolonial Focus.* Sheffield: Sheffield Phoenix Press, 2004.

Miller, Patrick D. *The Way of the Lord: Essays in Old Testament Theology.* Grand Rapids, MI: Eerdmans, 2004.

———. "Old Testament Exegesis in the Reformed Perspective: The Case of the Commandments." In *Reformed Theology: Identity and Ecumenicity II: Biblical Interpretation in the Reformed Tradition,* ed. Wallace M. Alston Jr. and Michael Welker, 217–229. Grand Rapids, MI: Eerdmans, 2007.

Moe-Lobeda, Cynthia D. *Healing a Broken World: Globalization and God.* Minneapolis, MN: Fortress Press, 2002.

Molyneux, Maxine. "Mobilization with Emancipation? Women's Interests, the State, and Revolution in Nicaragua." *Feminist Studies* 11/2 (Summer 1985): 227–254.

Moore, Carey A. *Esther.* Anchor Bible 7B. Garden City, NY: Doubleday, 1971.

Moore, Laurence. *Religious Outsiders and the Makings of Americans.* New York: Oxford University Press, 1986.

Moore, Stephen D., and Fernando F. Segovia, eds. *Postcolonial Biblical Criticism: Interdisciplinary Intersections.* London: T&T Clark, 2005.

Morgan, Edmund S. "Slavery and Freedom: The American Paradox." In *Colonial Southern Slavery,* ed. Paul Finkelman, 261–285. New York: Garland, 1989.

Mosala, Itumeleng J. "The Implications of the Text of Esther for African Women's Struggle for Liberation in South Africa." *Semeia* 59 (1992): 136.

Moss, J. Jennings. "Barbara Jordan: The Other Life." *Advocate,* March 5, 1996, 38–45.

Mouton, Elna. 2002. *Reading a New Testament Document Ethically.* Academia Biblica, no. 1. Leiden: Brill.

Nadar, Sarojini. "A South African Indian Womanist Reading of the Character of Ruth." In *Other Ways of Reading: African Women and the Bible,* ed. Musa W. Dube, 159–175. Atlanta: Society of Biblical Literature, 2001.

———. "'Texts of Terror': The Conspiracy of Rape in the Bible, Church, and Society: The Case of Esther 2:1–18." In *African Women, Religion, and Health,* ed. Isabel Apawo Phiri and Sarojini Nadar, 77–95. Maryknoll, NY: Orbis Books, 2006.

Nagel, Joane. *Race, Ethnicity, and Sexuality: Intimate Intersections, Forbidden Frontiers.* New York: Oxford University Press, 2003.

Nelson-Pallmeyer, Jack. *Jesus against Christianity: Reclaiming the Missing Jesus.* Harrisburg, PA: Trinity Press International, 2001.

Neusner, Jacob. *From Politics to Piety: The Emergence of Pharisaic Judaism.* 2nd ed. New York: Ktav, 1979.

———. *A Rabbi Talks with Jesus: An Intermillennial, Interfaith Exchange.* New York: Doubleday, 1993.

Newsom, Carol A., and Sharon Ringe, eds. *The Women's Bible Commentary.* Expanded edition. Louisville, KY: Westminster John Knox Press, 1998.

Nickelsburg, George W. E. *Ancient Judaism and Christian Origins: Diversity, Continuity, and Transformation.* Minneapolis, MN: Fortress Press, 2003.

Niditch, Susan. *War in the Hebrew Bible: A Study in the Ethics of Violence.* New York: Oxford University Press, 1993.

———. "Esther: Folklore, Wisdom, Feminism, and Authority." In *A Feminist Companion to Esther, Judith, and Susanna*, ed. Athalya Brenner, 26–46. Sheffield: Sheffield Academic Press, 1995.

Nissinen, Martii. *Homoeroticism in the Biblical World: A Historical Perspective.* Minneapolis, MN: Fortress Press, 1998.

Oberman, Heiko Augustinus. *Luther: Man between God and the Devil.* Trans. Eileen Walliser-Schwarzbart. New Haven, CT: Yale University Press, 1989.

Oden, Robert A., Jr. *The Bible without Theology: The Theological Tradition and Alternatives to It.* San Francisco: Harper and Row, 1987.

Oldfield, Gary. "School Desegregation after Two Generations: Race, Schools, and Opportunity in Urban Society. In *Race in America: The Struggle for Equality*, ed. Herbert Hill and James E. Jones Jr., 234–262. Madison: University of Wisconsin Press, 2003.

Orevillo-Montenegro, Muriel. *The Jesus of Asian Women: Women from the Margins.* Maryknoll, NY: Orbis Books, 2006.

Ozment, Steven. *The Age of Reform 1250–1550: An Intellectual and Religious History of Late Medieval and Reformation Europe.* New Haven, CT: Yale University Press, 1980.

Paris, Peter. "The Bible and the Black Churches." In *The Bible and Social Reform*, ed. Ernest Sandeen, 133–154. Philadelphia: Fortress Press, 1982.

Parker, T.H.L. *Calvin: A Biography.* Louisville, KY: Westminster John Knox Press, 2006.

Parsons, Michael. *Luther and Calvin on Old Testament Narratives: Reformation Thought and Narrative Text.* Lewiston, ME: Edwin Mellen Press, 2004.

Paton, Lewis Bayles. *A Critical and Exegetical Commentary on the Book of Esther.* International Critical Commentary. Edinburgh: T&T Clark, 1908.

Patrick, Dale. *Old Testament Law.* Atlanta: John Knox Press, 1985.

Patte, Daniel. *Ethics of Biblical Interpretation: A Reevaluation.* Louisville, KY: Westminster John Knox Press, 1995.

Pattison, Bonnie. *Poverty in the Theology of John Calvin.* Eugene, OR: Pickwick Publications, 2006.

Pelikan, Jaroslav. *Interpreting the Bible and the Constitution.* New Haven, CT: Yale University Press, 2004.

Perkins, Pheme. "The Gospel of Mark." *New Interpreter's Bible Commentary*. Vol. 8. Nashville: Abingdon Press, 1995.

Pharr, Suzanne. *Homophobia: A Weapon of Sexism*. Inverness, CA: Chardon Press, 1988.

Pinnock, Clark H., with Barry L. Callen. *The Scripture Principle: Reclaiming the Full Authority of the Bible*. 2nd ed. Grand Rapids, MI: Baker Academic, 2006.

Pixley, Jorge V. *The Bible, the Church, and the Poor*. Maryknoll, NY: Orbis Books, 1989.

Placher, William C. "Struggling with Scripture." In *Struggling with Scripture*, ed. Walter Brueggemann, William C. Placher, and Brian Blount, 32–50. Louisville, KY: Westminster John Knox Press, 2002.

Pleins, J. David. *The Social Visions of the Hebrew Bible: A Theological Introduction*. Louisville, KY: Westminster John Knox Press, 2001.

Pressler, Carolyn. *The View of Women Found in Deuteronomic Family Laws*. Berlin: W. de Gruyter, 1993.

———. *Joshua, Judges, and Ruth*. Louisville, KY: Westminster John Knox Press, 2002.

Prior, Michael, C.M. *The Bible and Colonialism: A Moral Critique*. Sheffield: Sheffield Academic Press, 1999.

Reid, Barbara E., O.P. *Taking Up the Cross: New Testament Interpretations through Latina and Feminist Eyes*. Minneapolis, MN: Fortress Press, 2007.

Rieger, Joerg. "That's Not Fair: Upside-Down Justice in the Midst of Empire." In *Interpreting the Postmodern: Responses to "Radical Orthodoxy,"* ed. Rosemary Radford Ruether and Marion Grau, 91–106. New York: T&T Clark, 2006.

Ringe, Sharon H. "Asian Readings of the Bible: A North American Feminist Response." *Biblical Interpretation* 2 (1994): 374–376.

Rivera, Mayra Rivera. "En-gendered Territory: U.S. Missionaries' Discourse in Puerto Rico (1898–1920)." In *New Horizons in Hispanic/Latino(a) Theology*, ed. Benjamin Valentin, 79–97. Cleveland: Pilgrim Press, 2003.

Rodd, Cyril S. *Glimpses of a Strange Land: Studies in Old Testament Ethics*. Edinburgh: T&T Clark, 2001.

Rogers, Jack. *Jesus, the Bible, and Homosexuality: Explode the Myths, Heal the Church*. Louisville, KY: Westminster John Knox Press, 2006.

Rogers, Jack B., and Donald K. McKim, *The Authority and Interpretation of the Bible: An Historical Approach*. San Francisco: Harper and Row, 1979.

Rogers, Mary Beth. *Barbara Jordan: American Hero*. New York: Bantam Books, 1998.

Rogerson, John. "Can a Translation of the Bible Be Authoritative?" In *Bible Translation on the Threshold of the Twenty-first Century: Authority, Reception, Culture and Religion*, ed. Athalya Brenner and Jan Willem van Henten, 17–30. London: Sheffield Academic Press, 2002.

———. "The Family and Structures of Grace in the Old Testament." In *Theory and Practice in Old Testament Ethics*, ed. M. Daniel Carroll R., 121–133. London: T & T Clark, 2004.

Rogerson, John, and Philip Davies. *The Old Testament World*. Englewood Cliffs, NJ: Prentice Hall, 1989.

Rowland, Debran. *The Boundaries of Her Body: The Troubling History of Women's Rights in America*. Naperville, IL: Sphinx, 2004.

Rubenstein, Richard L., and John K. Roth, *Approaches to Auschwitz: The Holocaust and Its Legacy*. Rev. ed. Louisville, KY: Westminster John Knox Press, 2003.

Ruether, Rosemary Radford. *New Woman, New Earth: Sexist Ideologies and Human Libertion*. New York: Seabury Press, 1975.

———. "Feminist Interpretation: A Method of Correlation." In *Feminist Interpretation of the Bible*, ed. Letty M. Russell, 111–124. Philadelphia: Westminster Press, 1985.

———, ed. *Feminist Theologies: Legacy and Prospect*. Minneapolis, MN: Fortress Press, 2007.

Russell, Letty M. "Authority and the Challenge of Feminist Interpretation." In *Feminist Interpretation of the Bible*, ed. Letty M. Russell, 137–146. Philadelphia: Westminster Press, 1985.

———. *Household of Freedom: Authority in Feminist Theology*. Philadelphia: Westminster Press, 1987.

Sakenfeld, Katharine Doob. "Ruth 4, an Image of Eschatological Hope: Journeying with a Text." In *Liberating Eschatology: Essays in Honor of Letty M. Russell*, ed. Margaret A. Farley and Serene Jones, 55–67. Louisville, KY: Westminster John Knox Press, 1999.

Sampley, J. Paul. "First Corinthians." *New Interpreter's Bible Commentary*. Vol. 10. Nashville, TN: Abingdon Press, 2002.

Sanders, E. P. *Jesus and Judaism*. Philadelphia: Fortress Press, 1985.

Say Pa, Anna May. "Reading Ruth 3:1–15 from an Asian Woman's Perspective." In *Engaging the Bible in a Gendered World: An Introduction to Feminist Biblical Interpretation in Honor of Katharine Doob Sakenfeld*, ed. Linda Day and Carolyn Pressler, 47–59. Louisville, KY: Westminster John Knox Press, 2006.

Scholz, Susanne. *Introducing the Women's Hebrew Bible*. New York: T&T Clark, 2007.

Schneider, Laurel C. "Changing the Missionary Position: Facing Up to Racism, Sexism, and Nationalism in G(LBT) Liberation." The Tenth Anniversary Gilberto Castaneda Lecture, Chicago Theological Seminary, May 3, 2007. http://www.ctschicago.edu/pdf/Casta%F1edaLecture2007.pdf (accessed December 2007).

Schneiders, Sandra M. *The Revelatory Text: Interpreting the New Testament as Sacred Scripture*. San Francisco: HarperSanFrancisco, 1991.

Schroeder, Joy A. *Dinah's Lament: The Biblical Legacy of Sexual Violence in Christian Interpretation*. Minneapolis, MN: Fortress Press, 2007.

Schüssler Fiorenza, Elisabeth. "The Will to Choose or to Reject: Continuing Our Critical Work." In *Feminist Interpretation of the Bible*, ed. Letty M. Russell, 125–136. Philadelphia: Westminster Press, 1985.

———. "The Ethics of Biblical Interpretation: Decentering Biblical Scholarship." *Journal of Biblical Literature* 107 (1988): 3–17.

———. *In Memory of Her: A Feminist Theological Reconstruction of Christian Origins*. Tenth anniversary ed. New York: Crossroad, 1994.

———. *Rhetoric and Ethic: The Politics of Biblical Studies*. Minneapolis, MN: Fortress Press, 1999.

———. "An Invitation to 'Dance' in the Open House of Wisdom: Feminist Study of the Bible." In *Engaging the Bible: Critical Readings from Contemporary Women*, ed. Cho

Hee An and Katheryn Pfisterer Darr, 81–104. Minneapolis, MN: Fortress Press, 2006.

Sherman, Max. *Barbara Jordan: Speaking the Truth with Eloquent Thunder.* Austin: University of Texas Press, 2007.

Shirer, William L. *The Rise and Fall of the Third Reich: A History of Nazi Germany.* New York: Simon and Schuster, 1960.

Skillington, V. George. *Reading the Sacred Text: An Introduction to Biblical Studies.* London: T&T Clark, 2002.

Smith, Andrea. *Conquest: Sexual Violence and American Indian Genocide.* Cambridge, MA: South End Press, 2005.

———. "Heteropatriarchy and the Three Pillars of White Supremacy: Rethinking Women of Color Organizing." In Incite! Women of Color Against Violence, *Color of Violence: The Incite! Anthology*, 66–73. Cambridge, MA: South End Press, 2006.

Smith, James P., and Barry Edmonston, eds. *The New Americans: Economic, Demographic, and Fiscal Effects of Immigration.* Washington, DC: National Academy Press, 1997.

Smith, Wilfred Cantwell. *What Is Scripture?* Minneapolis, MN: Fortress Press, 1993.

Southern, David. *Gunnar Myrdal and Black-White Relations: The Use and Abuse of an American Dilemma, 1944–1969.* Baton Rouge: Louisiana State University Press, 1987.

Sprinkle, Joe M. *Biblical Law and Its Relevance: A Christian Understanding and Ethical Application for Today of the Mosaic Regulations.* Lanham, MD: University Press of America, 2006.

Stackhouse, Max L. "Covenantal Marriage: Protestant Views and Contemporary Life." In *Covenant Marriage in Comparative Perspective*, ed. John Witte Jr. and Eliza Ellison, 153–181. Grand Rapids, MI: Eerdmans, 2005.

Steinmetz, David C. *Calvin in Context.* Oxford: Oxford University Press, 1995.

———. "Luther, the Reformers, and the Bible." In *Living Traditions of the Bible: Scripture in Jewish, Christian, and Muslim Practice*, ed. James E. Bowley, 163–176. St. Louis, MO: Chalice Press, 1999.

———. *Luther in Context.* 2nd ed. Grand Rapids, MI: Baker Academic, 2002.

———. "John Calvin as an Interpreter of the Bible." In *Calvin and the Bible*, ed. Donald K. McKim, 282–291. Cambridge: Cambridge University Press, 2006.

Stone, Ken, ed. *Queer Commentary and the Hebrew Bible.* Cleveland: Pilgrim Press, 2001.

Stone, Ronald H. *John Wesley's Life and Ethics.* Nashville, TN: Abingdon Press, 2001.

Stout, Jeffrey. *Democracy and Tradition.* Princeton, NJ: Princeton University Press, 2003.

Sugirtharajah, R. S. *The Postcolonial Bible.* Sheffield: Sheffield Academic Press, 1998.

———. *Postcolonial Criticism and Biblical Interpretation.* Oxford: Oxford University Press, 2002.

Talbot, Margaret. "Supreme Confidence: The Jurisprudence of Antonin Scalia." *New Yorker*, March 28, 2005, 40–55.

Tate, W. Randolph. *Interpreting the Bible: A Handbook of Terms and Methods.* Peabody, MA: Hendrickson, 2006.

Thompson, John L. *Writing the Wrongs: Women of the Old Testament among Biblical Commentators from Philo through the Reformation*. New York: Oxford University Press, 2001.

———. *Reading the Bible with the Dead: What You Can Learn from the History of Exegesis That You Can't Learn from Exegesis Alone*. Grand Rapids, MI: Eerdmans, 2007.

Thurman, Howard. *Jesus and the Disinherited*. Nashville, TN: Abingdon Press, 1949.

Tolbert, Mary Ann. "Afterwords: Christianity, Imperialism, and the Decentering of Privilege." In *Reading from This Place: Social Location and Biblical Interpretation in Global Perspective*, vol. 2, ed. Fernando F. Segovia and Mary Ann Tolbert, 347–361. Minneapolis: Fortress Press, 1995.

Troeltsch, Ernst. *The Social Teaching of the Christian Churches*. Trans. Olive Wyon. 2 vols. New York: Macmillan, 1931.

Turner, Philip. "The Ten Commandments in the Church in a Postmodern World." In *I Am the Lord Your God: Christian Reflections on the Ten Commandments*, ed. Carl E. Braaten and Christopher R. Seitz, 3–17. Grand Rapids, MI: Eerdmans, 2005.

Van Wijk-Bos, Johanna. *Ruth, Esther, Jonah*. Atlanta: John Knox Press, 1986.

———. *Ruth and Esther: Women in Alien Lands*. New York: General Board of Global Ministries of the United Methodist Church, 1988.

———. *Making Wise the Simple: The Torah in Christian Faith and Practice*. Grand Rapids, MI: Eerdmans, 2005.

Van Wolde, Ellen. "Texts in Dialogue with Texts: Intertextuality in the Ruth and Tamar Narratives." *Biblical Interpretation* 5 (1997): 1–28.

Vermes, Geza. *The Religion of Jesus the Jew*. Minneapolis, MN: Fortress Press, 1993.

Warrior, Robert Allen. "A Native American Perspective: Canaanites, Cowboys, and Indians." In *Voices from the Margin: Interpreting the Bible in the Third World*, ed. R. S. Sugirtharajah, 277–285. Maryknoll, NY: Orbis, 1997.

Weems, Renita J. *Just a Sister Away*. Revised and updated. New York: Warner Books, 2005.

Weinfeld, Moshe. *The Place of the Law in the Religion of Ancient Israel*. Leiden: Brill, 2004.

Welch, Sharon. *A Feminist Ethic of Risk*. Minneapolis, MN: Fortress Press, 1990.

Wesley, John. "Thoughts on the Present Scarcity of Provisions." In *The Works of the Rev. John Wesley A.M.*, ed. Thomas Jackson. Vol. 11, 53–59. London: J. Mason, 1830.

———. *The Journal of the Rev. John Wesley, A.M.* Ed. Nehemiah Curnock. 8 vols. London: Epworth Press, 1909–1916.

———. "Of Preaching Christ." In *John Wesley*, ed. Albert C. Outler, 232–237. New York: Oxford University Press, 1964.

———. "On the Original, Nature, Property, and Use of the Law." In *Sermons II: 34–70*. Vol. 2 of *the Works of John Wesley*, ed. Albert C. Outler, 4–19. Oxford: Clarendon Press, 1975.

———. "Upon our Lord's Sermon on the Mount, V." In *Sermons 1:1–33*. Vol. 1 of *The Works of John Wesley*, ed. Albert C. Outler, 550–571. Nashville, TN: Abingdon Press, 1984.

Wesley, John. "On God's Vineyard." In *Sermons III: 71–114*. Vol. 3 of *The Works of John Wesley*, ed. Albert C. Outler, 502–517. Nashville, TN: Abingdon Press, 1986.

———. "On Riches." In *Sermons III: 71–114*. Vol. 3 of *The Works of John Wesley*, ed. Albert C. Outler, 518–528. Nashville, TN: Abingdon Press, 1986.

West, Cornel. *Race Matters*. Boston: Beacon Press, 2001.

———. *Democracy Matters: Winning the Fight against Imperialism*. New York: Penguin Press, 2004.

West, Gerald O., ed. *Reading Other-Wise: Socially Engaged Biblical Scholars Reading with Their Local Communities*. Atlanta: Society of Biblical Literature, 2007.

White Crawford, Sidnie Ann. "Esther." In *Women's Bible Commentary*, expanded edition, ed. Carol A. Newsom and Sharon H. Ringe, 131–137. Louisville, KY: Westminster John Knox Press, 1998.

———. "Esther." In *New Interpreter's Bible*, vol. 3. Nashville, TN: Abingdon Press, 1999.

Wire, Antoinette Clark. "A North American Perspective." *Semeia* 78 (2001):145–150.

Witte, John. *Sex, Marriage, and Family in John Calvin's Geneva*. Grand Rapids, MI: Eerdmans, 2005.

Wong, Wai-Ching Angela. "Esther." In *Global Bible Commentary*, ed. Daniel Patte, 135–140. Nashville, TN: Abingdon Press, 2004.

Wright, Christopher J. H. *An Eye for an Eye: The Place of the Old Testament Ethics Today*. Downers Grove, IL: InterVarsity Press, 1983.

———. *Old Testament Ethics for the People of God*. Downers Grove, IL: InterVarsity Press, 2004.

Wright, N. T. *The Last Word: Scripture and the Authority of God—Getting Beyond the Bible Wars*. New York: HarperCollins, 2005.

Yee, Gale A. *Poor Banished Children of Eve: Woman as Evil in the Hebrew Bible*. Minneapolis, MN: Fortress Press, 2003.

Yoshino, Kenji. *Covering: The Hidden Assault on Our Civil Rights*. New York: Random House, 2006.

Zack, Naomi. *Thinking about Race*. 2nd ed. Belmont, CA: Thomson Wadsworth, 2006.

Zweig, Michael. *The Working Class Majority: America's Best Kept Secret*. Ithaca, NY: ILR Press, 2000.

———. *What's Class Got to Do with It: American Society in the Twenty-first Century*. Ithaca, NY: ILR Press, 2004.

Index